T0304457

Advance Praise for *Winning Judo*

"Once again, Steve Scott, the most prolific American writer for judo knowledge, has produced a new book on successful play, practice, and competitive judo principles for all levels of judoka. Careful reading is sure to expand one's thoughts, first on the important basics of our sport, second as it accompanies us throughout life's journey as we study our favorite sport."

—**Bruce Toups**, 7th dan,
former director of development, US Judo, Inc.,
US team coach and team leader to numerous international judo tournaments

"This is the type of book I wish I had when I started out in judo as a teenager. *Winning Judo* offers real-world advice to every judo athlete, from a novice starting out to an elite-level judoka looking for a competitive edge."

—**John Saylor**, 8th dan,
US National Judo Champion,
Pan American Judo Medalist,
Retired Head Coach of the US Olympic Training Center Judo Squad,
Director of the Shingitai Jujitsu Association,
Author of *Strength and Conditioning Secrets of the World's Greatest Fighters*, *Conditioning for Combat Sports* and *Vital Jujitsu*

"I have always enjoyed Steve Scott's works. His latest book *Winning Judo* reminds me of my extensive studies and training camps of judo and sambo in the former Soviet Republics. Just like the Soviet coaches and scientists did, Steve has broken down all aspects of judo training in this latest work. This book gives the judo athlete a comprehensive guide to training properly and helping to ensure competitive success on the mat, from local to international tournaments."

—**Gregg Humphreys**, 5th dan,
judo and sambo coach of Dynamo Grappling Concepts,
North American editor for Igor Kurinnoy's *SAMBO for Professionals* series

"Steve's passion in life has been to help his athletes and students achieve excellence in their lives, both on and off the judo mat. His coaching helped me win World and Pan American Games gold medals, so I can personally tell you that what is written in this book works. Steve's my husband as well as having been my personal coach for my athletic career, so I may be a bit biased, but this is a book that every judo or sambo athlete should own and read."

—**Becky Scott**, 7th dan, World and Pan American Games sambo champion,
US National judo champion,
US Olympic Festival judo champion,
US team coach for the World Judo Championships (under 21)

"This is the thinking woman (or man)'s book on judo. Whether you are a highly successful competitor or coach, a 'weekend warrior who has to be at work on Monday' or any other person who is interested in the whole of judo—history, vocabulary, and structure, this is the book for you."

—**Dr. AnnMaria DeMars**, 7th dan,
World and Pan American Games judo champion,
US National judo champion,
US Olympic Festival judo champion

"I've been in judo for over 50 years and have seen a lot of books, but when I first read Steve's book, *Winning Judo,* I reacted by like a little girl opening a present and found myself enthusiastically saying, 'That's a great idea' or 'That's really a cool drill' on just about every page I read. This book is packed with practical knowledge and information and every judoka reading it will benefit. Steve is not only keeping the sport of judo alive by his work, he is also part of judo's history."

—**Grace Jividen**, 7th dan,
World and Pan American Games sambo champion,
1992 judo Olympian,
world champion in judo for International Police and Fire Games,
US National judo champion

"*Winning Judo* is a must-read for anyone looking to learn the art of competitive judo. This comprehensive book is a treasure trove of expert insights and effective techniques. Steve Scott's passion and deep understanding of judo shine through on every page, making this book a valuable resource for both beginners and seasoned practitioners. I can't recommend *Winning Judo* enough for every aspiring judoka or grappler of any style."

—**Andrew Zerling**, martial artist,
award-winning author of *Sumo for Mixed Martial Arts*

"One-step judo book. Steve Scott has done it, everything you want to know about judo in one book. Steve is an amazing person, teacher, coach, and author. Like his book, he is amazing too."

—**Louis Moyerman**, 8th dan USA judo,
team leader 2000 Olympics and 1999 Pan American Games,
team manager for ten world events,
Liberty Bell Judo Classic tournament director of twenty-eight years

"*Winning Judo* is a 'Judo Bible.' Everything is in here. Throws, chokes, pins, and armlocks, from every position. Plus, training methods, strategy, theory, and coaching. Every competitor, or judo enthusiast, should have this book. I wish I had it when I was competing in the 80s and 90s. Steve Scott is the most dedicated coach in judo today, still producing champions."

—**Janet Trussell**, 5th dan,
World and Pan American Games sambo champion,
Pan American judo champion,
US National champion in judo, sambo, and freestyle wrestling

"*Winning Judo* offers a deep analysis on the various judo techniques, training drills and competition strategies. A must-read for athletes, parents, and coaches who practice the art of judo."

—**Donna Turk**, Pan American Games sambo silver medalist,
US National judo medalist

"Steve Scott's *Winning Judo* tells and shows both the elite and recreational judoka how to best prepare, train, compete, and win in competition judo. Judo competition is a complex and often daunting challenge, and *Winning Judo* is a guide you will use immediately and often to become a winner in today's sport of judo. I've trained an Olympian as well as other elite level athletes as well as recreational players and can tell you that this is bread and butter winning judo advice."

—**Tom Crone**, 7th dan, former member US National coaching staff, head coach of NorthStar Judo Club, author of Shichidan, *Judo Basics*

"*Winning Judo* by Steve Scott is one of the most thoroughly thought out and detailed judo books I have had the privilege to explore. Judo principles, concepts, tactics, strategies, and kinesiology can all be found in this book along with training, competition, and safety tips. This book is great for students, athletes, and coaches alike. Every grappler regardless of rank or style should have this book in their collection. I love the breakdown and usage of the Japanese terminology. The contents of this book are a testament of the wealth of knowledge and experience possessed by Sensei Steve Scott. I am grateful that he has taken the time and effort to share this wisdom with us all. I am looking forward to using this book as a reference guide for my own students and recommending it to all my fellow judo and jiu-jitsu peers."

—**Larry W. Keith**, Kodokan Judo 3rd dan, BJJ 1st degree black belt, author of *Takedown Secrets*, host of Takedown Confidence Summit, owner Dynamic Martial Arts, LLC

WINNING JUDO

Also by Steve Scott

The Judo Advantage

Sambo Encyclopedia

Triangle Chokes: Triangle and Leg Chokes for Combat Sports

Vital Jujitsu (with John Saylor)

Juji Gatame Encyclopedia

Winning on the Mat

Conditioning for Combat Sports (with John Saylor)

Tap Out Textbook

Groundfighting Pins and Breakdowns

Drills for Grapplers

Throws and Takedowns

Grappler's Book of Strangles and Chokes

Vital Leglocks

Championship Sambo: Submission Holds and Groundfighting

Championship Sambo (DVD)

Armlock Encyclopedia

Juji Gatame Complete (with Bill West)

Coaching on the Mat

WINNING JUDO

STEVE SCOTT

YMAA Publication Center
Wolfeboro, NH USA

YMAA Publication Center, Inc.
PO Box 480
Wolfeboro, New Hampshire, 03894
1-800-669-8892 • info@ymaa.com • www.ymaa.com

ISBN 9781594399848 (print)
ISBN 9781594399855 (ebook)
ISBN 9781594399862 (hardcover)

Editor: Doran Hunter
Cover design: Axie Breen
This book typeset in Adobe Garamond and Source Sans.
Illustrations courtesy of the author, unless otherwise noted.
20240322

Publisher's Cataloging in Publication

Names: Scott, Steve, 1952- author. | Saylor, John (Jujitsu master), writer of foreword.

Title: Winning judo / Steve Scott ; [foreword by John Saylor, 8th dan].

Description: Wolfeboro, NH USA : YMAA Publication Center, [2024] | Subtitle on cover: Realistic and practical skills for competitive judo: strategies that win for all grappling styles. | Includes bibliographical references.

Identifiers: ISBN: 9781594399848 (trade paperback) | 9781594399855 (ebook) | 9781594399862 (hardcover) | LCCN: 2024934530

Subjects: LCSH: Judo--Competitions--Training. | Judo--Training. | Judo--Physiological aspects. | Martial arts--Physiological aspects. | Wrestling--Physiological aspects. | Kinesiology. | Biomechanics. | Human mechanics. | Hand-to-hand fighting--Training. | Martial arts--Training. | Wrestling--Training. | BISAC: SPORTS & RECREATION / Martial Arts / General. | SELF-HELP / Safety & Security / Personal Safety & Self-Defense. | SPORTS & RECREATION / Wrestling.

Classification: LCC: GV1114.33.T72 S36 2024 | DDC: 796.815/3--dc23

Editor's Note: Throughout this book, readers will see mention of US Judo, judo's national governing body. This organization is also known as US Judo, Inc. and USA Judo. For our purposes, the terms are synonymous.

Printed in USA.

CONTENTS

Foreword xi

Introduction xiii

CHAPTER 1 **Some Background** 1

Why Do You Compete in Judo? 1

The Growth of the Sport of Judo 2

A Modern International Sport 3

Jigoro Kano's Three Principles 4

Maturing in Judo 5

Your "Judo IQ" 6

The Language of Judo 7

CHAPTER 2 **Basics Win Matches** 9

What Are the Basics? 10

Kuzushi: This Judo Stuff Works! 11

Types of Kuzushi 12

The Primary Elements of Physical Training in Judo 14

Judo Isn't Gentle 19

Technique and Skill: Function Dictates Form 20

Precision Judo 23

"Feel Your Judo" 23

Making Your Judo Work for You: Developing Your Own Style 25

Rate of Success 28

CHAPTER 3 **Factors of Success** 35

Judo Is Gripping and Movement 35

Control Judo: The Tactics of Judo 36

Strategy and Tactics 37

The Concept of Kobo Ichi 37

A Judo Contest Isn't a Game 38

Left-Side and Right-Side Techniques 38

Sportsmanship 39
The Rules 40

Scouting Opponents 42
Tactics of Keeping the Lead in the Score 43
Tempo or Pace 47
Body Space: Body Holes and Body Gaps 48
Position in Judo 49
Posture 50

CHAPTER 4 **Efficient Training Produces Effective Results** 61

Train Hard and Train Smart 61
Three Levels of Training Intensity 62

Training Outlines for GP, DP, and SP Intensity Levels 64
Age and Intensity of Training 67
Optimal Surplus in Judo 69
Conjugate Training 70
Cross Training 71
Training Diary 71
Training for a Tournament Is Like Rehearsing for a Movie 72
Stress in Training 72
Training Cycles or Periodization 72
Training in Waves 73
Injuries and Making Weight 74

Drill Training: Structure in Training 74
Two Types of Drills 75
Realism 76

CHAPTER 5 **Gripping and Movement** 95

Gripping in Judo 95

Everything Is a Handle 96

Take Control: Tactical Purpose of Gripping 96
Goals of Gripping and Grip Fighting 97

Some General Observations on Grip Fighting 105
Guidelines for Grip Fighting 106
Commonly Used Grips 109

Movement in Judo 117

The Movement Patterns in Judo 119
How Ayumi Ashi Works 120
How Taisabaki Works 120
How Tsugi Ashi Works 122
Some Guidelines for Effective Movement 123

CHAPTER 6 **Throws, Transitions, and Defense** 125

Nage Waza 125

Many Throwing Techniques Merge Together 126

Throws, Takedowns, and Transitions: Their Purpose 126

Success in Throwing 128
Control and Force 129
Physical Fitness for Throwing 129
A Throw Is a Tool 129
Double Trouble 130
Three Types of Throwing Attacks 130

The Four Stages of a Throw: Kuzushi, Tsukuri, Kake, and Kime 131
Kuzushi: Breaking Balance and Posture 134
Tsukuri: Building the Technique 136
Kake: Execution of the Throw 137
Kime: Finishing the Throw 138

The Movement Patterns in Judo 138
How Ayumi Ashi Works 140
How Taisabaki Works 140
How Tsugi Ashi Works 140

Analysis of Selected Throwing Techniques 141
Attacker's Legs Close Together: Forward Throwing Techniques 141

Ogoshi/Tsuri Goshi/Uki Goshi 142

Seoi Nage 145
Defining Features 146
Attacker's Legs Wide: Tai Otoshi/Kubi Nage 147
Defining Features 147

Knee-Drop Throwing Techniques: Seoi Nage, Seoi Otoshi, Hiki Otoshi 151
Defining Features 152

O Soto Gari/O Soto Gake/Harai Goshi 155
Defining Features 156
Throws Between the Legs: O Uchi Gari and Similar Throws 160
Defining Features 160
Attacker Is Supported on One Leg: Uchi Mata and Similar Throws 162
Defining Features 163

Foot Sweeps and Foot Props 166
Defining Features 166
Defining Features 169

Sacrifice or Bodyweight Throws: Hikikomi Gaeshi and Similar Throws 173
Defining Features 173

CHAPTER 7 **Transitions** 175

Three Types of Transitions from Throwing to Groundfighting 176

CHAPTER 8 **An Aggressive Defense** 191

An Aggressive Defense Wins Matches 191
More About Kobo Ichi: Counterattacks 192
Training for Defense 192

Lines of Defense 193

CHAPTER 9 **The Groundfighting of Judo** 201

Newaza, the Guard, Groundfighting, and Groundwork 201

Strategies for Groundfighting 203

Groundfighting Positions 209

Breakdowns and Turnovers 210

Osaekomi Waza 212
Position in Osaekomi Waza 213
The Anatomy of Osaekomi Waza 213
Position in Judo 217
Analyzing Selected Osaekomi Waza and Entries 217

CHAPTER 10 **Armlocks** 231

Control the Position and Get the Submission 232
An Explanation of "Position" 232
The "Setup" in Groundfighting 234
The Defining Features of Armlocks 234
Leg-Press Position 235
Analyzing Selected Kansetsu Waza and Entries 237

CHAPTER 11 **Chokes and Strangles** 257

Defining Features of Shime Waza 258
Strangles Start with the Legs 258

The Anatomy of Shime Waza 259
Using the Appendages in Shime Waza 260
Using the Judogi in Shime Waza 260
Position in Shime Waza 261
Applying the Strangle: Adding Torque 263
Analyzing Selected Shime Waza and Entries 264

Epilogue 279
References and Biblography 283
About the Author 285

FOREWORD

It's a great personal pleasure to write the foreword for Steve Scott's book *Winning Judo.* This book is aptly named, as it offers sound, practical advice on what it takes to be successful in the sport of judo. This is the kind of book I wish I'd had when I started my judo career, and it's also the kind of book that elite-level judo athletes and coaches will find enormously useful. For those who are looking for real-world advice on every aspect of training and competing in judo, such as cutting weight, drill-training, strategy and tactics, dealing with the stress of competition, and many other vital components of being a success in competitive judo, this book should prove to be a "go to" source of information for years to come.

Steve and I have been friends for many years and have coached together at many national and international training camps. We were the two coaches selected by the national governing body of judo to attend the USOC Coaches College at the US Olympic Training Center in Colorado Springs, Colorado, starting in 1984. I distinctly remember, after attending the daily classroom presentations by some of America's foremost coaches and sports scientists, sitting on the mat in the Olympic Training Center's dojo comparing notes with Steve. We were both young and upcoming judo coaches and excited about how we could have a positive impact on judo in the United States. It was during these conversations that I realized Steve had the technical and organizational ability to coach judo athletes so that they would be able to meet their full potential, both as athletes and as human beings. Through the years, he's proven me right. Steve has developed national- and international-level athletes in judo, sambo, and other grappling sports at his Welcome Mat Judo Club as well as international judo champions when he worked as the national coordinator and head coach for the under-twenty-one program with our national governing body. I worked closely with Steve at many national training camps held at the US Olympic Training Center and had more opportunities to discuss coaching judo with him. But, more importantly for those who read this book, Steve's practical experience as a coach at all levels of competition—from local judo tournaments to being the coach for the US team at the World Junior (under-twenty-one) Judo Championships, Pan American Judo Championships, and many other international tournaments—is reflected on the pages of this book.

When reading this book, you will notice that Steve has developed what I consider to be a complete system of attack (as well as defense) organized into progressive groups of skills. He peels back one layer after another to get to the core at what an athlete needs for success in the sport of judo. It's this focus on progressing from one level of skill development to the next and how to make it work for each individual athlete that has made him a successful coach, and that is what's presented in this great book.

One last thing. Everything in this book is based on sound principles of sports science that have proven successful at all levels of competitive judo. What you will see on these pages is both fundamentally sound and technically innovative, providing a reliable source of information.

—**John Saylor**, 8th Dan
Former Coach, US Olympic Training Center Judo Squad
US National Judo Champion and Pan American Medalist

INTRODUCTION

The purpose of this book is to provide a realistic and practical guide to winning in competitive judo. The information contained on these pages can be used by experienced judo athletes as well as those who are starting out in the sport. In addition to explaining how to use or apply a particular technique, tactic, or drill, the reasons that technique, tactic, or drill works will be analyzed. All of this discussion aims at helping you be successful in the sport of judo.

Judo is based on sound principles of movement and biomechanics. It's a sequence of skills based on functional efficiency. Judo is also a tough and demanding sport that reveals the character of the person doing it.

Everything on these pages is based on a lifetime of experience, education, training, experimentation, and observation. I am fortunate to have gotten involved with judo during a time when many technical innovations were taking place. This was during the 1960s when growth took place in all aspects of judo, especially in competitive judo. Back then, judo was emerging as an international sport, and this led not only to the development of innovative techniques but also to innovative training methods, all absorbed from the wider audience that judo was attracting. Judo retained its value as a method of physical education but gained new prominence as a sport. As a sport, judo has proven to be one of the most challenging ever invented. As a method of physical education and means of personal growth, judo continues to fulfill Jigoro Kano's vision of his invention, Kodokan judo.

I wish to express my sincere thanks to my wife Becky Scott and to my great friends John Saylor, Dr. AnnMaria DeMars, Ken Brink, Tom Crone, and Dr. Phil Rumaboa for the technical expertise, advice, and input that they gave me in the writing of this book. The photographs for this book were provided by some consummate professionals; Terry Smemo, Mark Lozano, Sharon Vandenberg, Jorge Aldovar Garcia, Jake Pursley, and Joe Mace offered their considerable skills graciously and I sincerely thank them. The publisher of this book, David Ripianzi, was instrumental in getting this book written. David urged me for about a year to start this project, telling me that there was some more to say about judo and he was right. Doran Hunter, the editor of this book, did his usual masterful work in keeping me focused. Barbara Langley, our publicist, was a pleasure to work with again as was the entire staff at YMAA Publication Center. Additionally, the athletes and coaches who train at Welcome Mat with me have contributed much to the quality of this book. I appreciate their input, time, and patience in demonstrating the skills presented on these pages.

It's always been my belief that, in any book, the author is having a discussion with the reader. Hopefully, if I'm successful as a writer, the words and images presented on these pages will elicit both thought and action on your part. Books are marvelous tools in that you can come back at a later date and gain another perspective or insight you didn't have before. This is certainly the case for me. There are books I have read, reread, and then read even more for many years. These books represent a valuable reference source as well as a source of inspiration to delve further into a subject. Books make us think and, of course, the purpose of this book is to make you think. Hopefully, you'll come back time and again to ponder what is presented in this book further and we can continue our "discussion" for many years to come.

—Steve Scott
Kansas City, Missouri

CHAPTER 1

Some Background

We all start somewhere and with somebody. It's where we end up that counts.

—John Saylor

This short first section examines some fundamental topics that every athlete who aspires to be successful in judo should consider. This section starts out with a personal question about the reasons a person has for competing in judo and moves onto a variety of subjects that provide a background for appreciating the difficulty of achieving success in the sport of judo.

Why Do You Compete in Judo?

This is a question you should ask yourself; and after asking it, think about it and give yourself an answer. There's no "right" or "wrong" answer, there is only your answer. There may be one reason or there may be many reasons why someone competes in a demanding sport like judo. But it's important that you consciously tell yourself the reasons why you're doing what you do so you can go about doing it better.

Every species on earth has to compete to survive and humans are no different. Some like to compete more than others and they like to compete with each other in different ways. It's human nature to want to prove oneself, to be tested and prevail. There are different kinds of tests. Some people like to climb mountains and some people like to throw others on a mat. If you're reading this book, the odds are good that you are not a mountain climber.

The Growth of the Sport of Judo

To have a better appreciation for gaining success in competitive judo, it's a good idea to know how judo developed into the modern Olympic sport that it is today. What follows is a brief history of judo's journey from the early years of Kodokan judo to today's international sport.

The sport of judo as we know it today was developed from Japanese jujutsu to become Jigoro Kano's Kodokan judo in 1882. It was from this foundation established by Kodokan judo that judo developed as a sport, growing and evolving in the twentieth century. The late 1800s and early 1900s were the time when the concept of "sport" as we know it now was beginning to develop. Many of the sports we do today were born during this period, including judo.

With the onset of the industrial revolution, life generally improved for most people from their earlier condition in agrarian societies. One benefit of the improved living conditions was having more leisure time. Also, more people lived in cities and had more interaction with others. Humans, as the competitive beings that we have always been, developed new methods of recreation and sport.

Jigoro Kano's timing couldn't have been better. His Kodokan judo was at the vanguard of the popularity of sports in the late 1800s. The modern Olympic movement was developing at this time, and in 1894 Pierre de Coubertin spearheaded the founding of the International Olympic Committee. In 1896, the first modern Olympics were held. Jigoro Kano saw the Olympics as an opportunity to further his new innovation in jujutsu: Kodokan judo.

Kano developed a relationship with de Coubertin that was both professional and friendly. Both men shared the same vision of using sport to improve the lives of people around the world. For his part, Kano worked to advance the Olympic movement in Japan as well as promote a wider acceptance of physical education in general. Part of this effort was getting judo accepted as part of the Japanese school curriculum. Along with his efforts to advance judo, Kano was a founder of the Japanese Olympic Committee, and in 1912 at the Stockholm Olympics he was the flag bearer in the opening ceremony representing Japan with its first two Olympic athletes who competed in track and field.

Jigoro Kano died in 1938 on a ship at sea while he was on a trip to promote judo as an Olympic sport. Even in death, his trip was successful. Through his efforts, judo was to be included in the 1940 Olympics in Tokyo. This didn't come to pass because war broke out and the Tokyo Olympics were cancelled. But Kano's vision of judo becoming an Olympic sport didn't die. It just took twenty-four more years for it to happen with the inclusion of judo in the 1964 Olympics in Tokyo.

Jigoro Kano worked tirelessly to advance the cause of judo and show that sport could be a way of improving people's lives. He was an innovator and genius who gave the world a gift that has enriched the lives of millions of people, including you and me.

A Modern International Sport

The sport of judo as we know it today gained momentum in the 1950s and into the 1960s with the growing interest, organization, and technical development by nations outside of Japan, especially in Europe. In 1951, the International Judo Federation (IJF) was formed, and in 1956 the first World Judo Championship tournament for men was held in Tokyo. In 1964, judo was included as a demonstration sport for men in the Tokyo Olympic Games. Athletes from twenty-seven nations competed in the first Olympic judo event in 1964 in three weight categories and an open category.

In 1972, the International Olympic Committee (IOC) accepted judo as a regular part of the Olympic program of events at the Munich Games, but only for men. With the growing number of women competing in judo starting in the 1970s, there was a groundswell of support internationally for women's judo to be included in the Olympics. In the 1988 Seoul Olympics, women's judo was included as a demonstration sport. In 1992 at the Barcelona Games, the IOC accepted women's judo as a regular part of the Olympic schedule of events. Judo was now truly a sport in which everyone could participate.

Judo had become a sport with an international following. To both the general public as well as to many members of the judo community, judo wasn't simply a Japanese martial art anymore. Success in competition took on a greater degree of importance than it ever had before.

But to many people's way of thinking, it's not an "either-or" situation. Judo is still more than simply a sport to many of us. Coaches continue to teach judo to students using the principles laid out in Kodokan judo by Professor Kano. These principles apply to the teaching of all students at every level but can provide additional and specialized training for those interested in pursuing competitive judo. The accelerated focus on judo as a competitive sport has actually improved the technical quality of *what* students are taught as well as *how* students are taught, whether they compete in judo or not.

With its increasing international popularity, every aspect of judo was subject to development by exponents outside of Japan. Starting in the 1950s, a new field of study, sports science, was emerging internationally. Every Olympic sport, including judo, was now being analyzed and studied in an effort to develop faster, stronger, and more technically skilled athletes. A judoka was no longer simply a skilled proponent of judo; he was now a judo athlete. People started searching for improved athletic performance in judo using biomechanics, sports psychology, and other methods of sports science.

This new breed of athletes and coaches viewed winning in the sport of judo as an ultimate expression of judo ability and skill. To many people, earning a black belt was important, but winning a gold medal was just as important.

Judo is now a sport practiced worldwide in something close to 190 nations. Jigoro Kano's dream of making judo available to everyone has been realized. But a paradox has arisen. Judo has grown in popularity primarily because of its sport aspect and not as much as a method of education as Kano had envisioned. To Jigoro Kano, inclusion in the Olympic movement represented international acceptance for judo, not just as a sport but as an ideology for the improvement of humanity. He was an idealist who cautioned against only focusing on the specialized training of sport judo to the exclusion of other aspects of Kodokan judo.

But all of this brings us back to the purpose of this book. When a judo athlete enters a tournament, the goal is to win. This statement may be blunt to some, but it's true. It is less than honest to enter any competitive activity for any other reason. And the desire for a person to win in the sport of judo does not diminish his love or commitment to the activity of Kodokan judo as established by Jigoro Kano. The training necessary to win in the sport of judo can prepare a person for more to come in his life, both on and off the mat.

Jigoro Kano's Three Principles

The often-quoted phrase "judo is more than just a sport" is true. Before delving into the specifics of finding success in sport judo, it's important to point out that judo, as a sport, is only one aspect of Jigoro Kano's invention. If a person only pursues judo as a competitive activity, he is missing out on the totality of what judo is. This totality is encompassed in the three core principles of Kodokan judo that were established early in its history by Jigoro Kano that remain relevant today.

Rentai-ho: The first principle is rentai-ho, or judo as a method of physical education. Judo is first and foremost a just such a method. The connection to physical education is listed first because education does not just mean the training of a specific skill but rather an understanding and appreciation of the reasons why a person does that skill. This basis in physical education provides the logical and rational groundwork for every aspect of technical development in judo. Judo, as a sport, would not be possible without this foundation of physical education.

Shushin-ho: The second principle is shushin-ho, or judo as a means of ethical training and character development. A person who studies judo should be a positive addition to this world. Shushin-ho also relates directly to sport judo because this principle is the foundation of sportsmanship. Without the concept of sportsmanship, there is no sport.

Shobu-ho: The third principle is shobu-ho, or judo as a method of sport and self-defense and is the subject of this book. This is the principle that focuses on achieving technical success and applying it to sport or self-defense.

That the focus of this book is the sport aspect of judo doesn't diminish judo's vital role in physical education, character development, and self-defense. Nor does it take away from the fact that millions of people practice judo simply because they like studying an interesting activity. As stated earlier, without a firm foundation based on education, judo could not have developed into the technically complex and diverse sport it has become. Jigoro Kano is not only recognized as the founder of Kodokan judo, he is regarded as a founding father of physical education in Japan as well as a founding father of the Olympic movement in Japan. Through judo, his vision of uniting education and sport has been realized.

Maturing in Judo

For those who are serious about judo and stay in it for a long period of time, there are two general stages of development in the career and life of a judoka: kyogi judo and kogi judo.

The first phase, kyogi judo (also called gedan judo or "lower-level judo"), is when a judoka focuses entirely on the immediate concern of gaining success in competitive judo and the development of the technical and tactical skills necessary to do so. The term kyogi implies a narrow or limited level of understanding or appreciation of judo. This doesn't mean that a judo competitor isn't technically skilled at what he or she does; what it means is that this is a specialized and narrow focus on one aspect of judo and that aspect is success in competition. For those who focus on competitive judo, the kyogi level of involvement in judo takes up the bulk of their time, effort, thought, and training in judo. This is natural, and there's nothing wrong with the focused and narrow pursuit of judo as a competitive sport as long as we realize there is more to come for us in our judo careers.

That "more to come" is kogi judo (also called jodan judo or "higher level judo"), which is a broader understanding, study, and appreciation of the totality of judo. Kogi judo is the maturation of a judoka, and it takes a long time for this process of growth to come about. We build and develop a maturity in our judo based on our early experiences as competitive judo athletes. As we progress in our training, we widen our understanding and appreciation of the many technical and tactical applications of judo. But it shouldn't stop there. These lessons on the mat are hard earned and enable us to reflect on how our experiences in judo give us a wider and more comprehensive view of life in general. If we make the effort, we not only mature in our judo; we mature as human beings as well.

When a person makes the decision to pursue judo as a competitive sport, that person's life will change forever. Judo is a tough sport, and the road to success has many road bumps and detours. Few people ever become rich or famous doing judo, and the ones who do have certainly earned it.

Not everyone will stand on the podium with a medal draped around his neck, but the effort is worth it if for no other reason than because it was so difficult to accomplish.

Your "Judo IQ"

Judo isn't for dummies. It's a complex activity made up of many technically difficult movements. The technical complexity of judo is similar to the technical complexity of gymnastics. Gymnastics is a highly technical and difficult sport, but a gymnast does not have to apply these technical skills against a resisting, fit, and equally skilled opponent as is the case for a judo athlete.

In addition to knowing *how* to do a technique, an athlete must understand *why* the technique works and *when* that technique works best against resisting and fit opposition with a good rate of success. The ability to do this is what people call a "fight IQ" or a "sport IQ." We can make "fight IQ" more specific and call it "judo IQ." Your judo IQ is knowing how and when to use every tool you have in your toolbox of technical and tactical skills against a variety of opponents and in a variety of situations. Someone with a good judo IQ has the ability to see the weaknesses or strengths of opponents and develop the techniques and tactics needed to beat them.

The Language of Judo

Japanese is the international language of judo. Japanese terminology will be used throughout this book and, whenever necessary, an accurate English translation will be provided. This is done for two primary reasons. First, the Japanese conceived judo and they thought and spoke in the Japanese language. The technical theories that have worked for many years (and continue to work) were conceptualized initially in the Japanese language. To best appreciate and understand both a fundamental technique or movement and its underlying principles, one must have an accurate and clear understanding of how and in what context it is described. Almost all of the names used to denote and identify the many techniques of judo are descriptive in nature and are from the Japanese language. If you understand what the name of the technique actually means, you'll have a better understanding of the technique. Secondly, Japanese terminology provides a generally accepted nomenclature for judo. As stated at the onset of this paragraph, Japanese is the international language of judo. For example, when someone uses the word "randori," it is universally understood what it means. Every activity or subject has its own jargon and judo is no different. The intent isn't for anyone to have to learn or speak the Japanese language, but knowing the lingo will open doors for you and give you a good understanding not only of how something is done but why. So while the ability to speak Japanese isn't required, the ability to "speak judo" is.

You have to play a long time to be able to play like yourself.

—Miles Davis, Jr.

CHAPTER 2

Basics Win Matches

This section of the book focuses on the importance of fundamentals. No one has ever walked onto a judo mat and immediately became an elite-level athlete. Natural athletic talent is helpful, but judo is a sport made up of many complex skills that require serious effort and a lot of time to develop for anyone who aspires to be a champion. Anyone who thinks otherwise will have a short and limited career in judo.

During the course of his career, a judo athlete will train at a variety of dojos and with a variety of coaches. But every judo athlete starts his career somewhere and with somebody. This first exposure to judo is critical. Initially learning, practicing, and applying biomechanically efficient technical skills in judo is vital for long-term success at the sport. These technical skills are the basics of judo. There is a progression of technical skill as well as a progression of understanding and appreciation of judo for every successful judo athlete. For all of this to take place, there must be a solid foundation of technical skill provided by a judoka's initial coach.

Elite-level judo is simply the basics performed to their full potential. No judo champion ever skipped learning the fundamental skills of judo. Basics do indeed win matches. Not only are the technical fundamentals of throwing and grappling necessary for an aspiring judoka, learning and understanding the theories and philosophies of why Kodokan judo works are also necessary. To begin, let's examine the basics.

What Are the Basics?

When beginning anything (including judo), learning the basics sets the foundation for more advanced study, application, and appreciation of that subject. But what are the basics of judo?

They are skills and movements that focus on the gross motor skill of applying a technique or movement in judo. These gross skills don't require a lot of intricate or refined physical actions on the part of the beginner. They are simple, direct, and don't require higher levels of critical thinking.

Basics are also skills readily learned by a beginner, giving him a real sense of accomplishment in a relatively short period of time. These are skills a beginner can apply on a non-resisting partner initially. These gross motor skills progress to fine motor skills as the student progresses. What often takes place in skill progression is that a student will apply the skill he initially learned and apply it in a more practical or realistic situation. These basic skills are lead-up skills that logically progress to more advanced application of the initially learned skill and then on to more complex and intricate patterns of movement.

Throwing techniques such as koshi guruma (hip wheel), ogoshi (major hip throw), uki goshi (floating hip throw), kubi nage (neck throw), and o soto gari (major outer reap) are techniques that focus on gross motor skills and don't require a great deal of intricate movement for a beginning student to grasp them.

From these basic techniques, the coach can add another layer of technical skill and progress the students to the next level of ability. For example, koshi guruma (hip wheel) is a good lead-up skill in order for a student to learn ippon seoi nage (one-arm back carry throw). Another example is starting a student with kubi nage (neck throw) and progressing on to tai otoshi (body drop). One thing leads to another in a logical progression of adding more layers to the initial technique or skill.

Pinning techniques such as kesa gatame (scarf hold) or mune gatame (chest hold) are good examples of techniques that take a relatively short amount of time for a beginner to understand and apply successfully. From these initial pins, a student can quickly progress in his or her learning and acquire the ability to turn a training partner over and secure the pin. From this set of skills, the coach can add another layer of skill and teach beginners how to escape from these pins. This sequence of learning starts with the coach teaching a technique that doesn't require a lot of fine motor skills to learn or master. As the students developed skill, understanding, and confidence in the technique, another layer of skill can be added. This also applies when teaching shime waza (strangling techniques) or kansetsu waza (armlock joint techniques). A coach should make sure to initially teach the technique in an" ideal" or non-moving situation, showing the mechanically correct way to perform it. In other words, the coach should not show an intricate rolling movement or other setup skill to make the technique work; he should simply focus on the core mechanical skills of the technique and teach it to beginners by focusing on how and why the technique works in an ideal or non-resisting situation.

Basic skills are also movements and behaviors that do not require a long attention span to learn. Beginners have shorter attention spans than intermediate or advanced judo students. This is true for both children and adults. It takes time and much repetition for a student to develop an attention span required to learn, understand, and apply more advanced and complex technical skills in judo.

Another important aspect of the basics in judo is for beginners to learn how to practice safely. Ukemi (falling safely) is an important part of learning how to do judo and is more important than some people may think. If a judoka knows that he has the skill to land safely when being thrown, that judoka will be a better training partner for others. The ability to land safely on the mat gives a beginner confidence, which allows him to be more willing to take falls in practice and engage fully in training. There is a definite correlation between having good ukemi skills and having good throwing skills. When someone knows what it feels like to be thrown, he understands better how to apply that throw. Ukemi develops a kinesthetic awareness or "feel" for how to perform a throwing technique.

A major part of teaching the basics is for the coach to instill a good work ethic in beginning students. Good etiquette on the mat (and off) is important. If disciplined and mature behavior is expected and taught from the onset of a judo student's career, this mature approach to learning and training will enable him to better learn more advanced skills of judo. Expressions of respect like bowing on and off the mat and being on time for practice are important basic behaviors that are necessary for success in judo. The old saying "there is no learning without discipline" is true.

Kuzushi: This Judo Stuff Works!

Years ago, one of my young students came to judo practice and excitedly told me, "This judo stuff works!" It was this "judo stuff" that enabled him to throw a neighborhood bully and defend himself. That young student grew up to become a successful judo athlete who continued to prove that "this judo stuff works" against a variety of opponents during his long career. The point of the story is this: judo really does work. It works because it's based on sound mechanical principles as well as on the forces of gravity and how the human body moves based on the forces of gravity. Gravity works and gravity always wins.

Every technique, action, or movement used in judo is based on a core principle: the principle of kuzushi. Kuzushi translates to "breaking" and means controlling an opponent's body and movement, breaking his posture and balance. Kuzushi is the initial action that makes it possible to take further control of an opponent and successfully increase, control, and apply the force necessary to throw an opponent. Every movement in judo is based on kuzushi. Kuzushi is controlling the initiation and direction of force; how you make force happen and where you send or guide that force in order to successfully apply a technique. It's the breaking of an opponent's posture and balance and then taking control of the situation. The principle of kuzushi works both in throwing techniques as well as ground fighting techniques.

Types of Kuzushi

There are six distinct types of movement that create kuzushi, all based on natural body movements. These are the first movements in the initial action of a technique that enable further application of the technique. Every judo technique uses one (or more) of these types of movement. Knowing these elements can be helpful to you when you want to work out some technical answers as to why, how, and when a specific technique works. For the sake of clarity, the term tori (taker or thrower) will be used and uke (receiver of the technique) will be used to explain them.

Explosive and Continuous Force: This is one application of kuzushi where an immediate, sudden, and explosive concerted force flows directly in an accelerated action to break and control uke's balance. After an explosive action that starts an application of force, tori continues to apply that force in a specific direction. Doing this increases the force being applied. Just like a boulder rolling down a hill and increasing its speed as it rolls, a defender's body can be controlled by an initial strong and sudden application of force that can be made stronger by continuous control by the attacker. This form of kuzushi is simple and effective. This application of kuzushi is best illustrated by the Kodokan principle of "happo no kuzushi" where there are eight directions a human body can be moved in order to break and control balance and then apply a technique as momentum is accelerated.

Yielding and Adapting to an Opponent: Pull when an opponent pushes you and push when he pulls you. This is one of the most well-known applications of kuzushi, but it's important to remember that the first part of it (yielding) requires the second part of it (applying your own force) for it to work. This type of kuzushi works well when both the attacker and defender are moving in a straight line. A judoka need only take one step to initiate this action for it to work. In this type of kuzushi, tori will react to uke's movement, and it is the opposite of the next type of kuzushi I describe.

Using a Reaction: This is a situation where a tori will initiate a movement, forcing his opponent to react. When the opponent reacts, tori will adapt to the situation and yield to the opponent's initial force and then move in such a way that he will apply his own force, creating more momentum. By doing this, tori is multiplying force and directing it where he wants it to go. This increased momentum breaks and controls an opponent's balance and enables him to be thrown. In other words, tori does something to make uke react, and when he does, tori takes advantage of the situation. This is called "hando no kuzushi" in Kodokan judo, meaning "break balance by creating a reaction."

Taisabaki-Circular Movement: One of the most popular and effective movement patterns used in judo is taisabaki (moving an opponent in a circular pattern). Taisabaki works because tori moves uke in a circular direction and stands in the middle of the circle. Exactly in the same way the hub of a wheel works, tori acts as the hub. Tori moves in a small circle with uke moving in a wider circle around him. The judoka (tori) moving in the smaller circle has more balanced movement because he is controlling the judoka (uke) moving in a wider circle. A good example is for a judoka to use the taisabaki movement pattern to pull his opponent closer to him and load the opponent up and onto his hip, then apply a throwing technique such as seoi nage (back carry throw) or tai otoshi (body drop).

Upper Body/Lower Body Movement: In this application of kuzushi, the upper half of a judoka's body moves at a different speed and in a different direction than the lower half of his body. One of the most common ways that this application of kuzushi is used in when using foot sweeps, such as okuri ashi barai (send after foot sweep). Tori initiates the action by both judo athletes gripping each other and facing each other with tori moving uke in a lateral (side) direction (with the attacker moving to his right and with the defender moving to his left). As both judo athletes move, momentum increases and the attacker uses his left foot to sweep the defender's right ankle. The defender's feet are swept out from under him quickly. When this happens, uke's feet are moving faster than his upper body is moving; his feet are moving in one direction (to his left side) and his upper body is moving in the opposite direction (to his right side) as his body moves through the air. The uke's body is literally upended and he is thrown off the mat and through the air. What takes place is the velocity of the defender's lower body moves faster than the velocity of his upper body in the opposite direction.

Sacrifice/Body Weight: These are the throwing techniques where the attacker falls to the mat in order to throw his opponent. In Kodokan judo terminology, this type of a technique is called a sutemi waza, which translates to "sacrifice technique." The attacker uses the weight of his body to start the process of kuzushi and "sacrifices" his own body's balance to break and control his opponent's balance. In practical terms, tori will move his body under the center of gravity of uke, using the weight of his own body to break uke's balance, which enables tori to continue to use his body weight to form or develop the technique that will throw the opponent. Tomoe nage (circle throw) is a classic example of using this type of kuzushi. Tori and uke are facing each other with both gripping each other. Tori steps in deeply with his base leg (his right leg) as he swings his hips between uke's legs and deeply under the defender's center of gravity. As he does this, tori places his right foot at uke's waistline to provide a fulcrum that uke will go over. At this point, tori's body is formed in a round position and the weight of his body swinging under uke's body creates the necessary momentum to throw uke forward and over the head and rounded body of the tori.

The Primary Elements of Physical Training in Judo

In any field of study, there must be some kind of structure so that the contents of that particular area of study can be logically understood, taught, learned, and ultimately passed on to others. Additionally, that structure or framework must allow for innovation to take place. It must be fixed yet flexible so that the activity (in this case, judo) has room to grow. Judo has such a framework and is comprised of three physical (and a fourth mental) fundamental elements that have not changed to any significant degree since judo's founder Professor Jigoro Kano conceived them. These elements are kata, randori, and shiai. Like any other vital activity, expansion of the original ideas has added to the effectiveness of both the technical aspect of judo and to the teaching of judo, but Professor Kano's original theories and concepts have stood the test of time and provide a useful framework for teaching and learning judo. Like any form of physical education, judo has taken on and included new things, yet it's managed to retain the original concepts that make it unique. When Professor Kano introduced these ideas in the late nineteenth and early twentieth centuries, they were groundbreaking in terms of teaching jujutsu and martial arts. Jigoro Kano was heavily influenced by Western concepts of education and used them in formulating a core methodology in the teaching and learning of judo. These three elements are present in every form of physical education and sport, not just judo, and provide a good blueprint for how to get the most out of your training.

Kata

The first element is kata. Kata is structured training. The word "kata" means "form or shape." In a practical sense, kata is structured learning and is any movement or activity designed to increase performance in a skill. Early in judo's history, Professor Kano realized that a systematic, structured approach to developing technical skill was necessary. His answer was kata and the structure it brought to training. His approach to kata included the historical approach of feudal jujutsu where kata was the repository of the techniques of a particular jujutsu school and took the concept further. Kano was rightly critical of the poor training methods used in the jujutsu schools of Japan during the late 1800s. His goal was to replace these crude teaching methods with a systematic and orderly methodology that would prove to be more efficient and effective. That systematic methodology is kata.

There are ten recognized kata in Kodokan judo. Each has a specific purpose that enhances learning in that specific area of judo. These are drills that are used to develop the technical skill as well as understanding of how the technical skill should be used for the person doing them. To many people, kata is something a person must do as a requirement for a rank promotion, or it's used for demonstration purposes. But kata wasn't intended to be a demonstration. It's a means of exploring all aspects of learning technical skills and how they should be applied in judo and in teaching it in an organized way. Kata also provides the structured training necessary for learning judo systematically and effectively, not only explaining how a technique works but also why it works.

Using the concept of kata for its functional application, any drill or exercise that provides structured, organized learning and skill enhancement for the student is a kata. Most, if not all, sports have some kind of kata. The structured and systematic learning (kata) describes the drill training used in other forms of sport and physical education. Compare kata, randori, and shiai used in judo to the sport of football. In a football practice, the coach runs the players through various drills. Some drills emphasize skill development, others emphasize physical fitness, while still others are situational where the team rehearses the actual plays they will use in a game. This is kata (structured training and learning) in every sense of the word. The team will also scrimmage during practice, giving them a chance to try out what they have rehearsed in the drills. Some scrimmages are more controlled than others, depending on the needs of the team. This is randori. On Saturday, the team plays in an actual game against an opposing team. This is the test (shiai) for both teams. The point here is that every form of physical education or sport, judo included, relies on kata, randori, and shiai; and it is kata that provides the structure necessary for the other two elements to be successful.

Randori

The second element is randori. Randori is free practice. This is the phase of training where judo athletes can freely attack and defend. Randori is training, not a contest. It's a time when an athlete can experiment with new techniques or refine old ones. Randori is like a controlled scrimmage in football. A coach or senior team member should always supervise randori.

Jujutsu, which is the forerunner of Kodokan judo, emphasized the use of "kaho" or the method of training that relied strictly on the use of kata. The rough and tumble techniques of the many jujutsu schools made it all but impossible to practice them in any form other than a pre-arranged series of movements. There was no such thing as randori in most jujutsu schools. According to martial arts historian and author Donn Draeger in his book *Modern Bujutsu and Budo*, when Professor Kano studied Kito-ryu jujutsu, he was introduced to what was called "ran o toru," which means "to take freedom of action." The word "ran" means something that is disorderly or random; in other words, the opposite of "kata," which represents structured form. While kata emphasizes structure of movement, randori emphasizes freedom of movement. This was a form of training that developed into what we now recognize as randori. This concept of "ran" or "freedom" that he learned from the Kito school led to his concept of "randori" or "free exercise."

While randori is an enjoyable aspect of training and often takes up a good portion of a judoka's training time, if judo athletes limit their training to doing only randori, they are limiting themselves severely in their technical development. One needs kata (form or structured training) to learn and refine the skills necessary to be able to effectively use randori as a method of training. Likewise, judo athletes need randori (free practice) to learn how to put their techniques to work in a functional and practical way. So, in a very real sense, kata and randori depend on each other to provide a well-balanced approach to learning and training in judo. There are times in training where a judo athlete emphasizes randori and may have practices made up entirely of randori, but this is part of an overall development program and shouldn't be the only method of training. Simply making it a habit of showing up to the dojo and only doing "fighting judo" won't make anyone a complete judoka and certainly won't make anyone an elite-level judo athlete. It's the same as a football team only scrimmaging in practice and never learning their plays.

For everyone to have the most productive (and safe) training experience, there are some basic rules everyone should observe when doing randori: 1. Randori is training. It's not a tournament. Look for the people on the mat who will make you work hard and extend yourself. Don't look for the people you can beat. The only way you will improve is to train those who will push you and make you better. That said, it's also important to randori with people of equal skill and experience as you. This is where you will find a good opportunity to see what your strong points are as well as your weak points. 2. Every round of randori should have a purpose. In each round of randori, make it a point to have some aspect of your technical or tactical skills that you want to emphasize. 3. There are different types of randori and some are more intense than others. This goes along with having a specific purpose for each round of randori. 4. Randori should always be supervised by a coach or senior member of the club or team. 5. Do not beat up on your training partners. Take care of each other. The best piece of training equipment in a dojo is a good training partner. Always remember that if you get a reputation for beating people up, you will quickly run out of training partners, and there will always be somebody tougher than you. 6. Don't limit your randori training to only standing work. Make sure you work both standing techniques and ground techniques. 7. If the mat is crowded, watch out for others so that you don't crash into them while workout out. 8. Randori is dependent on other structured training such as kata and drill training. Doing only randori doesn't provide the technical well-rounded training needed for skillful judo. 9. Listen to the advice of your training partners as well as your coach. Sometimes, the best coach you can have on the mat is a good training partner. 10. There are times when randori gets intense. Don't lose your temper and never show anger or emotion during training. Everyone, at one or more times in his or her career, takes a beating in randori. If someone is giving you cheap shots, give them back. Don't expect every training partner to be a nice guy. Anyone who has ever trained seriously in judo knows there are some training rooms and some training camps where randori gets intense. If you are known as someone who gets emotional, it can be like sharks attracted to blood in the water. This is why a rule of randori is that it should be supervised by a coach. A good coach will stop a problem as it develops, but if there's no coach to supervise what's going on, it's up to you to be mature enough to handle yourself and the situation.

Randori should be enjoyed. Mixing it up on the mat is fun. It's been said that "randori is cheaper than a psychiatrist." Randori is indeed a really a good way to release frustration and go home after practice sweaty and in a better mood.

Shiai

The third element is shiai. Shiai is the testing of oneself. The phrase is made up of two Japanese words. "Shi" means "to test" and "ai" means to mutually meet. It's generally accepted that a shiai is a competition, but the word implies "testing" more than simply fighting or competing. Participating in a judo tournament is certainly a test of a person's physical, mental, and emotional abilities. The stress of competition tests anyone taking part in it. Most judo tournaments aren't an isolated bout or fight where a judoka faces only one opponent but often a day-long affair where a judoka must be prepared to face multiple opponents. Each opponent provides a new challenge. So, realistically speaking, a judo tournament really is a test.

Jigoro Kano believed that the character of each of his students was the ultimate "shiai" or test. The idea of "kogi" judo, or a total approach to the study of Kodokan judo, was the goal of Kodokan judo rather than "kyogi" judo, or the exclusive sport-combat approach to training. So while standing on top of the podium is the immediate goal, becoming a stronger, better human is the ultimate goal. The process of training and competing (and all the effort and sacrifice that come with it) is the vehicle to become something better than what you started out as. This is why it's called shiai: it really is a test and not simply a game or a fight.

A Word About Mondo

There is a fourth element in the education of a judoka called mondo. Mondo translates to having a dialogue and is often used as a question-and-answer period, usually held during the end of a training session. Mondo isn't included in the physical aspects of training but instead is the mental preparation necessary for success in judo. For a competitive judo athlete, mondo can include studying video of opponents and discussing strategy and tactics with his or her coach.

Winning at the sport of judo relies on a firm foundation. An athlete's development is taken in steps, not leaps and bounds. These physical elements of kata, randori, and shiai (along with the mental preparation of mondo) form the philosophical and educational underpinning for successful judo. A program of structured training and learning, interspersed with a good amount of free practice and, once in a while, a test to see how well the progress is coming along, is a good formula for success as a judo athlete.

Judo Isn't Gentle

The phrase "judo" is often interpreted to mean "gentle way." But to paraphrase the great martial arts writer Donn Draeger, "Judo isn't gentle." What it is (as is the case in any martial discipline that uses the principle of ju, such a jujitsu) is adaptable, flexible, using strength in the most efficient way possible, yielding when necessary, and then applying force when it's needed. Gentle is, indeed, one of the meanings of the word ju (as are the above-mentioned words as well), but it's taken "ju" too far out of context and has implied that the activity (and the sport) of judo is "gentle," which it isn't. As Donn Draeger stated in his book *Modern Bujutsu and Budo*, "When the principle of ju is wrongly interpreted, there is an obvious conflict between theory and practice. In many ways, these erroneous opinions still influence modern day judo..." One of these erroneous opinions is that physical strength or fitness isn't necessary for "good technique." On the contrary, good technique relies on speed, strength, flexibility, excellent coordination, and cardio-vascular fitness (among other things). Good technique doesn't develop in a vacuum. It's the result of hard physical and mental effort. A physically fit body will have better judo technique than a body that's not physically fit.

The concept of "ju" also implies a lot more than simply yielding or using an opponent's strength against him. It's also using one's own strength in the most efficient way possible under given circumstances. It's being prepared to use strength when necessary. Not brute force, but force that is best suited to getting results. Geof Gleeson, in his book *All About Judo*, contends that ju has an even wider meaning. Control of a situation and how to best assess a situation are factors that make up ju. These have direct implications for winning in competitive judo. A successful athlete must make the best assessment of a situation (through coaching, training, and experience) and then control the situation so it's advantageous to him. Professor Kano was influenced greatly by his training in the Tenjin Shinyo school of jujutsu where the body is subordinate to the mind, which makes it necessary for the mind to be flexible and able adapt to any given situation, which, in turn, enables the body to be flexible and able to adapt as well. This ties in directly with Gleeson's view of ju.

Judo, by its very nature, is eclectic, adaptable, and functional. Without a doubt, the concept of ju implies a functional approach of using what it takes to get the job done. It's utilitarian in nature. Ju is using an opponent's strength, movement, balance, mental capacity, emotional state, the rules of the sport, or anything else against him and using your own strength, movement, balance, mental capacity, emotional state, and knowledge of the rules to give you the edge and defeat him. The concept of ju is neither good or bad; it's simply a tool. If you understand it and use it in a competitive judo match better than your opponent, you will most likely beat him. If he uses it better than you, he'll beat you.

Technique and Skill: Function Dictates Form

We often hear the phrase that a person has "good technique." What that really means is that the person is skillful in applying a technique. The words technique and skill are often used in the same way with little thought as to what each word actually means, but it's important to know the difference and how they are connected with each other. A technique is a particular movement or series of movements in judo. Skill is how you make a particular technique work for you and is the practical application of a technique. The goal for anyone who wants to be successful in judo is to have effective skill when applying techniques with a high rate of success against fit, resisting, and skilled opponents.

Technique: A technique is a distinct movement pattern in and of itself and is the structure, shape, form, or appearance of a movement. Much like a frame of a house that has a distinct look or design, a technique has a distinct look or design. It's the generally accepted way of performing a throw, hold, choke, or armlock.

For instance, when someone thinks of o soto gari (major outer reaping throw), a specific, distinct movement comes to mind that everyone recognizes as that particular throw. However, there are so many ways of performing o soto gari in so many situations by so many different people that the throw often takes on a new shape and purpose depending on the size or strength level of who applies it and the circumstances where and when it's applied. All the factors that make up how the thrower actually applies the technique (and the success of his efforts) determine how skillful the whole action really is.

Skill: If a technique is done skillfully, it's done in the most efficient manner possible to achieve the goal at hand or get the job done. This is how a technique, which is a distinct movement pattern, in and of itself, becomes a skill. Because of this, the aesthetics of the technique are determined by its function and by its success. Scores in the sport of judo are awarded based solely on effectiveness and results. We don't get style points like they do in some other sports. So, if beauty is in the eye of the beholder, a skill that works looks a whole lot better than one that doesn't. Because of this, function dictates form. The bottom line is that if a movement isn't functional, it should be modified so that it is. There must be a practical and functionally efficient reason for every movement of the body when performing a skill in judo. If a movement of any type is done only for aesthetics, then there is no reason to perform it if you want to win on a consistent basis against skilled, fit, and resisting opponents. Shawn Watson, one of my most successful (and skillful) athletes, once remarked, "It's only pretty if it works!" In addition to being effective in competition or randori, applying a technique with efficient skill gives a judoka a satisfying feeling. Doing something well is a reward in itself.

Skill Mastery: When it's said that a judoka has mastery of skill in a specific technique or movement, it doesn't imply that the person is a high-ranking judo sensei. Mastery means that the person has a proficient and practical ability to apply a particular technique or movement. To have mastery of a skill is to have command over all of the parts, as well as the whole, of a particular technique. For example, a judoka can have mastery of skill in uchi mata (inner thigh throw) but not have the same level of skill in another technique. Every experienced judo athlete has his own "style," and in order for a person to be good enough to have his own style, he must have a mastery of skill in a variety of different technical areas. Later in this section, there will be an examination of how to develop your own style as a judo athlete. Judoka can be said to have "mastered a skill" when they can consistently perform a technique or movement in the most efficient way and under conditions similar to an actual judo match and do it with a high rate of success. Repeating something, anything, creates a habit, and doing something habitually creates permanence. Permanence means that a specific method of applying a specific technique is fixed in the athlete's brain. Both practical experience and sports science say that it takes 10,000 repetitions or hours to create permanence in a technique or movement. Whether the exact number 10,000 is accurate or not depends entirely on the individual circumstances of an athlete. It may not take exactly10,000 repetitions or hours of training for skill mastery, but there is no doubt that it takes thousands of repetitions and hours of focused practice for mastery of skill in anything, especially a technically complex sport like judo. So, for mastery of a judo technique, the key is to create permanence through the most efficient application of the skill that the judoka wants to master and then repeat it correctly thousands of times.

Tacit Knowledge: In acquiring any kind of skill or set of skills, especially in a technically complex sport like judo, something called tacit (or unspoken) knowledge is developed; it's a "feeling" that is hard to explain or put into words and is easier to demonstrate than explain. This is one aspect of an old judo adage called "feel your judo." There will be more on feeling your judo in the next section and other parts of this book. But suffice it to say here that people learn by watching and imitating what others show to them and then repeat it over and over. The human brain is suited for this type of learning. This is why it's important for a coach to teach a beginner the most mechanically efficient (correct) way of doing a technique.

As stated previously, a correctly performed technique that is repeated thousands of times become a habit and permanently fixed in the brain. A good way for an aspiring judo athlete to think about learning skills is that it's "on-the-job training." There is a similarity between a beginning and intermediate judoka (brown belt and lower) and an apprentice in a trade or craft. The apprentice learns from the journeyman or master craftsman, watching and repeating what he is taught. After thousands of hours of on-the-job learning, the apprentice develops the practical skill and knowledge to become a journeyman. This is very much the case in learning judo.

Develop Good Habits: Someone can have good skill when doing a technique or have bad skill when doing a technique, so the word "skill" doesn't always refer to an efficient movement or a good result. It simply defines how the technique is applied and performed. This is why learning the correct and most biomechanically efficient method of basic skills is so important early in a judoka's career. When people perform a movement repeatedly, it becomes a habit. A habit is an acquired behavior pattern that has become an involuntary behavior or automatic response. A habit can be good or bad. Bad habits are hard to break, and the time and effort in correcting them impedes an athlete's future technical development. This is why developing good habits early in a judoka's career is essential for progressing to more advanced levels of skill development.

Risk Factors: Some techniques are riskier than others. Throwing techniques such as tai otoshi (body drop) where the attacker has both feet on the mat are less risky than techniques where one leg supports the attacker's body, like uchi mata (inner thigh throw). A judo athlete must weigh the risk factors. A throw like uchi mata is popular because it is so adaptable and has such a strong ballistic effect. This high impact of attacking an opponent with uchi mata often overshadows the risk factor of attacking an opponent even though the thrower is standing on only one leg. So a judo athlete must consider the risks involved when selecting the technique he chooses to use as well as the pattern of movement used in applying this technique.

Precision Judo

In the same way an archer attempts to hit the bullseye with an arrow, a judoka wants to execute his techniques with skill and precision. Judo techniques applied in a functionally efficient manner are what my great friend and fellow coach Bob Corwin called "precise judo." From the very start of a judoka's study in judo, the focus should be placed on skillful technical development. Precise judo is achieved for a judo athlete when the basic application of a technique is learned correctly and adapted to work in the most efficient (and precise) way possible for the person doing it. Don't take short-cuts in learning and developing techniques. Doing something "good enough" takes only minimum effort. Minimum effort always leads to minimal results. Pay attention to details. The great basketball coach John Wooden said, "Small things make big things happen." This describes what precision judo is. To a judo athlete, a judo technique is the same as a bow is to the archer. It's a tool, and if the tool needs to be modified to get an optimal result, then it is important to modify it so it works as reliably and precisely as possible.

"Feel Your Judo"

As I mentioned above, there is an old phrase that says a good judoka will "feel his judo." This is what is known as kinesthetic awareness. It's a person's ability to sense the movement and position of his own body and sense the movement of an opponent's body. When a person tenses or compresses the muscles, the muscles communicate sensory information about movement, body space, and posture. This ability to feel your judo comes from performing skills thousands of times. Repetition leads to an automatic reflex or response that can be enhanced to the point of an almost intuitive response (what this author calls an advanced automatic response). The definition of an intuitive response is a response to some type of stimulus without involving thought or reason. In other words, it's doing something without thinking about it like scratching your face when it itches. An intuitive response can be either good or bad. In some things in life, it's best to go with your intuition, but often in sports (especially a technically complex sport like judo), it isn't often the best thing to do without sufficient training.

Learning how to perform a technical skill correctly and then repeating it thousands of times (and in a variety of situations) produces an automatic response or reflex. An automatic reflex is a trained reaction to a situation so that the person reacts in the optimal (efficient and effective) way to that situation. Repetition of a movement enables a person to have a heightened sense of awareness and permits him to instantly determine if a movement is efficient or not. This is an advanced automatic response and is the reason a skilled judoka will "feel" his judo. As mentioned above, it's generally accepted that it takes somewhere around 10,000 repetitions of a movement for it to become an advanced automatic reflex. That's why the jazz musician Miles Davis, Jr. said, "You have to play a long time to be able to play like yourself."

Reading an Opponent

Kinesthetic awareness also permits a judo athlete to "read" an opponent, based on both the judo athlete's visual (what he sees) as well as tactile (what he feels) observation. For those who have been around judo long enough, the ability to read or anticipate what an opponent will do is developed. Just as a baseball player can "see the stitches of a baseball," a judoka can see how an opponent moves and calculate his or her best response to that movement. Based on the movement patterns, posture, pace, and tempo of movement, a judoka can anticipate how and when an opponent will move. This is a critically important skill when scouting an opponent and something every serious judo coach should strive to develop. So it's a good idea to watch a lot of judo both in person and by watching videos and develop the skill of "reading" an opponent.

Ukemi: Safety in Throwing

Ukemi, the method of breaking falls and landing safely, is a time-tested and valuable set of skills. Jigoro Kano literally invented the concept of taking falls safely in practice. Prior to Kano, jujutsu had no formal method of landing or being thrown without injury. Another method of safety is having good partners in training and being a good partner in training. Cooperative training partners are important in developing well-executed throws (as well as any phase of judo). Being able to land safely gives you more confidence that you won't be injured when taking a hard fall. If you haven't learned how to fall safely, make sure you learn good breakfalls before attempting any of the skills presented in this book. From a competitive point of view, knowing how to safely, turn out, turn in, or otherwise escape from being thrown is an important skill, but a skill that is reserved for advanced judo athletes. Cartwheels, roundoffs, and other tumbling skills are helpful in learning how to keep from being thrown on the back. However, before an athlete attempts these skills, he must learn and master ukemi and be skilled and confident in flying through the air from an opponent's throwing technique. A word of caution is necessary at this point. Never land in a bridge position (arching the back and landing on the head and feet) when being thrown. A trophy isn't worth a broken neck.

There are those who believe that teaching judo athletes to do ukemi is the same as teaching a football player to get tackled. "Breakfalls teach losing" is a phrase that has been used by some coaches in past years, and while the focus of this book is about being successful at competitive judo, knowing how to land safely when thrown is important. Just about every viable form of sport or physical education has a safety factor so that the sport can be practiced with a minimum of injury. Judo is no exception. Additionally, when you practice throwing with a partner who is confident, relaxed, and can take a good fall, you will perform your throw better and get more benefit from the training session.

Crash Pads: Another Layer of Safety in Throwing

Along with skill in ukemi, using crash pads significantly reduces the number of injuries in training. In addition to providing a softer landing for athletes when taking hard falls, using crash pads permits judo athletes to throw each other with full force and to do more repetitions in training. The use of crash pads has grown in popularity over the years and now just about every good dojo has one or more crash pads that are used on a regular basis. There are numerous drills that can be used for throwing on crash pads, but whatever drills are used, the real advantage of crash pads is that a judoka can do more throws, do them with full force, and do them safely.

Making Your Judo Work for You: Developing Your Own Style

It doesn't matter what the activity or subject is, we human beings have a capacity to adapt something and personalize it so that it works best for the person doing it. This is what "style" is about. It takes quite a bit of time, experimentation, and thought for an athlete to develop his own style and way of doing judo so that it works for him on a regular basis. The best way to find out what techniques work best for you is to learn the basics and spend a lot of time developing them in randori. When developing your own style, here are some things to consider.

"Trial and Error": The best way to develop your style or refine what you already have is by trial and error. Experiment in the dojo and be open to trying anything that will help you. A good way to use this trial-and-error approach is the subject of the next item.

Randori: Often, the best way to find out which techniques work for you is to do a lot of randori. Randori permits a judo athlete to be creative and explore new things. What takes place is that you will find a technique that feels like a natural fit during randori training. From this initial "feel" you can develop that technique a bit more and do some more randori and try it out. Finding a technique that seems and feels natural is much like finding the right spouse. It may take some trial and error to find something that works or it may occur and develop more quickly.

Input from Coaches and Teammates: Sometimes, the best "coach" a judo athlete can have is a teammate who offers good advice. Ask fellow teammates, as well as coaches, for their input on how you are progressing.

Fitness Level Affects Judo Style: An important factor in determining your own style is your physical fitness. Elite-level judo is not possible with an unfit body. Judo techniques aren't magic; they are based on biomechanical principles. In order for the human body to apply complex and skilled techniques against fit, resisting, and skilled opposition, it must be physically capable of doing it. The stronger and fitter a judo athlete is, the better his or her technical skill is. The foundation of technical skill is fitness. An athlete doesn't rise to the occasion; he rises to his level of preparation.

Be Honest: Be honest with yourself about your strengths and weaknesses and be realistic in finding what works best for you. If you are not naturally gifted in quick reflexes or fast foot speed, work on improving these areas, but at the same time, develop skill in techniques that develop from a slower pace or tempo. Improve the physical attributes you lack and develop a range of technical skills that work best given your level of physical ability.

Things Change: What may work for a judo athlete at an early stage of his career may not work for him at a later stage of his career. Injuries often determine how a judoka adapts his style. That slick foot sweep you once had may not be so slick after several knee surgeries, so if you want to continue to compete, you will have to adapt and find something to replace the technique that isn't working any longer.

Changes in the contest rules are something else to consider when developing your own style. After the International Judo Federation changed the rules and no longer allowed grabbing or touching an opponent's legs, judo athletes had to adapt to the new rules and either modify the techniques they were using or discard them in favor of something else.

Success Determines Style: Another factor in determining your personal style is your own success. If it becomes common knowledge that you use a specific technique with regular success, your opposition will eventually learn this and adapt to it. This means that if you intend to continue to use that technique, you will have to add something to it. This is what is called "adding layers" to your judo. An example of adding layers is that your opponent knows you have a strong uchi mata (inner thigh throw) and they adapt by defending against it. You now must add some layers to that uchi mata in order to be successful with it again. One way is to use another technique as a combination or feint in order to hit in with your uchi mata. Another layer that can be added is to change the way you grip your opponent or use a different movement pattern to set up your uchi mata.

Weighing the Risks: A judo athlete must weigh the risk factors in deciding how he wants to develop his judo style. Some techniques are riskier than others. Throwing techniques such as tai otoshi (body drop) where the attacker has both feet on the mat are less risky than techniques where one leg supports the attacker's body such as uchi mata (inner thigh throw). A throw like uchi mata is popular because it is so adaptable and can end the match quickly, with the opponent thrown flat on his back. This high impact involved in attacking an opponent with uchi mata often overcomes the risk that comes with attacking an opponent even though the thrower is standing on only one leg. It's a matter of weighing the risks against the rewards.

Personality in Judo: The personality of a judo athlete often determines the style of judo he uses during a match. My good friend John Saylor once said, "No matter where you go, you always take yourself with you." This is certainly true in judo, because you take yourself, which includes your personality, on the judo mat when you compete. Judo style is often a reflection of the judo athlete's perspective in life. People who are risk-takers in their daily lives are often risk-takers in a judo match. A risk-taker doesn't have to have an outgoing personality; there are quiet people who like to gamble and take risks just as much as outgoing people. However, an outgoing personality often does have a wide-open style of judo when competing. On the other hand, dour people generally have a pedantic or overly careful style of judo when competing. Those who have analytical minds often have an analytical approach to competing in judo; and these people often make good coaches later in their careers.

Be Open-Minded: Be open to trying anything that will improve your judo. When developing your own style, don't do conventional things. Experiment in practice to see what works for you and don't be afraid to change something so that it does work for you. If a variation of a technique is based on sound biomechanical principles and it works for you, then do it. If you only follow conventional wisdom, you will only get conventional results.

Rate of Success

An important factor for every judo athlete is the rate of success of what he is doing. This is the frequency and regularity with which a technique has a successful outcome. If a technique or movement often results in a score or leads to a scoring situation, that technique or movement has a high rate of success. It's doing the right thing at the right time during a judo match.

A judo athlete may have a specific technique that he uses in a specific situation with good results and he knows he can count on it when he needs it. Finding what to do in a specific situation or which technique works best for that situation takes time and effort. A good way to determine what works best in specific situations is, during randori, to be mentally aware of what you do in specific situations. Take videos of your matches to see how you react to situations, and work on what you can do to gain the advantage in that situation. This is similar to having a tokui waza or "preferred technique" in a specific situation. This is a skill or series of skills that are your "go to" moves and have a high rate of success when you use them. The rate of success plays a key role in the tactics you will use in a match. If you know you can count on a specific technique or movement in a specific situation, then you can work to create that situation during a judo match.

Tokui Waza Is Plural

As discussed elsewhere in this book, the phrase "tokui waza" translates to favorite or preferred technique. But it's rare for a successful judo athlete to have only one tokui waza. Think of your tokui waza as a plural rather than a singular thing. A judo athlete will usually have a tokui waza for a particular situation or may even adapt his tokui to a specific opponent. Whatever an athlete's tokui waza may be, there have to be a variety of different ways to apply it. For example, a successful judo athlete may win a lot of matches with juji gatame (crossbody armlock), but he or she will have more than only one way to get opponents in position in order to apply juji gatame. The juji gatame is the end product of what people see. What people often fail to see is how, when, and why that tokui waza works and works with a high rate of success.

It takes planning for a tokui waza to work. A good way to think about developing your tokui waza is to imagine that it's the hub or center of a wheel. Each spoke that comes from that hub is a situation or a follow-up technique comes naturally as a result of your tokui waza. Again, let's say that your tokui waza (hub in the wheel) is juji gatame; one spoke will then be how to apply juji gatame if your opponent is in the turtle position on all fours. Another spoke will be how to apply juji gatame if your opponent is lying flat on his front. Yet another spoke in the wheel is how to finish your opponent with juji gatame after throwing him. There may be a lot of spokes in your wheel or there may be a few, but the point is that every tokui waza is the result of a series of events or situations that take place in a judo match.

The Tactics for Tokui Waza: Tactically, a successful judo athlete will have a tokui waza for a specific situation. So, it's important to make that situation happen as often as possible in order to apply his tokui waza.

Let's say that you have an effective ko uchi makikomi (minor inner wrapping throw) that works well for you on a regular basis. Let's analyze why. What are the conditions or situations that are in place when you throw your opponent with ko uchi makikomi? What grip are you using? What direction is your opponent moving? How fast is the pace of the action? Which hip are you leading with? What stance is your opponent in when you attack? At what point during the match does your ko uchi makikomi best work; is it immediately after gripping your opponent's jacket or is it after you have attacked with another throw?

The next step is to get on the mat with your coach and teammates and work on creating the situation or situations that make this throw happen, and then drill on them so that you make them happen on a regular basis. The next step is to work on creating these situations in randori against a variety of training partners. After this, work on creating these situations so they happen in local and regional competition. At this point, it's time to use your ko uchi makikomi against opponents of equal skill and fitness in national and international competition.

Be Adaptable with Tokui Waza: You may have to adapt a technique based on what takes place during a match or who your opponent might be. An example of this is that your tokui waza is juji gatame, and when opponents are positioned on all fours in groundfighting, you may prefer to roll opponents in one direction to secure the armlock. But in the course of rolling an opponent over, he resists in such a way that you have to reverse the direction of the roll and take him the other way.

Another way of adapting your tokui waza is that you may use a particular throwing technique as your tokui waza but have the ability to use it on both the right and left sides. Here's an example of what I mean. One of my athletes used uchi mata as his tokui waza.

He won a lot of matches with it. One of the reasons he won a lot of matches with it was because he would use it equally well as a right-handed throw as well as a left-handed throw. But what really confused his competition was that the uchi mata he used from his right side differed from the uchi mata he used from his left side. The right-sided uchi mata was more of a "classic" lifting-pulling type throw and his left-sided uchi mata was more of a leg-style spinning attack. Based on what his opponent during the match, he would attack with either the right side or left side.

Another way of adapting your tokui waza is to use it in combination with another technique, either using the additional technique as a setup for your tokui waza or using your tokui waza to set up the other technique. An example is that your tokui waza is ko uchi makikomi (minor inner wrapping) and you use ippon seoi nage (one-arm back carry throw) as a fake attack to elicit a response from your opponent. As your opponent avoids the initial ippon seoi nage attack, you use ko uchi makikomi to throw him.

Strategy and Tactics

Strategy is your overall plan, and tactics are how you make that overall plan work. Strategy is a more concrete plan of what you want to achieve, and tactics are more fluid with respect to how you go about achieving it. Strategy and tactics depend on each other. A strategy is only as good as the tactics used to make it happen. But tactics without a strategy are nothing more than reacting to what your opponent does. A successful strategy is determined by your strengths and weaknesses; it should stress your strengths and limit your opponent's chances to exploit your weaknesses. For example, suppose you have a high rate of success using foot sweeps. For these foot sweeps to be used, you must create and maintain a fast tempo of action during the course of the match. Because you like to use foot sweeps using a fast tempo, your cardio-vascular fitness is excellent. Knowing this, your strategy is to attack often with foot sweeps and, in doing so, deplete your opponent's energy.

So, tactically, you will set a fast tempo for the match and attack with a foot sweep at least once every twenty seconds. In your training leading up to this tournament, you know that even if your foot sweep doesn't throw your opponent but only takes him to his knees, you are skilled at following through and transitioning into a pin or armlock from this situation. Going back to your strategy, now suppose you have a back-up plan by using your foot sweeps as an initial action in order to elicit a response from your opponents. You also know you have a strong uchi mata (inner thigh throw). Tactically, this is achieved by faking a foot sweep in order to get your opponent to react by moving the foot you have attacked, and as he does, you attack him with your uchi mata. So, even if you are a novice, know what you want to do and how you want to do it every time you enter a tournament.

Enthusiasm Breeds Success

Before someone becomes a champion, he must *want* to become a champion, and for a person to excel at anything, he must first want to participate in judo and enjoy it. Enthusiasm is the seed that grows into the desire to achieve success.

Enthusiasm will take someone a long way. The initial enthusiasm of starting and studying judo develops into a new level of enthusiasm that enables a person to pursue judo on a more advanced level. It's rare that someone walks onto a judo mat for the first time with the intention of becoming an elite-level judoka. What takes place is a growth in the level of enthusiasm that leads a person to progress to more advanced levels. Enthusiasm is the mental and emotional desire required to take something to the next level, and that next level is the physical act of participation. The physical and mental act of participating in an activity, especially a physically challenging activity like judo, is where a person's enthusiasm is first tested. At each step along the way, a judoka's enthusiasm and growing desire for advancement are the determining factors of his or her success.

It takes a conscious and deliberate decision to pursue judo as a competitive sport. People who are good at judo enjoy doing difficult things. To become a champion in judo, a person takes this attitude to an even higher level of enthusiasm (one that may not be shared by family or friends). In the United States, judo champions get little (if any) public recognition. It's different in other countries such Japan, France, Korea, and elsewhere, but even in these countries where judo is popular, other sports such as football (soccer) offer greater rewards, both financially and in terms of public recognition. So, a judo athlete's initial enthusiasm is often tested by the fact that success in judo won't bring a great deal of public recognition. Realize that this is a maturing process that enables a judo athlete to place personal satisfaction over public recognition. As a judo athlete, you may not become rich or famous, so it's even more important to love what you are doing.

This is being discussed here because it's important that everyone who aspires to be a champion in judo should understand a basic fact of life in judo: the life of a judo athlete can be difficult. Every judo athlete must make a personal assessment of himself on a regular basis, and it is that tremendously important element of enthusiasm that keeps a person going.

Humility Is the Seed of Success

If there is one attribute absolutely necessary for success in judo, it's humility. Humility is the virtue that is the underpinning of all the others, such as enthusiasm, discipline, and being honest with oneself. A humble athlete who is honest with himself is more capable of objectively recognizing what he needs to improve and then doing what is necessary to achieve it. It's the ability for a person to put things in perspective both on and off the mat. This perspective is the ability of an athlete to identify both his weak points as well as his strong points and is based on a foundation of humility.

Discipline is the outgrowth of humility and is necessary for success not just in a demanding sport like judo but in any aspect of life. Discipline is another way of saying "self-control." It's a learned habit. It is the ability to control one's emotions, thoughts, and actions. When we are children, it is our family and teachers who teach us discipline. As we grow older and mature, we learn how to use and apply self-control. It's this self-control that dictates how we conduct our lives, both on and off the mat. Few sports are as difficult as judo, which requires a widely diverse set of technical skills and requirements for physical conditioning. The training regimen a judo athlete must follow for success at any level of judo requires an immense level of discipline.

Humility is also what makes us keep life in perspective and teaches us that just because we are accomplished at one thing doesn't mean we are accomplished at everything. A person may be a national judo champion and a fifth-degree black belt, but when he needs his car repaired or needs medical attention, he goes to the people who are accomplished in those fields. That black belt or gold medal won't fix a car or mend a broken arm.

Humility is not the same as being weak-willed. We all make mistakes and must learn from them. A person can be humbled by personal misfortune and yet have the capacity to use the experience to do what is necessary to make improvements. A weak-willed person will simply accept his fate and try to prevent it from happening again or simply give up and do something else.

Confidence is a direct result of humility. Like discipline, confidence is a learned trait. Confidence is not the same thing as being cocky, arrogant, or boastful. It's the result of many hours of being on the mat and honestly making the effort to improve. Confidence is believing in yourself even if others don't.

Judo is a great way to learn humility. Everyone who has ever done judo for any length of time knows that the pounding we take in randori keeps a person humble. There's always someone on the mat willing to serve us a slice of humble pie by throwing us repeatedly.

The One More Willing

A judo match is a test of willpower. A story from the Old West makes this point well. Bat Masterson was a famous lawman in America's Wild West days and was the subject of many popular dime novels that told of the exploits of famous lawmen and outlaws. One time, an author of one of these dime novels asked Bat Masterson what gave him the edge over the bad guys he had dispatched in his career as a lawman. "Was it your fast draw? Was it your aim?" asked the writer. Bat Masterson answered, "It's not that I'm faster than my opponent, and it's not that I have better aim. I'm just more willing." What Bat Masterton meant was that he was more willing to do what was necessary to win the duel. A judo contest may not be a duel on the dusty streets of the Old West, but it is still a duel and a test of wills. A judo athlete must be more willing than his or her competition to do what's necessary to win.

Make your judo work for you.

—Maurice Allan

CHAPTER 3

Factors of Success

This section of the book focuses on the factors that make for a solid foundation of technical and tactical skill in competitive judo. The previous chapter stressed the importance of basics and this chapter will examine how each judo athlete can adapt and personalize the basics to work in the most effective way for him.

Judo Is Gripping and Movement

Fundamentally, judo is a contest of gripping and movement. If you control the grip, you control the movement. While there are unlimited permutations of what can take place in a judo match, it really all comes down to gripping and movement. The athlete who has the better grip will control how his opponent moves around the mat. This is what I call "control judo."

The basic strategy of control judo has two tactical applications: 1. Control and nullify an opponent's ability to move about the mat freely and prevent him from launching an attack. Shut him down as much as possible. 2. Increase your ability to move about the mat freely and increase your ability to launch your attack. In other words, make your opponent fight your kind of fight. Control and nullify his movement. Prevent him from getting the grip he wants. By doing this, you increase your chances of doing what you want in the match. Effective grip fighting limits your opponent's mobility and his ability to fight the kind of match he wants to fight.

In any field of endeavor, whether it's a judo contest, a business operation or armies fighting in a war, a basic precept of every successful judoka, businessman, or general is to control and limit an adversary's ability to be successful. The ultimate goal for a judo athlete is to be able to be as free as possible to apply his skills and win the contest. To do this, he must be physically and mentally fit enough to accomplish the task as well as be technically skilled enough to accomplish the task. But just as important, he must make sure that his opponent doesn't have the opportunity to apply his skills. By no means is this to imply that an athlete resorts to cheating. It means that a key factor of success in a combat sport like judo, an athlete not only must apply his own skills, but he must limit his opponent's ability to apply his skills.

Control Judo: The Tactics of Judo

Control judo is simple in concept but takes work to accomplish. Control as many aspects of every situation as possible and use them to your advantage. Control the grip and control the opponent's movement. Control the clock and use the allotted match time to your advantage. Control as many aspects of the contest as possible for as long as possible during the match. It's not always possible to win by a resounding ippon, and because of this, an athlete will have to rely on his tactical ability to win a tight, hard-fought match. Control judo is tactical judo. When it comes down to who will stand on top of the podium, this is important.

The most physically gifted athlete, the toughest guy in the tournament, or the athlete with the best technique doesn't always win. In a competitive match, where the contestants are equally matched, the athlete who knows how to get the tactical advantage is often the winner. Knowing how to fight hard is important, but it's just as important to know how to fight smart. A tactically aware judo athlete should never want a "fair fight." That's not to say that the mat officials should be unfair to an opponent, but what it does mean is that a tactically smart judoka should do everything possible to have an advantage as often as possible in every aspect of the match. The goal for a judo athlete is to control as many aspects of a match as possible, imposing your will and forcing your opponent to fight on your terms, not his.

Strategy and Tactics

Strategy is what an athlete wants to accomplish and tactics are how he does it. Strategy is the planning and preparation required to win. When training for a tournament, a judo athlete's efforts are focused on developing a strategy and using the necessary tactics to carry it out. Specifically, it's the overall fight plan. But a strategy must be flexible. Your opponent has a strategy too, and because of this, your fight plan must be adaptable. The famous German general Helmuth von Moltke was noted for saying, "No plan survives first contact with the enemy." Heavyweight boxing champion Mike Tyson put it another way: "Everybody has a plan until he gets hit in the face." So, when developing a strategy, remember to make it realistic and make sure it's flexible.

What makes a strategy realistic and flexible are the tactics. Tactics are the practical application of strategy in a match and doing what it takes to win. They are adaptable and may change as situations dictate. For example, an athlete will have a different tactical approach if he's ahead in the score than if he's behind in the score. The best place to develop tactics is in the dojo during training. Use situational drills where you place yourself in different situations and work on how to react to them. During drill-training and randori, work on setting training partners up tactically in order to apply your tokui waza (preferred techniques).

The Concept of Kobo Ichi

Kobo ichi is the epitome of applying strategy and tactics. Kobo ichi is based on the practical theory that attack and defense are one in the same thing and the priority is determined by the circumstances of any given situation. This means that offense and defense are used interchangeably as the situation unfolds. Here's an example for our purposes: a judoka using a hip block and cut-away defense stops his opponent's throw and then immediately launches his own counterattack. Another example is when a judoka attacks his opponent with a forward throwing technique, but the opponent avoids the attack and hops around in a defensive movement. As this happens, the attacker changes the direction of his throw and uses a technique to throw his opponent in the opposite direction from the initial attack.

The reason for this is that kobo ichi is based on the concept of "ju" (flexibility or adaptability), which we discussed in an earlier section. And because of this, the concept of kobo ichi is different than "the best defense is an offense." In actual practice, the concept of always being on offense isn't realistic. No one constantly stays on offense in any sport, especially in judo. Knowing when (and how) to switch from defense to offense or switch from offense to defense is an essential element in effective, successful judo. When training in the dojo, make it a point to practice how to block an opponent's attack and then counter with your attack. Work on how to react if an opponent blocks your attack and how you adjust to defense if he counters with his attack. Kobo ichi is a practical principle that every successful judo athlete should understand and use.

A Judo Contest Isn't a Game

As discussed above, judo tournament is called a shiai. Shiai is a phrase that translates to "a mutual test." It's a test between two athletes. It's a test of physical skills and tactical skills. It's also a test of which athlete is more willing to win. A judo contest is personal. It's one-on-one competition. Unlike basketball, baseball, or hockey, there's no teammate to blame when the team loses. It's just you and your opponent on the mat. Not only is it one-on-one competition, judo is a combat sport. Just like in wrestling or boxing, a judo match is personal combat that takes place under a set of mutually agreed and understood rules. There may be rules to the sport, but make no mistake about it, slamming an opponent onto his back or making him submit to a choke or armlock is exhilarating. It's also humbling when you're the person who got slammed on his back or had to tap out because of an opponent's submission technique. It's personal, and it takes a lot of personal humility and strength to win graciously and lose graciously. Being able to take the credit for victory or accept the blame for defeat are necessary for everyone who aspires to be a champion in judo. In a very real sense, a judo match is a fight, but it's a fight under a mutually agreed and understood set of rules. But, at the heart of the matter, it's still a fight and not merely a game.

Left-Side and Right-Side Techniques

About 90 percent of the world's population is right-handed. Many judo athletes rely heavily on right-sided throwing techniques because that is the way they have been taught initially. It's been my observation that as judo athletes progress from local to regional to national and on to international levels of competition, the number of judo athletes who use left-handed techniques tends to increase. I'm sure there are statistics to back this up.

The ability to use techniques both right-sided and left-sided equally well is a skill that will win a lot of matches, but it's not common to see someone with this ability. What often takes place is that some judo athletes will have the ability to use a limited number of specific techniques on both sides, and these are often their tokui waza (preferred technique). This was discussed in the section on tokui waza earlier in this book. Most athletes who do this will usually have one or two throws they apply as right-sided attacks and have one or two throws they apply as left-sided attacks. The reason most people can't perform every technique equally well on both sides is that learning throwing techniques is not an easy task, even when learning only on one side. Many people who want to switch sides in throwing select throws they're good at on their normal side and train on using it from the opposite side. With all of this said, the best advice is if you do not already have some throws you are able to do from your opposite side, get busy and start working on some.

Groundfighting is a different matter. Learning grappling techniques is a lot easier for most people, and as a result, most people learn pins, chokes, and armlocks from both the right side as well as the left when they start their study of judo and have equal skill in doing them.

Sportsmanship

This subject has been touched on previously, but it is worth examining at length now. An important factor to understand when thinking about strategy and tactics is sportsmanship, so let's focus in on why sportsmanship is a vital part of winning. Rules, as established by the governing body conducting the tournament or match, must be accepted by everyone who participates and are in place to ensure that sportsmanship is maintained. Referees and officials are vital to the entire process. They ensure that sportsmanship is the overriding theme of the event. The most important way they do this is to enforce the rules and do it in as objective a way as possible. Without sportsmanship, any sporting event, especially a combat sport like judo, deteriorates into nothing more than a free-for-all.

Sportsmanship is "ethics applied to sports." Without some kind of guiding ethical beacon, there is no possible way to compete with other human beings safely and in a fair manner. This is why sportsmanship is so important.

Maturity: When Jigoro Kano developed Kodokan judo, his intention was that judo should contribute to society in a positive way. Character development and the development of a mature human being are integral parts of what judo really is. Judo coaches teach people—and in many cases, children—how to fight. Judo is an efficient personal combat activity, and if coaches don't instill discipline and maturity in their students and athletes, then all that judo really becomes is an effective method of grappling and fighting where the most aggressive and dominant athletes survive. The amoral ethics of evolution will govern the result, and only the strongest and most aggressive will prevail. As mentioned previously, discipline is a learned trait, and sport is an ideal tool for instilling discipline in young people. Through the accepted rules and mores of sportsmanship, athletes, coaches, parents, and anyone else connected with the activity have a certain expected standard of behavior to exhibit. Without good ethical training, athletes (especially those athletes in combat sports or sports where aggressive behavior is required for success) become predators. Sport, and judo in particular, would not survive from generation to the next without a definite set of ethics and sportsmanship.

Reacting to Winning and Losing: Expect to win and when you do, act like it. When the referee raises his hand in your direction after you've won a match, bow to your opponent and be gracious in your behavior. No theatrics or fist pumping are necessary. Likewise, if you lose a match and the referee raises his hand in the other direction, bow and accept what just took place with dignity, even if you thought you won the match. Reacting poorly only makes you look immature. If there's been a discrepancy or mistake by the mat officials, let your coach handle it. A judo tournament is a shiai. That means it's a test—a test of not only your skill but also of your character. Years after a judo athlete ends his career, how he conducted himself both on and off the mat will be remembered as much as how many medals he won. The sportsmanship displayed by an athlete is a direct reflection of his or her character. It's best to be respected by your peers, both during your career and after it's over.

The Rules

The rules of any sport literally dictate how the sport is played or conducted. The rules place emphasis on what the governing body of the sport wants the athletes to do and the image the governing body wants the public to see. Through the years, the contest rules for judo have changed numerous times, and with each rule change, how coaches and athletes prepared for competition changed as well. An athlete must know how to win within the confines of the rules of the sport and the place to learn this is on the mat in the dojo. Coaches must "coach by the rulebook and not by the textbook." This isn't to imply that information contained in textbooks is bad, it simply means that if an athlete or coach doesn't know the rules or how to use the rules to his advantage, he will be at a disadvantage in the face of opponents who do.

It's the responsibility of both the athlete and his coach to have a thorough knowledge and understanding of the contest rules of judo. Knowing how to use the rules to win is very much part of an athlete's fight plan for both a strategic approach and on the tactical level. It doesn't matter if you win a major tournament by an ippon or a small margin, you still win. The best way to prepare to win tactically is to practice on it on the mat. Tactical training and knowing how to use the rules to your advantage in preparation for any judo tournament are important. A good way to do this is for a judo athlete to put himself in specific situations during randori. For instance, tell yourself you are behind in the score by a waza-ari and you have a specific amount of time to tie the score or throw for an ippon. Another example is for you to have your partner use a specific grip on you that has been giving you trouble so that you have to work on breaking that grip and taking control of the situation. Take any situation that actually occurs in a judo match and use it in training. This type of situational drill training is helpful in both tactical and technical training.

There are some techniques in judo that aren't permitted in the current contest rules, but that doesn't mean that a judoka should not learn them for a more complete understanding of judo. For instance, the standard way of applying kata guruma (shoulder wheel) isn't allowed in the current IJF (International Judo Federation) contest rules because the attacker uses his hands to grab the defender's legs. Grabbing an opponent's legs with the hands isn't permitted in the current IJF rules, so when preparing for a tournament, the judo athlete must either adapt kata guruma to avoid grabbing the opponent's leg or avoid doing kata guruma altogether. But grabbing the opponent's leg while doing kata guruma is still the standard application of the throw. So, while it's necessary to avoid grabbing the leg of an opponent when doing kata guruma in competition and when training for competition, it's important for a judoka to know the standard application of the technique. This is a matter of knowing when to use it. It's important to be able to separate what is necessary to do to win in competitive judo from what is necessary to do for a total study and understanding of Kodokan judo.

The rulebook doesn't care who wins. You can either use the rules in your favor or have the rules used against you. That's the nature of competitive sports, including judo. Think of the rules as another tool in your toolbox. If you know how a tool works, you will know how to make it work better for you. The better you know the rules, the better chance you have of using them to your advantage. On the other hand, if you don't have a thorough knowledge and understanding of the rules, the chances are that an opponent who does will use the rules against you to win.

Scouting Opponents

Knowing the opposition is vital to success in any form of combat, whether it's a war or it's a judo match. The better an athlete knows his opposition, the better chance he has of winning. In today's age of computers and the internet, a smart athlete or coach can scout the opposition more easily than ever before. When scouting an opponent, there are some specific questions you should try to answer. The questions presented below represent my personal list, but feel free to change or add to the list as you see fit.

1. Is he a right-sided or left-sided player? What attacks does he make from the right and what attacks does he make from the left?
2. Does he come straight at you, move sideways or work at angles? How many steps in one direction does he take before he shifts or changes direction?
3. Does he try to get the initial grip or does he hang back and counter your grip?
4. What is his primary grip? His grip often tells you what throw he relies on the most. Does he focus on trying to control your shoulders, or does he work more loosely and try to control your arms? Does he set his primary grip up with a setup grip, or does he go for his main grip without any setup grip fighting?
5. Does he have an upright posture or a bent-over posture? Does his posture and tempo change if he is ahead in the score as well as if he's behind in the score?
6. What's his best throw? What does he do best in groundfighting?
7. What's his tempo standing? What's his tempo in groundfighting? A fast tempo in groundfighting often tells you that he likes armlocks, and a slower tempo often tells you he works slower for a position and prefers pinning.
8. Does he like to get close to you in the grip fighting, or does he prefer to stay away?
9. Is he a counter fighter, or is he aggressive?
10. How does he act when he's leading in the score, and how does he act when he's behind in the score?
11. What's his fitness level? Does he fatigue and fade after a specific period of time?
12. Are most of his attacks in the early part of the match or in the later stages of the match?

Once you've scouted the opposition, use the information and plan and train accordingly on the mat before the tournament. Simply knowing how an opponent fights isn't enough.

You have to know how to beat him and then do what is necessary to make sure you do, indeed, beat him!

Tactics of Keeping the Lead in the Score

If you are ahead in the score, do everything possible to keep your lead and win. If you are behind in the score, do everything possible to catch up and take the lead and win. That's easier said than done, so let's look at how to do it. The athlete who is ahead in the score and attempting to keep his lead is what the great British coach Geof Gleeson called "front fighting," and the athlete who is behind in the score and attempting to catch up and win is "back fighting." Knowing how to keep your lead when ahead in the score and how to catch up or take the lead when behind in the score is vital to winning in judo and should be taken into consideration when training.

Your Competition: In a judo match, you aren't only competing with your opponent. You are competing with the mat officials and with the time clock. It's your job to accomplish what you want to accomplish within the confines of what the match time allows and in doing so, satisfy the mat officials that you are the athlete who deserves to win.

Front Fighting: When ahead in the score the most important thing is keep your lead, build on it if possible, and win the match. Waste as much time as possible on the clock. Don't take chances, but just as important, don't make it obvious that you are wasting time. Do not try to "finish off" an opponent, attempt a big throw, or do anything that will blow the lead and allow an opponent to win. A gold medal isn't tarnished if you win by a small margin instead of slamming your opponent for an ippon. It's still a gold medal. Take your win any way the rules allow. Unless there is a valid reason for winning a match by an ippon score, don't blow a lead in the score to finish off an opponent.

Penalties: Sometimes, it's okay to draw a penalty to keep the lead in the score. If an athlete is up by a waza-ari with a short amount of time left in the contest, he can afford to get a shido penalty in this situation and still win the match. A thorough knowledge of the contest rules will help an athlete know how to use them in his favor, especially in determining how to use the rules tactically during a match. In the dojo, practice keeping your lead and practice catching up and taking the lead. Place yourself in specific situations or assign a specific score in randori. Work on fighting when behind in the score and work on fighting when leading in the score.

Circle and Make Space to Keep the Lead: Seconds count when keeping the lead (or catching up) in the score. An effective way to keep your lead in the score and kill some time on the clock is to do the following. After a break in the action and the referees calls to resume the match, as you move forward toward your opponent, move at an angle (not directly toward hm) and move in a circle around him. As you move, make probing movements with your hands and arms in an attempt to nullify his grip and establish your own grip.

Grip Fighting: An effective way to waste time without getting penalized is for you to engage in grip fighting with your opponent, but make sure that when doing this you keep as much space between your body and your opponent's body as possible. An effective grip to keep space and kill time is to use a low sleeve grip against both of your opponent's arms. As you do this, pull down (toward the mat) on his sleeves and move laterally (never back away). This double slow sleeve grip is a long grip that creates space and kills time but is also a good grip to use when attacking a knee-drop throw.

One-Hand Grip: Your opponent needs to have both hands gripping onto you in order for him to attack you. Don't let your opponent get both hands on you. Make him become a one-handed fighter. One way to do this is to engage your opponent in a prolonged grip-fighting battle, all the while making sure you prevent him from gripping you with his power hand (his tsurite). He needs his power hand holding onto you in order to launch an attack. Kill his power hand and make him a one-handed fighter.

Tempo: When protecting your lead, speed up the tempo of how fast you move about the mat. It may sound counterintuitive as conventional thinking may say to slow things down. But you don't want to slow things down when you are winning, you want the clock to keep ticking away as fast as possible and get the match over with. As you move at angles and make probing attacks from long range, move quickly. Every few seconds, make an attack. This leads to the next tactic.

"Safe" Attacks: When leading in the score, use "safe" attacks. Safe attacks are designed to make you look good (and busy) to the mat officials. Mat officials are wise to the "flop and drop" knee-drop seoi nage (back carry throw). Conversely, a knee-drop throwing attack using a double sleeve grip is often an effective technique. And, when using a knee-drop throw, continue driving with your feet on the mat to drive through. Doing this not only makes it look like you're actually trying a throw, you might even turn your opponent onto his back for a score.

Don't try anything risky that could be countered by your opponent. If you are winning, keep the lead. Do not attempt to throw your opponent for an ippon because your opponent will be waiting for it and may counter you. Using safe attacks is particularly important when competing against an opponent who is as equally skilled as you or has been a frequent opponent. In situations such as this, the judo athlete with the better tactics will win the match.

Sell the Attack: This works for when you are leading in the score as well as when you are behind in the score. It is an old tactic, but it works. Use a kiai (spirit shout) when attacking, especially when using a sacrifice throw like yoko tomoe nage (spinning or side circle throw) or when using a knee-drop throw. An example of how this works is when one of my athletes was in the world team trials and in a tough semi-final match. There was no score on the scoreboard with about thirty seconds left in the match. My athlete attacked with a tomoe nage (circle throw) and used a kiai as she did. As she rolled under her opponent (still yelling loudly), she continued to push and drive with her foot and leg at her opponent's belt line and rolled her opponent onto the opponent's side. It wasn't a particularly strong attack, but the kiai was enough to "sell" the technique to the referee who awarded a score for the throw. From this point, my athlete immediately got behind her opponent and attempted to dig her foot and legs in to apply a strangle. Time ran out and she won the match. This was tactical judo at its finest. She looked busy, used her kiai to sell the score to the referee, and milked the score in groundfighting to waste time on the clock. This was enough for her to win against a tough opponent.

Milking the Score: This means that when you are leading in the score, a good way to waste time is to follow through to the mat from every throwing attack and work to get behind your opponent or the top position. Look busy and continue to work for a breakdown or turnover. If your first breakdown doesn't work, move quickly to another in order to prevent the referee from calling a halt to the action. Do everything possible to make it appear that you are working to apply a scoring move on the mat and prevent the referee from calling a halt to the action. Milking the score in this way can turn a knockdown (or even a possible score) from a throw into a longer groundwork session, killing time on the clock.

Grinding the Opponent: As an offshoot of milking the score in groundfighting, make every effort to wear your opponent down and fatigue him. Groundfighting can be used grind an opponent down and make it the most miserable time of your opponent's life with you on the mat. Continue to look busy, but also continue to apply pressure on your opponent and make him tired. When the referee does call a halt to the action and get you standing again, your opponent will have a little less energy than he had before.

Don't Look for a Score: When making an attack, whether it's an attack to waste time or a real throwing attack, don't look at the referee to see if he called a score. It's obvious that a judo athlete who does this is begging for a score to be called and will only make the referee watch you more closely to see if you're making false attacks.

Combination Attacks: In keeping with using safe attacks as a tactic for maintaining the lead in the score, you are able to waste a good amount of time by using a series of combination attacks. Probably none of these combination attacks are good enough to score points, but they are good enough that your opponent must respond by avoiding them.

Tactics of Getting the Lead when Behind in the Score

Tactics are a lot less complicated when an athlete is losing than when he is winning. Basically, when an athlete is losing, he has to do anything possible (allowed within the rules) to win.

Don't Give Up: If you are behind in the score, you haven't lost; it just means that you have more work to do. This isn't meant as a pep talk but as a statement of fact.

Stay Calm: When an athlete is losing, it's essential that he stays as calm as possible, understand his situation, and then do what he needs to do to catch up and take the lead. Keeping your cool is important, especially in this situation. When an athlete is behind in the score, he's at a psychological disadvantage. If you understand this, you will deal with it better. Don't appear panicked or make erratic hand or body gestures. Looking flustered or getting emotional won't win the match.

Stay Standing: In most cases, an athlete has a better chance of scoring points with throwing attacks rather than ground attacks even if a judo athlete is stronger in groundfighting. With limited time on the clock, it's generally easier to score points in standing judo than on the ground. The faster pace and greater freedom of movement that come with standing up allows for more attacks (in most cases) and more opportunities to score than in groundfighting.

Opportunities: Look for every opportunity to score on your opponent, and whenever possible, create an opportunity to get a score. Sometimes, you get lucky, and getting lucky usually results from seeing an opportunity and taking advantage of it.

Get Close to Your Opponent: When behind in the score, your job is to get close enough to your opponent so that you can attack him. If he knows how to keep his lead, he will work to create as much space between you and him as possible. Use aggressive grip fighting to get closer to him.

Make Your Opponent Appear to Be Stalling: Apply continuous pressure and force your opponent to back up. Relatedly, do not run or rush toward him in a straight line, but move at an angle and grip him. As you do this, launch an attack.

Grip and Go: One way to apply more pressure on your opponent is to immediately attack as soon as you get your grip on his jacket. In many cases, the instant you and your opponent grab each other, the judoka who's leading will be not be moving. This is one of the best times to launch a throwing attack if you are behind in the score.

Fitness: Fitness is a key element in tactical judo and especially so when an athlete is losing the match. If an athlete has the gas in the tank to mount an aggressive series of attacks, he has a better chance of catching up in the score and going on to win the match.

Tempo or Pace

Tempo (also called pace) is how fast or slow the two bodies of the athletes move about the mat in a judo match. Different athletes fight at different tempos, and a feature of every judo match is a contest between the two athletes to see who controls the pace of the match. Usually, lighter athletes fight at a faster tempo than heavier athletes. However, there have been some outstanding lightweight athletes who have had impressive careers slowing down opponents and making them fight at a slow tempo. Setting the tempo to suit the immediate needs of the situation makes for a good part of the strategy of many intelligent judo athletes. An athlete may alter the tempo of the match as necessary. The tempo of the match is as important in groundfighting as it is in standing judo. A good example is that, often, armlocks come out of a fast tempo in groundfighting. The momentum needed to roll an opponent over or set him up to lever (pry) his arm free often comes from a fast-paced attack. In standing judo, some throws simply work better from a fast tempo. Okuri ashi barai (send after foot sweep) is a good example. The fast foot movement sets up the sweeping action when the throw is applied. On the other hand, some throws such as ura nage (rear throw) often come out of a slower tempo. While this isn't always the case, it's often true. An intelligent athlete will work on varying the pace of the action in practice during drill training and randori so it can be varied during an actual match as needed.

Controlling the tempo requires excellent physical fitness. The athlete who controls the tempo of the match might initially set a blistering pace, slow it down as tactically necessary, and then speed it up again as needed. This ability requires that the attacker (controlling the tempo) not only move his body about the mat but also dictates how his opponent's body moves about the mat as well. In other words, he's moving and controlling two bodies, and this is why fitness is vital.

In some cases, the location where the athletes are on the mat dictates the tempo of the match. An example is that when the athletes are very near the edge of the boundary, the action may slow down to avoid going out of bounds. Knowing this and using it as a tactical tool can benefit an intelligent athlete.

Body space often dictates the tempo of the match. A wide body space between the two athletes often indicates a slow tempo in a match. This takes place when the athletes are not inclined to give much of an advantage to each other and this results in a slow tempo. They may be in a low, crouched, and defensive posture, but this is not always the case. As a general rule, however, it is. Often, when the athletes are in an upright posture and leading with their hips, they can more freely move (and thus attack and defend) and this results in a faster tempo. Some bad poetry might help you to remember how tempo fits into an overall winning strategy: if you want to do good judo, control the pace, control the space, and control the place.

Body Space: Body Holes and Body Gaps

Body space is the distance between the bodies of the two athletes. It's that area that is available for attacking, defending, and moving an opponent, all with the intent of controlling what takes place in that body space. Often, the distance between the two bodies dictates the tempo of the match, both in standing and groundfighting. Take advantage of the small openings or spaces in an opponent's defense that occur both in standing situations and in groundfighting. In order to take advantage of body space, it's important to know how to create it when you need to and close it when you need to. In throwing techniques, you need enough space between your body and your opponent's body to enable you to fit your body into position in order to throw him. I've often called this space the "hole" that your body can fit through to make your technique work. When you "create a hole" you use the combination of your gripping and controlling your opponent's movement so that enough space opens in order for you to develop your throw.

This hole is what is called ma-ai or "mutual distance" in many martial arts, and knowing how to use this distance in the most efficient way at the right time is a skill that is developed from doing a lot of randori and situational drill training. Knowing how to look for a hole is also a skill that must be developed by randori training; it's that instant when you see your opponent has moved in a way that makes him vulnerable to your attack.

In groundfighting situations, a hole can be created for the attacker to give himself enough space to fit his body in the best position for a pin, choke, or armlock. In groundfighting, a hole big enough for a judoka to fit his body into is called a "body gap." Think of it this way: there is a small crack in a rock that is just big enough for you to get your crowbar into but not big enough for anything else. So, you use your crowbar to jam in that crack and make it wide enough so that it is useful to you. Now, more to the point, a good example of a body gap in groundfighting is that it is the space between the upper leg and the calf when an opponent is on all fours (on elbows and knees). This gap can be used by the attacker to work in his hand or arm, get a good handle onto the opponent's arm or leg, and create a bigger opening in order to start a breakdown or turnover that will result in a scoring technique. In just about every situation in groundfighting, body gaps develop. Having the tactical intelligence to spot them only comes from a lot of groundfighting randori.

Position in Judo

Judo is a series of positions logically linked to each other, often taking place in sequential order. One thing almost always leads to another. How an athlete puts himself in position in relation to his opponent and where it's located on the mat at any given point in the match can enable an athlete to create openings and opportunities that can lead to a successful conclusion to the match. Position is important in both standing situations and groundfighting. The goal is to always try to be in a position where you have an advantage over your opponent and continually try to improve your position to dominate him. Mobility and the ability to move fluidly from one situation to another are important parts of being in a good position and controlling an opponent's position. Conversely, continually attempt to limit an opponent's movement and nullify anything he might do. There will be more on what position is and how to use it in specific situations throughout this book.

Posture

Your posture and your opponent's posture dictate much of what takes place in a judo contest. Through training on a regular basis, you develop the ability to change your posture to fit the immediate needs of the action in a contest. In most cases you will use a strong upright posture, but in some circumstances you will need to use a defensive posture.

An effective posture to use is an upright posture where you "lead with your hips." In other words, if you are a right-sided judoka, you will move about the mat with your right hip slightly leading. Always have your lead hip in position so you have freedom of movement and are able to attack or defend as the situation arises. Do not extend your lead foot or leg out in front of your lead hip. Always try to keep your lead leg and foot in a direct line under your lead hip. It's important to point out that your hip action starts your body rotation and turning when launching an attack with a throwing technique. All of your attacks start with your hips. To the untrained ear, saying this makes no sense, but it's important to know why it works and know how to make it work in a real situation.

By leading with your hips, you're better balanced whether you're moving or standing still and are more balanced when you move your feet. You're in better position to attack and defend. This fluid movement allows you to go immediately from defending against an opponent's attack to turning it into an attack of your own. This is a working definition of kobo ichi, or the concept of an aggressive defense and an adaptable, constant offense. A good way to develop this skill is to work a lot on hip block drills and grip-fighting drills. When leading with your hips, you will generally assume the shizentai, or upright, natural posture. This posture allows you to keep your hips close enough to your opponent to attack and defend as the situation warrants.

Many athletes who come from a wrestling background have a strong tendency to bend over at the waist and have their hips much too far away from their opponent. This position may be good for amateur wrestling, where they "shoot" takedowns from far away with the primary goal of getting behind their opponent and not throwing him onto his back. If your hips are too far away from your opponent because you are using a bent-over, crouched posture, he will see your attack coming and avoid it. By leading with your hip, you place the center of your body (your hip area) in the most efficient position for launching an attack or for defending against your opponent's attack. To be able to lead with your hip, your posture must be upright with a straight (not rigid) spine. The most advantageous posture to use on a regular basis is shizentai.

Stance: Aiyotsu and Kenka Yotsu

How a judo athlete stands relative to his opponent is another aspect of posture. Much like a boxer who assumes a stance during the course of a bout, a judo athlete will have a preferred stance during the course of a judo match. And just like in boxing, a "southpaw" or boxer who uses a left-handed stance will give problems to his opponent using an orthodox right-handed stance. So, not only is the stance important from a technical aspect, it's important from a tactical aspect as well. A major part of grip fighting is trying to maneuver an opponent into a posture that is weak for him, giving you the opportunity to launch your attack as well as to prevent him from launching his own attack.

There are two primary stances a judo athlete will use. One is aiyotsu and the other is kenka yotsu. The word "ai" translates to "mutual or harmonious" and "yotsu" translates to "circumstance." What this means is that both judo athletes are leading with the same side (a right-sided judoka versus a right-sided judoka). The word "kenka" translates to "non-mutual" and it takes place when the judo athletes are leading with opposite stances (a right-sided judoka versus a left-sided judoka). A judo athlete who takes a right-sided stance will lead with his right hip and a judo athlete who takes a left-sided stance will lead with his left hip. In most cases, the judo athlete who uses a left-sided stance will tend to apply left-sided throwing techniques, and the judo athlete who uses a right-sided stance will tend to apply right-sided throwing techniques.

An old phrase used in judo is to "be in position." This means that for a throwing technique to be most effective, the judoka doing it must first use the most efficient stance and posture possible for the particular technique being used. In every case, the stance that a judoka takes determines how the throwing technique the judoka uses will be applied.

Aiyotsu: Each judoka has a similar side stance. Generally, if a right-sided athlete is competing against another right-sided athlete, they face each other using an aiyotsu posture.

Kenka Yotsu: One judoka leads with his right hip and the other leads with his left. Generally, when a left-sided judo athlete faces a right-sided judo athlete, the kenka yotsu posture is used.

Shizentai and Jigotai

There are two primary postures in judo: shizentai (natural posture) and jigotai (defensive posture). Shizentai is an upright posture where the attacker's placement of his legs and feet are in a direct line under his hips. Do not step too far out in front of the hips and do not have your feet placed too close together; foot placement should be directly under the hips for the most efficient control of movement. For shizentai to be most effective, the judoka's body should not be rigid or stiff and should be relaxed so that the judoka can reflexively react to an opponent's movement. The judoka's head should be upright and not looking at the opponent's feet or at the mat. The whole purpose of shizentai is to provide a balanced posture that can quickly initiate an attack or react to an opponent's attack.

Jigotai is a low, crouching posture often used as a temporary maneuver based on the situation. Every judo athlete uses jigotai when necessary. An important element for jigotai to be effective is that the person doing it should have a straight back and not bend over at the waist. In other words, lower the level of your body with your bent or flexed knees and use them like springs on a car, bending and straightening as necessary. With a straight back, the weight of your body is better distributed as opposed to being bent over at the waist, with the head and shoulder too far in front of the hips. (Remember, even when using jigotai, your hips lead and control the direction of your movement.) There is a difference between a useful jigotai position and a crouched, bent-over posture. Never bend over at your waist with your head and shoulder far out in front of your hips. When doing this, the body is weak in a forward direction as there is too much weight in the head and shoulder areas. The body is also weak to the rear because there is too much weight placed on the heels and buttocks. This crouched, bent-over position also places the hips too far away from the opponent, and the opponent will quickly see any attack coming from the person using this bent-over posture.

This shows an example of shizentai (natural posture) where one or both judo athletes have an upright posture. The hips of both athletes are close to each other, allowing for an immediate attacking action or defensive action.

This shows an example of jigotai (defensive posture) where one or both athletes are bent over. Notice that the hips of both athletes are far away from each other in an attempt to prevent the opponent from initiating a throwing technique. Bending over in this defensive posture will draw a penalty from the referee, but every judo athlete must use jigotai from time to time as part of his or her tactical approach to preventing an opponent from attacking.

"Own the Mat"

The location on the mat where the action takes place during a match is important from a tactical point of view. Try to "own the mat" when in a match, keeping your opponent where you want him to be as much as possible. Keep your back to the center of the mat and keep your opponent moving about the perimeter of the mat with his back to the boundary line. This way, you have as much room as you want and can better move your opponent to the edge of the mat when you need to or keep him in bounds when necessary. From a tactical standpoint, if you are ahead in the score, it's often a good idea to move your opponent to the edge of the mat with his back facing the edge. This invisible boundary line restricts his movement and allows you to control both the tempo of the match and the space between you and your opponent. In other words, putting him on the edge with his back to the line restricts his movement and allows you more freedom of movement. This is also a time when you control him with effective grip fighting and shut him down, prohibiting him from mounting an effective attack. Another effective form of front fighting is to milk the score. Most of these tactics blend into each other so review the previous section above about "milking the score" to keep the lead.

Making Weight

It should be made clear that I am not a nutritionist, just a coach and former judo/sambo athlete who's made plenty of mistakes in cutting weight but who has fortunately learned from those mistakes. My advice is based on both my education and experience. So, first of all, the most important thing to know when losing weight in order to compete in a specific weight class is that cutting weight is not normal. Cutting weight is not healthy and certainly not the same thing as when someone wants to lose weight to improve his or her health. When cutting weight, you, as an athlete, are losing a specific amount of weight in order to compete in an artificially contrived weight category with other athletes doing the same thing.

Judo is a sport with weight categories, and because of this, athletes will lose weight in order to compete in the weight category they think will give them the best chance of winning. When losing weight to compete, remember that you don't get a gold medal for making weight; you get a gold medal for winning the tournament. For a judo athlete who is already physically fit and relatively lean, losing a large amount of weight will weaken him. The idea that an athlete has the physical advantage if he drops to a lower weight class is more often a myth than a reality. This is especially true for judo athletes in the lighter weight categories. Athletes in the lighter weight classes have less body fat than judo athletes in the heavier weight classes. It's physically more difficult for a judo athlete to drop from 160 pounds to 145 pounds than it is for a judo athlete to drop from 260 pounds to 245 pounds. This is because lighter athletes usually have a leaner body mass than heavier athletes. In other words, lightweights have less body fat that heavyweights. This is basic stuff, but something that must be remembered when you want to lose weight to make a specific weight category. If you are competing at an elite level, it's advised that you get your body composition tested professionally before you start your training cycle for a major competition. This will tell you not simply how much you weigh, but how much of what you weigh is muscle tissue, essential fat, non-essential fat, bone, and organ tissue. Based on this information, you and your coach can make more informed decisions on whether or not you should lose weight in order to compete at a lower weight class. And if you decide to drop to a lower weight class, you'll have a better idea of how much of your actual body weight is non-essential fat that can be shed.

If you are training for a tournament and have to lose weight during your training cycle, lose the weight gradually, with the goal to be on weight at least one or two days before you have to weigh in. Again, this advice is based on you having an accurate knowledge of your body composition. As a general rule, try not to lose more than two pounds daily. Dropping excessive weight on the night before or on the morning of the weigh-ins dehydrates drastically, which is a major problem. The rapid and excessive loss of water from the body sets you up for diminished and erratic motor skill function as well as mental and emotional fatigue. The reason an athlete feels tired when cutting a lot of weight is because he *is* tired, both physically and mentally. And by no means should you use diuretics or any drug in order to lose weight. These drugs are banned by the International Olympic Committee for good reason; they are dangerous and harmful to your health.

Water Breaks During Practice: In past years, taking a water break was considered a sign of weakness. Better education of coaches has changed that. During training, athletes naturally perspire. As the intensity of training increases, the need for sufficient hydration intensifies. Hydration is the process of absorbing water as well as introducing additional fluid into the body. Water is the main component of the human body, accounting for about 73 percent of lean body mass according to the *Journal of Athletic Training* published by the National Athletic Trainers' Association. During a workout, sweating (and its evaporation) is the primary way the human body regulates its temperature. Athletes whose sweat loss exceeds the amount of fluid taken in during a training session can become dehydrated, and as a result, they become overheated. Being overheated could lead to heat exhaustion, and heat exhaustion leads not only to diminished performance but also serious health risks. If athletes lose more than 1 or 2 percent of their body weight during a training session, their training session will be compromised and possibly diminished. In the same way a car engine needs water in its radiator, athletes need water in their body.

Take a water break about every ten to fifteen minutes (depending on the intensity of the workout), then get on with the workout. Water should be your primary source of hydration, especially during a workout. Avoid carbonated beverages. Don't take salt pills to replace the sodium lost while sweating from training. The fluid you take in replaces the sweat and urine lost during training. If you are prone to sweating a great deal, make sure you drink sufficient water. It's a good idea to drink water throughout the day, actually; consider it part of your training. It's also advised that you drink six to eight ounces of water ten to twenty minutes before a training session and not to go into a judo practice thirsty. After practice it's a good idea to rehydrate with water. Satisfy your thirst but don't overdo it. Drinking too much water dilutes the sodium in your blood and this can cause headaches, nausea, or other side effects. Athletes who are cutting weight should be especially aware of proper hydration during training. Losing body weight that is excess body fat is the goal, but losing body weight that is water isn't.

Strategy and Tactics Training: During the training cycle (the specific period of training) for a tournament, the athlete and coach should spend some part of every workout working on the tactics necessary to win. The overall strategy of what the athlete wants to accomplish are made up of specific tactics that make it happen. During training, the athlete should put himself into specific situations that will actually take place in a match. This situational drilling is necessary for the athlete to react reflexively and instantly to what takes place in the contest. Strategy and tactics training is also a good time to review video of anticipated opponents and develop specific tactics suited to these opponents. Moreover, it's a time for coaches and athletes to work on how the coach will offer mat-side coaching advice during the tournament. In my career as a coach for national and international judo and sambo athletes, I developed specific verbal and nonverbal (hand) signals with my athletes. Key words can be used to designate specific things. The athlete should know to always look over to the coach as well as to look at the time clock when the referee calls a break in the action. This is the time that the coach can communicate with the athlete. There will be more on this a bit later, but what is important is that the athlete looks to the coach for advice and that the coach provides useful advice to the athlete. In order for this to happen, the coach and athlete must practice this during the training sessions leading up to the tournament.

Training Environment: Where you train and the conditions in which you train should be considerations when preparing for a judo tournament. Your training environment should match the conditions where you will compete. If the upcoming tournament is in a large, air-conditioned auditorium, then there is nothing wrong with training in an air-conditioned dojo or training room. Some coaches insist on turning up the thermostat in a dojo while preparing a team for a tournament, but doing this hasn't improved the performance of my athletes. The location where training takes place, however, isn't the only factor in a training environment; the stress placed on athletes during training is also an important aspect. The best way for an athlete to handle stress in a tournament is for the athlete to encounter it during training. This topic is also discussed in the section on periodization, so just a few points will be made here. Randori (free practice) simulates what takes place in a judo tournament. The intensity of randori should be increased as the training cycle gets closer to the tournament. In addition to increased intensity in randori, a judo athlete should compete in local tournaments during his or her training cycle to sharpen technical and tactical skills. Judo athletes only fight as hard (or as smart) as they train, and this is why the training environment is so important.

Preparations During the Tournament: Judo tournaments are day-long affairs, and being prepared for staying all day in a gym takes some planning. First of all, a judo athlete needs fuel to make it through the day. A well-planned breakfast of easily digested carbohydrates along with good hydration is usually the best thing on the day of the tournament. This is especially true if the athlete has been cutting weight in order to make a weight class. It's usually difficult to get away from the tournament and eat lunch, so it's a good idea to pack some high-carbohydrate snacks and drinks. Make sure someone brings a cooler with bottled water as well. It's also a good idea to include a small first-aid kit. Athletic tape is always a necessity, so make it a point to bring several rolls of it. Most large tournaments now have a visible clock for the match time, but just in case, bring a stopwatch. It's the responsibility of both the coach and the athlete to make sure that both a blue judogi and a white judogi are brought along, as well as a spare uniform of each color as a back-up.

Mat-Side Coaching

A coach's job isn't finished when the training is over and the tournament starts. When the tournament begins, the coach takes on another task and that task is mat-side coaching. From my own experiences coaching athletes in local tournaments as well as coaching athletes in world championships, it's important to an athlete that the coach be there for the big wins as well as the big losses.

Winning on the mat takes a team effort. An athlete needs a reliable and skilled coach or teammate at the side of the mat during a match. That second set of eyes from the coach at mat-side may see a weakness in an opponent that the athlete can't see because he's involved fighting him. In this case, the coach at mat-side may make the difference between winning and losing.

Communication from Mat-Side: At mat-side, a coach should give clear, precise instructions to the athlete. The coach should not go into a long discussion or give complicated instructions. The athlete on the mat needs information that will help him win. Ultimately, it's up to the athlete if he chooses to use the instructions or information from the coach or not. He's the one fighting on the mat. If the coach calls out to perform a specific move and the athlete knows that, for whatever reason, it won't work, it's ultimately up to the athlete to make the decision. This is only true with experienced, skilled athletes who have been working with their coach and have the experience and technical skill to decide what to do under the pressure of competition. Another important thing to remember is when coaching at mat-side, coaches should not "overcoach." Make sure what is said to the athlete is worth listening to. Coaches or teammates standing by the side of the mat who yell non-stop, shouting one thing immediately after the other at their athletes during the course of a judo match, do absolutely no good for those athletes.

During the training cycle leading up to the tournament, the coach and athletes will develop specific phrases or words for techniques, movements, or actions (both technical and tactical) that only the coach and athletes know. Hand signals are also useful for communication. These phrases must be short and to the point using only one or two words. Upon hearing the phrase from me at mat-side, athletes would make a small gesture with their hand (that I would look for) to let me know they received the instruction and if they thought it would work or not.

Tips on Mat-Side Coaching: The following is a list of items on how to coach mat-side more effectively. Some of these items have been mentioned previously, and you may also have items to add to the list.

1. Prepare in the dojo. Work on strategy and tactics as part of your training. If you have special signals or phrases, this is the time to work on them so the athletes will be able to know them and use them in the tournament.
2. Know the rules. Coach by the rulebook. I've seen coaches who were ignorant of the rules (or a specific rule in question) and argue with the referees. As a result, they lose every argument every time. Also, it's a good bet that if a coach doesn't know the rules, his athletes won't know the rules either.
3. Come prepared for the day. Bring water, food, a first-aid kit, extra judo uniforms, and anything else that might be needed during the tournament.
4. Bring a stopwatch just in case there isn't a visible timer or clock.
5. Pre-match instructions are important. The coach (or senior teammate) should talk to the athletes before the tournament and to each athlete before each match. If a "rah-rah" talk is needed, do it. It works for some athletes in many situations, but if you do, mean what you say. Generally, this is a good time to offer any last-minute information the athletes can use. Often, a quick discussion of the upcoming match that keeps things positive helps.
6. Don't overcoach. At the same time, a coach shouldn't ignore his athletes either. It's difficult to say which is worse, the coach who shouts, talks, and yells too much or the coach who sits there like a spectator and never offers any advice or information.

7. There should be only one coach at mat-side. Too many people shouting at an athlete only confuses the situation, and some people simply offer dumb advice the athlete might hear.
8. Advice should be clear and to the point. When you offer mat-side advice, make it clear, understandable, and concise. Don't confuse your athlete with useless banter or garbled language.
9. Don't be a cheerleader. Offer encouragement, when necessary, but keep to the job at hand. When the match is over, don't get too excited. You can congratulate him and be happy, but don't overdo it. Be professional and a gracious winner. Likewise, if your opponent loses, don't blame the officials or make disparaging remarks about the opponent (even if your athlete got a bad call). You may not like the outcome of the match, but don't be a sore loser.
10. When the referee calls a break in the match, the athlete should look over to the coach for advice.
11. Do not berate, scold, or verbally abuse during the course of the match. If you need to discipline the athlete, do it after the match and don't do it in public. Never use profanities when speaking to your athletes, referees, or anyone at the tournament. Never physically abuse an athlete, fellow coach, referee, or spectator. Anyone who does this should be barred from coaching.
12. Don't irritate the officials. They control the match; you don't. You can't coach if you've been thrown out of the gym.
13. Be polite to the officials. You're at the tournament to help your team win. A referee will be more likely to give your athlete the benefit of the doubt if you treat him with respect. Referees are human too.
14. Sometimes your athlete is wrong. If your athlete deserves a penalty, don't argue when he or she gets one. If the referee made a technically incorrect call and you have a basis for a review, then by all means ask for a review. But when you do ask for a review, make sure you have a good argument to justify it.
15. Sometimes your athlete loses. In every match, there is a 50-percent chance one athlete will win and the other will lose. If your athlete gets thrown for ippon, don't argue the call (unless you believe you are correct on technical grounds).

16. Video the matches. Have another coach, teammate, or parent video the matches for later study and analysis.
17. Be professional in your behavior and in how you dress. Look and act professional. Stay in the assigned area for coaches. Don't ever walk onto the mat unless specifically asked by the referee.
18. You are there for your athlete. Represent him or her to the best of your ability.

The items listed have a proven record of success, but there may certainly be other items that can be added. Make sure, as a coach, that you don't do or say anything that will harm the sport of judo. You are a representative of judo as much as you are a representative of your team. We are all in this together, and none of us are getting rich or famous for what we do, so we might as well enjoy it and make it as positive an experience as possible.

CHAPTER 4

Efficient Training Produces Effective Results

Never miss practice.

—Jigoro Kano

This section of the book focuses on efficient training methods. Training is the activity of improving a person's capacity for a specific task or behavior. It's a process, and the more efficient the process, the more effective the result of that process will be. This process of training is called practice. Practice is a systematic or repeated performance for the purposes of becoming proficient at something. It is more than simply showing up and rolling around on the mat. There has to be a reason for everything that is done in training.

Train Hard and Train Smart

There is no "secret" to being successful in a difficult sport like judo. A judo athlete must train hard and train smart. In other words, everything done while training on the mat (and off the mat) must have a purpose and be focused in order to train in the most efficient way to achieve that purpose. This is what is meant by "training smart." Showing up and working hard at practice is laudable, but it's not enough for an athlete who wants to excel at competitive judo. There must be a reason for everything done in training, and everything must be geared toward a specific goal. On the other hand, training smart isn't a replacement for training hard. These concepts must be mutual to get optimal results from training. If a judoka truly trains "smart," he or she will invariably train "hard." An athlete will push himself harder if he understands the purpose of what he is doing in a training session because will then know why he is doing something and therefore be better able to discern how to get the best results from his training. This is a smart, informed, and objective approach to training.

A judo athlete must be prepared both aerobically and anaerobically much more than athletes in many other sports (more on aerobic and anaerobic training later). A sprinter trains to run fast in a straight line. A powerlifter trains to lift heavy weights. A gymnast must train so he or she has control over his or her own body in order to perform physically complex technical skills. But a judo athlete also trains to perform physically complex technical skills, and he has to train so that he attains control over not only his own body but also control over his opponent's body.

Three Levels of Training Intensity

There are three levels of development and preparation in judo training.

General Preparation (GP) or "Accumulation Phase": This level of intensity is what most of us do on a regular basis. It's the normal workout we get when we go to the dojo. Judo is first and foremost a method of physical education and this is when we accumulate technical knowledge and skills as well as physical fitness through judo training. Some workouts will be harder than others. For some people, practicing judo once or twice a week is enough; others may wish to train more often during the week. Training at this level doesn't prevent a judoka from entering judo tournaments and enjoying competitive judo if he or she wishes. But competitive judo isn't the entire focus of training at this level. For a majority of judo enthusiasts, this level of training is sufficient for a well-rounded education and training experience in judo.

Directed Preparation (DP) or "Intensification Phase": For those so inclined to pursue judo as a competitive activity, the next phase of training is more intense. Directed preparation consists of the methods used that are in some way more focused on success in competitive judo. It's during this level of training that a judoka will engage in more off-mat training in order to increase his or her aerobic and anaerobic fitness to supplement training on the mat in the dojo. When on the mat, the focus is now on developing the technical and tactical skills required for success in competitive judo. A judo athlete will spend more time training on the techniques that he specializes in (his tokui waza or favorite techniques). This phase of training is when randori becomes more purposeful (and intense) with the judo athlete working to perfect his skills against resisting training partners. The drill training during this phase is also more focused on the skills the judoka specializes in, and it's during this part of training that situational drills are used regularly to simulate what takes place in an actual judo match.

This is the phase when it's necessary for a judo athlete (and his coach) to carefully organize and structure the overall training program. On some days, the judo athlete will be on the mat doing judo, and on other days the judoka will be off the mat training either in the weight room for strength or working on aerobic conditioning outside or in the gym. This is also when a judo athlete makes the decision to lose weight in order to compete in a lower weight category, and part of his training is in the management of his body weight and daily weigh-ins. In other words, the judo athlete has made a conscious decision to intensify and direct his training for success in judo competition.

Specific Preparation (SP) or "Transformation Phase": This level is extremely specific and aimed at a judo athlete's unique needs for success in competitive judo. This is when a judo athlete will transform the general and directed training of the previous two phases into specific skills that are unique to the athlete. To be successful, a judo athlete must have an organized plan of training. There may be some days that the athlete will be in the gym on the treadmill for aerobic training in the morning and on the mat for focused judo training in the afternoon or evening. It's during this phase that randori is more specialized and focused with the training partners providing varying levels of resistance and intensity that are supervised by the coach. Now is the time to strengthen movement patterns of your whole technique or specific parts of it. For instance, if you specialize in uchi mata (inner thigh throw), you will see an improvement in it by using rubber resistance bands or tubing, a throwing dummy, or resistance drills with training partners.

Incorporate training that duplicates the fatigue and physical stress of a judo match. Exercises and drills that put the judo athlete under more stress than he will encounter are used during this phase of training. This level of intensity is difficult to maintain for long periods of time. Often, specific preparation is part of an athlete's training cycle (periodization). There is more on periodization later in this section.

Training Outlines for GP, DP, and SP Intensity Levels

There will be a different type of practice or training session for each of these three levels of intensity. What follows are three general outlines, one for each of the three typical levels of intensity.

General Phase Typical Practice: This training session is aimed at the general judo student and focuses on providing a well-rounded learning and training experience. The duration is from sixty to ninety minutes and is divided into nine specific areas of education and training: 1. Juniundo, the warm-up phase after bowing in. This includes the general exercises and calisthenics for warming up the muscles, as well as providing some minor cardiovascular exercises, strength exercises and drills, coordination exercises and drills, as well as functional flexibility exercises and drills. This can include a quick mat game as part of the warm-up from time to time. 2. Ukemi, the practice of breakfalls and falling safely. 3. Newaza uchikomi, structured drill training on groundfighting skills such a breakdowns and turnovers to pins, strangles, and armlocks, drill training on escapes from pins, armlocks or strangles, as well as working on transition skills from standing to the mat. 4. Tachi waza uchikomi, the repetition practice for throwing techniques, both non-moving (static) and moving (dynamic). This includes drill training on grip fighting and defensive skills. 5. Nagekomi, throwing practice done with or without crash pads. 6. Kata, the time during a training session when the coach teaches a new skill or adaptations on an existing technical skill. 7. Randori, the time allotted for free practice. Every round of randori should have a purpose done under the supervision of the coach. Usually, for a ninety-minute workout, the time allotted for randori should be about fifteen to twenty minutes. This includes randori and randori-like drills and games. 8. Mondo, the time for questions from the students and answers from the coach discussing general judo knowledge or specific topics chosen by the coach. 9. Shumatsu undo, the cool-down period consisting of light stretches, mat games, or other activities to end practice on a good note with everyone going home tired and happy after bowing out.

Directed Phase Typical Practice: This is a more intense and focused training session aimed at the competitive judo athletes in the club or program. The training should be to-the-point and strenuous. The "90/10 rule" (where there is 90 percent activity and 10 percent active rest) is in effect. This workout will go about sixty to seventy-five minutes. (As I have often told my athletes, the workout will be "short and not-so-sweet.") Usually, there is no need for the coach to spend time working with the entire group on a technical skill; his time will be spent in offering coaching advice as needed to each athlete on the mat during the drill training and randori periods. This training session is divided onto seven segments: 1. Junbiundo and ukemi, with the exercises and drills for both the warm-ups and breakfall practice relevant to what will be done later in the training session. For example, there is no need for a long period of ukemi training if the group of athletes will be taking a lot of falls later in the workout. 2. Newaza uchikomi, with the emphasis on having each athlete on the mat focus his drill training on the breakdowns, turnovers, and other groundfighting skills that he specializes in or wishes to make improvement in doing. 3. Tachi waza uchikomi, with the emphasis on grip fighting randori, drill training on defenses against throwing techniques, and dynamic (moving) uchikomi with the athletes using their tokui waza (favorite techniques) in realistic situations. 4. Nagekomi, using the crash pads for the development of full power into the throws in addition to throwing practice without the crash pads in realistic, moving situations. (Note: the coach, when necessary, should make technical or tactical suggestions to the individual athletes during the course of the workout.) This is also a time when the athletes will work on transition drills from standing to groundwork in order to finish an opponent with a pin, armlock, or strangle. 5. Randori, with the emphasis on functional preparation that includes situational randori drills. 6. Shumatsu undo or cooling-down exercises can consist of a mat game or some light stretching exercises. 7. Mondo or chalk talk with the emphasis on discussing tactics, scouting upcoming possible opponents, and other factors relative to the team.

Specialized Phase Typical Practice: This training session will take place during a training cycle during periodization training, so outlining a "typical" workout is a bit difficult, but the focus of this training is for each judo athlete to specialize in the technical and tactical skills he or she needs. This type of training session is intense and focused, usually lasting about forty-five to sixty minutes. This type of training isn't for a weekend warrior. Depending on when the training session is done during a training cycle, the level of intensity in this session is high. Mandatory water breaks for rehydration are required for every athlete on the mat about every ten to fifteen minutes. Training at this level is for serious judo athletes who have progressed from the general phase of training and the directed phase of training. The focus is on winning and honing the technical and tactical skills that regularly set the judo athlete up to have the best opportunity of winning. In addition to the focused technical and tactical skills, every aspect of physical and mental training is focused on what each specific athlete requires to win. Training sessions at this level of intensity should either focus on groundfighting or standing/transition work. For example, a morning session for groundwork and an afternoon/evening session of standing/transition work should be done on a daily basis.

Groundfighting Practice: A groundfighting training session like this is divided into five segments: 1. Junbiundo (warm-ups) should be specific to what the judo athlete will be doing in each particular training session. If the training session emphasizes groundwork, then the warm-ups should reflect that and focus on exercises and drills to prepare the athletes for groundwork. 2. Newaza uchikomi drills should be specific to each athlete on the mat. Each athlete will work on the breakdowns, turnovers, and other forms of entry at varying levels of resistance from training partners (as determined by the coach) on pins, strangles, and armlocks. The coach will add stress and urgency to the drills by timing the drills so that the athletes must perform specific breakdowns or turnovers within specified time periods. This is tactical training for groundfighting, as the current judo contest rules permit limited time for a judoka to set up a move in newaza. During this phase of training, the coach will offer advice to each athlete as necessary in order for the skill being worked on to be more efficient and effective. During this phase of training, the coach will use situational drills where he places the judo athletes in a variety of situations and have them work. An example is placing Judoka A in a bad or inferior position in relation to his training partner with the goal of Judoka A working out of the bad situation, improving it, and then working to secure control. Another example of a situational drill is for the coach to place the athletes in common situations that occur in groundfighting and then have them work to take control of the situation. 3. Newaza randori will consist of both short, intense bouts of groundfighting randori lasting one minute as well as longer bouts of groundfighting randori lasting two to three minutes. The shorter bouts of randori will focus on quick, intense rounds of activity with the focus on overwhelming an opponent. The longer bouts or rounds of randori will be intense, but the focus will be on increasing each athlete's fitness level. Usually, in a forty-five-minute training session, three to five rounds of one-minute randori and five to ten rounds of two-minute randori are done. 4. Shumatsu undo or cooling down exercises such as light stretching or having the athletes do a quick back, neck, arm, or lower leg massage on each other. A light mat game can also be done (but make sure no one is injured in a mat game). 5. Mondo or the time for a chalk talk to discuss an overall strategy and the specific tactics that will be used to make that strategy work. This is a good time to discuss upcoming opponents, as well as any other topic the coach thinks pertinent to the group.

Standing/Transition Practice: A standing/transition training session is divided into eight segments with one drill flowing into the next drill so that the entire training session is one set of drills followed by another (make sure to have adequate water breaks every ten minutes): 1. Junbiundo exercises and drills should relate specifically to the work that will be done later. In this case, the warm-up exercises should be some cartwheels, roundoffs, and other gymnastic movements as well as some rolling breakfalls. The athletes will get plenty of ukemi practice later when they throw each other, so don't place much emphasis on ukemi (if any at all) during the warm-ups. 2. Grip fighting randori drills should follow with the emphasis on having each individual athlete work on getting the grip or grips that work best for him. Grip fighting randori should be intense at this level of training. 3. Defense skill drills should follow with each athlete working on defense against throwing attacks on both the right and left sides. Several rounds of defense drills should be followed by "defense randori" where the focus is for the athletes to block and negate the attacks of their partners. 4. Moving uchikomi drills should follow with the emphasis on having each athlete use the movement pattern or patterns he intends to use during the upcoming tournament. Much like an actor rehearsing lines for a play or a movie, the judo athletes will "rehearse" their throws using moving uchikomi drills. 5. Transition drill training should include having each judo athlete transition from a throw to an immediate pin, choke, or armlock. These drills should be cooperative in nature so that each judo athlete can quickly and efficiently move from a standing situation or a throw immediately into finishing an opponent with a pin, armlock, or strangle. 6. Nagekomi drills both using crash pads and without using the crash pads should be done next with the emphasis on each athlete focusing on his or her tokui waza (preferred technique or techniques). This phase of the training session should be structured so that each athlete will perform about one hundred full throws on the crash pads (depending on when in the training cycle this session takes place; the intensity of training will subside the closer it gets to the actual tournament). 7. Randori will consist of rounds that are equal to the time limit of the actual matches in the tournament. In other words, it the time limit is four minutes in the tournament, then the time limit for randori will be four minutes. The rest periods between rounds of randori should only be long enough for the athletes to get rehydrated. 8. Shumatsu undo should consist of light stretching and the athletes should give each other quick massages. 9. Mondo should be a chalk talk on strategy and tactics as well as any new scouting information that might be available on upcoming opponents.

Age and Intensity of Training

As already mentioned, specialization is necessary for a person to become an elite or world-class judo athlete. There is a "shelf life" for every judo athlete. This shelf life is the period of time that a judoka is mature enough physically, mentally, and emotionally to be best able to train and compete at a high level. If a judoka starts specializing at a young age and too soon, he or she will burn out and never fully realize his or her potential. From my personal experience as a coach, as well as staying updated on reliable research in education, it's my belief that intense and specialized training for young children in any sport, especially a technically complex and physically demanding sport like judo, does more harm than good for the child. It's not simply my opinion that starting a child too soon in specialized training is detrimental, there is an abundance of research supporting this statement. Starting a child in judo at the age of four or five is too young generally. There are always children who are physically mature for their age, and these are the kids who will dominate the other children in tournaments. From my experience and observation, an overwhelming percentage of children who start judo at the ages of seven or younger end up quitting judo within a few years, usually never to return. Children are "adults in training." The goal should be for a child to participate in a variety of educational and sports activities and mature into adulthood. Judo can be one of many positive and beneficial activities for a child.

If a child starts judo at the age of eight or nine, the focus should be on doing judo as a method of physical education, character development, fun, self-defense, and sport. The technical skills taught to this age group should be geared toward teaching movement, coordination, fitness, and mechanically correct fundamental judo techniques. Success in competitive judo should not be stressed; instead, the emphasis should be on a general judo education. In addition to their judo education, children should experience and participate in a variety of other sports. For proper maturation (physically, mentally, and emotionally) a well-rounded approach should be taken with children at this age level. Kids should play basketball, baseball, soccer, or take gymnastics classes in addition to doing judo. If a child (and not the parents pushing the child) is naturally competitive, the coach should permit him to compete in club, local, and regional judo scrimmages, and tournaments. But the emphasis isn't on winning medals or trophies at this age; the emphasis is on teaching the child physical education through judo. This level of judo education should last for several years, up to the age of about twelve years old.

At the age of twelve or thirteen, and if the child shows interest in approaching his judo training more seriously and wants to compete in the sport of judo, the child can advance to a more intermediate level of intensity. This is the time when a child no longer goes to "judo class" but instead goes to "judo practice." The focus is still on a good overall judo education, but at this level of intensity, the child is more directed toward training for competitive judo. This is a good time for a young judoka to start competing in national judo tournaments or attend training camps. Although a child can start to specialize in judo at this age, he or she should continue to play other sports as well. This variety of sports and activities (including such things as music or art lessons) prevents a budding judo champion from burning out during this period in his life. A child may be really good at judo, but he's still just a kid, so it's a good idea to let him mature into a young adult.

At the age of fifteen or sixteen, a young person is mature enough to advance to more specialized competitive judo training. In some cases (and we all know one of more of this type of young judo athlete), a teenager with several years of judo training can compete successfully against local and regional-level adults. Some teenagers have won the senior national championship or qualified to compete in the world championships or Olympic games. These teenage years are when a young judoka makes his or her move into more elite levels of competition.

On the other hand, someone who starts judo at a later age and wishes to compete in the sport of judo can certainly fulfill his potential if he is already mature enough to understand what he's getting into. One of my successful black belts (who later became a coach) started judo at the age of twenty-five. While he was talented physically, he caught on quickly to the skills of judo and (most of all) had a tremendous work ethic.

The "shelf life" mentioned earlier for a judo athlete will last as long as the judoka enjoys the life of a judo athlete and can overcome the injuries suffered during the course of a career. Some athletes may need to take a break from judo for a short period of time and then get back on the mat. Everyone is different. And there's nothing to stop former judo athletes from coming back and getting on the mat on a regular basis and competing simply because they enjoy it.

Optimal Surplus in Judo

How many times have you seen a top-level judo athlete finish a forward throw even when his hip wasn't in the perfect textbook position to throw his opponent or pry an opponent's arm straight after finishing a turnover into an armlock? Many times, the overwhelming strength of your finish will compensate for minor technical flaws or overcome an opponent's attempt at defense. The ability to finish a technique from an unfavorable position is one of the hallmarks of a champion. Champions have an optimal surplus of physical and mental qualities necessary for success.

Optimal surplus means that an athlete has more of the psychological, physical, and technical qualities than actually needed for a sport. Only through an optimal surplus of physical, technical, tactical, and psychological preparation can an athlete achieve a high rate of success. This optimal surplus doesn't happen by accident; it's developed through training.

A judo athlete must be physically strong enough to "drive through" and finish a technique. This is why strength training is crucial for success in judo. Style points aren't awarded in judo. While a clean, precise technique is desired in order to beat an opponent, the reality of competitive judo is that a judo score is based solely on the results of what a technique has produced. A common occurrence in competitive judo is when a judoka throws his opponent and continues to drive into the action of the throw in order to finish the throw so that the defender ends up flat on his back. What might have been a waza-ari score has been turned into the ippon win. This capability comes from having the physical strength to do it, but it also comes from training "smart" in the dojo. Practicing how to finish (or drive through) is a skill learned and refined in the dojo.

The ability to finish a technique from a less-than-ideal position or situation comes from a judoka voluntarily putting himself in unfavorable positions during training. This is what is known as situational training. In a "situation drill" the judo athletes put themselves in a difficult or unfavorable position many more times than they would actually occur during a judo match (or even in randori). You can invent a drill for everything (and every situation) that happens in a judo match. There will be more on situation drills later in this section.

Conjugate Training

This form of training was made popular in the United States by the great powerlifting coach Louie Simmons based on work done by Soviet sports scientists and coaches in the 1950s through and including the 1970s. Conjugate means "joining together" and describes exactly what conjugate training does. It joins or integrates different exercises, movements, drills, and skills as well as the most effective time to use these exercises and movements so that training is more effective. For our purposes in judo, conjugate training means using a variety of drills, exercises, and movements at the most productive time in an athlete's training schedule. This is not only what exercises to use, but when to use them in a specific training session (or the best time in an overall training cycle) for the most effective results.

Conjugate training encourages the judo athlete to vary his workout routine on the mat. An example is that on Monday, judoka did uchikomi (repetition for throws) training with his partner in a non-moving drill, doing ten sets of ten repetitions for each set on his three favorite throws. On Tuesday, he changed his uchikomi training so that he did moving uchikomi with partners in a variety of movement patterns, doing five sets of five movement patterns. The judoka did uchikomi at both practices but did them in a different manner. Basically, he repeated the same movement patterns but in different ways to provide more practical and realistic situations in training.

Adaption: The human body (as well as the mind) adapts to the stress placed on it. This is called "adaption" and is your body's physiological (and psychological) response to training after repeated exposure. As the body adapts to the stress of one type of training, that type of training becomes easier to perform. It can get boring doing the same workout routine every practice, and this can quickly lead to staleness in training. Conjugate training "shocks" the body and keeps it guessing. By using a variety of skills, drills, and exercises, the body doesn't have a chance to get used to the demands placed on it. Simply put, by using conjugate training, you can plan how to vary your training sessions and when the best time is to practice these variations.

Cross Training

Training in other grappling disciplines is recommended for every judo athlete as long as it is remembered that the purpose of cross training is to supplement a person's judo skills and fitness. The purpose of cross training isn't to supplant or replace what you are doing but to add another layer of skill to what you are doing. Objectively look at how the skills or techniques from other grappling disciplines can be absorbed into your style of judo. Too often, an inexperienced judoka who cross trains in something else thinks he must stop what he is already doing in judo and change his style completely over to what he is cross training in. So, if you want to get the most benefit from cross training, you should have a good foundation of judo skill, and confidence in that skill, before you do.

Training Diary

A good way to "train smart" is for you to keep a training diary and write down any and all information about your on-mat training as well as your off-mat training. This is a good place to keep track of your eating habits as well as how much you weigh (especially if you are cutting weight to make a weight category). You can refer to this training diary when you need some ideas on what worked for you in the past (and what didn't work for you in the past). In a very real sense, your training diary is your personal history of what you did and how you did it in your judo career.

Training for a Tournament Is Like Rehearsing for a Movie

Much like an actor who rehearses for a role in a movie, a judo athlete must rehearse for a judo tournament. For an actor, just learning and repeating the lines in the script isn't good enough. He has to actually bring those words in the script to life for the audience watching the movie. The audience must forget who the actor is and believe (even for a while when watching the movie) that the actor delivering those lines is actually the hero or villain saying them. The actor must deliver his lines so that everything he says is believable. The same thing goes for a judoka. Instead of lines in a script, the judoka learns the technical and tactical skills needed to win judo matches. But that's not enough. The judo athlete must have the ability to turn these skills into the real thing and make them come to life on the mat. He must focus his training on the execution of his technical and tactical skills in such a way that he makes a believer out of everyone who sees him. Maybe winning an Oscar isn't in a judoka's future but standing on top of the podium can be.

Stress in Training

More stress must be placed on the athlete in training than he will encounter in an actual tournament. There is an old saying: "train hard and fight easy"—but no fight is easy. The mental and emotional factors in an actual judo match have to be replicated as much as possible in training, but only actual experience in competition will prepare a judo athlete for what takes place on the mat in a tournament. That said, the goal is to replicate as many aspects of an actual match as possible in training so that the athlete is prepared as completely as possible to deal with them successfully. This training intensity must be gradually increased through the efficient use of training cycles (periodization) leading up to the time of the tournament so that the athlete peaks at the right time in preparation for the event.

Training Cycles or Periodization

The word "periodization" is another way of describing training cycles. It's the practice of dividing the process of training into specific periods or blocks of training. Each period of training has a purpose and lasts a specific amount of time. These periods build on each other progressively from the start of a training cycle to its culmination immediately before a tournament. Each period has a specific purpose that progresses to the next level. These different periods should work together so that the athlete using them is trained in the most efficient manner possible and attains the most effective results possible. What follows is a recommended approach to using periodization for judo.

Training in Waves

It is humanly impossible to train at 100-percent capacity at every training session during the entire year. This is why cycling your training is important. Training in "waves" (called undulating periodization) is the type of training where the volume of your training and the intensity of your training go up and down during a training cycle. The idea is for the body to adapt to the varying types of training, allowing for recovery from an intense training period and then progressing on to a more intense period of training.

Training in waves is preferred for judo because we have no established "season" in judo. Because of this, there is no "off season" in judo for an athlete to stop training completely and recover. There are times during the year that have fewer major events, and in reality, this is about as much of an "off season" a judo athlete has in order to rest and recover. Because of this, a judo athlete must endeavor to remain in at least 50-percent condition during the time of the year he isn't in intense training. This base of conditioning is necessary for training in "waves" to be most efficient. Just like a wave in the ocean, the intensity rises and falls and then the cycle repeats.

Each year, an athlete and his coach must schedule the upcoming major events (both competitions and training camps) the athlete plans on attending. From this, smaller events should be considered as part of the overall training plan for the athlete. The goal for the athlete is to progressively increase his fitness and technical skills to coincide with the major events in which he competes.

An example of this is for an athlete to prepare for a large tournament in early March starting about the second week of January. The athlete will increase his or her aerobic capacity with off-mat training in addition to working on general and non-specific strength training. The on-mat judo workouts should focus on drill training and improvement in technical skills with moderate intensity in randori. This type of training should last about four weeks. At this point, about late February, the athlete should compete in a local judo tournament in order to get back into a competitive frame of mind. After competing in the local tournament, the athlete will back off in the training intensity for a week. This is the first "wave" in the training cycle. After this week of rest (not stopping training, just lessening the intensity so that the body can recover from the initial wave), the athlete will start his next wave of training, only this time, the wave will start at a higher level of fitness and technical skill than the first one did. At each succeeding training period or wave, the athlete will focus on more intense training and specific fitness/strength training for the major tournament of the year. Usually, there will be periods or cycles of three-to-five-week training waves for a judo athlete during any given year with each wave leading up to a specific tournament.

Injuries and Making Weight

Injuries are inevitable, so the best advice is to adapt and learn to train to being as close to 100 percent of your capacity as possible, even with an injury. If an athlete is injured, he or she must get it treated as quickly as possible. Ignoring injuries only weakens an athlete's body. If unattended, one injury will lead to another. On the other hand, judo is a tough sport, and the bumps and bruises that come along with it are part of what we do.

Making weight is also part of what we do, even for heavyweights. During an athlete's career, he should make every effort to control his body weight. Don't allow yourself to become too heavy during an off-time from major competitions. Doing so just makes training all the more difficult during a training cycle. When losing weight for a tournament, make your weight cuts gradually. Losing weight too fast weakens the entire body. Remember, your goal isn't to make weight; your goal is to win the tournament.

Drill Training: Structure in Training

Every practice must have structure. Drill training is this structure. Drill training is the most efficient method of teaching and reinforcing desired behavior in any sport, including judo. An efficient (and effective) practice session is comprised of one drill leading to another. Drill training eliminates to a great extent the goofing off that can take place in a practice session. Through an intelligent use of drill training, judo athletes will learn skills more readily, and the coach can regulate the training times better, avoiding boredom in practice. Drill training can prevent a group of athletes from going stale because it provides for a variety of situations in training.

Drill training is efficient because the drills can vary so much that they provide a variety of training situations that can be structured. Drills permit a coach to conduct a practice session on a small mat area with only a few athletes. Drills provide the coach and athletes the opportunity to isolate specific or general skills and get the athletes to focus on performing them. Just about any situation that takes place in judo can be made into a drill. A drill can be designed for every facet of judo action or reaction. Drills can be done as static (non-moving) or dynamic (moving) and can be done in ideal situations or in realistic situations.

Two Types of Drills

Generally speaking, there are two types of drills: skill drills and fitness drills.

Skill Drill: This type of drill emphasizes the teaching and reinforcing of technical or tactical skills. This drill has its name because this is the process of the athlete learning and practicing a skill with the intention of improving it. There are two types of skill drill. First is a closed-ended drill where the athlete learns and reinforces a specific skill in a specific manner. This is also called a "fixed drill" where the athlete works on a specific skill repeatedly so that is becomes an automatic reflex or movement. This is the type of drill used for beginners learning a new judo throw or pin, but it is also the type of drill necessary for an elite-level athlete to develop specific skills. In this case, the skills being learned and reinforced in a skill drill may be fine-motor skills that can "sand off the rough edges" of a movement for an elite-level judoka. When learning the fundamental of any skill, or when a new skill or concept is introduced to elite-level judo athletes, using closed-ended skill drills should be used so that specific techniques or tactics can most efficiently be learned and developed into an automatic response.

A good example of a closed-ended or fixed drill is uchikomi. Uchikomi is repetition practice where judo athletes perform many repetitions of a specific skill so that the skill becomes an automatic reflex.

The second type of skill drill is an open-ended drill (also called a situational drill). This type of drill is when a judoka is presented a situation and must adapt to it based on already-learned technical or tactical skills. A situational drill is when an athlete practices specific situations that actually take place in a judo match. A coach can develop realistic situational drills by carefully observing situations that come up in an actual judo match and placing his athletes in them during practice.

Fitness Drill: The second type of drill is a fitness drill. These drills emphasize physical development, strength, functional flexibility, coordination, and all movement conducive to the development of functional technical and tactical skill.

An important rule when doing fitness drills is that they must directly relate to judo. This is especially true in junbiundo (warm-up exercises) and shumatsu-undo (cooling-off exercises). The warm-up should directly relate to what is being done later in the workout. If the team is focusing on groundfighting in a particular training session, the warm-ups for it should focus on exercises that strengthen and enhance newaza skills.

There is a carry-over value for every drill. Some skill drills provide excellent fitness training in addition to their intended purpose.

Realism

Drill training should be as realistic as possible. Realism in practice does not mean that the athletes fight each other at 100-percent effort all the time. Some people mistake realism for non-cooperation in practice. Realism means that the judoka performing the drills should cooperate so that maximum learning takes place. Some drills require total cooperation (often this is the case in closed-ended drills where the athletes learn a new technical or tactical skill) while others call for varying degrees of cooperation. For instance, a group of judokas can randori, with both partners giving 50-percent effort. In another type of randori, one partner can go 100 percent while his partner goes only 50 percent with the intent of providing the first partner opportunities to apply his skills. Randori like this prevents the randori training from becoming a free-for-all and provides a purpose for each round of randori. Another example of this type of drill training is when working on breakdowns or turnovers in groundfighting. Drills for breakdowns and turnovers can be done in varying levels of realism so that the first level is total cooperation and the final level is total resistance. However, total resistance in any drill is not all that productive because there should always be an element of surprise. In a drill, uke (the person receiving the technique) knows what tori (the person doing the technique) is going to do. If uke offers 100-percent resistance because he knows what to expect, that is not realistic. Drill training takes cooperation on the part of both athletes who are doing the drill so that the most efficient training takes place.

Time Is Valuable: the 90/10 Rule

Every minute on the mat in training is valuable. What is called the "90/10" rule is where the athletes are engaged in some type of productive activity at least 90 percent of the time and are engaged in active rest for 10 percent of the time. Productive is the key word here. Every minute spent on the mat should have a purpose. Rest when necessary and make sure to stay hydrated during practice. Taking a quick rest break and a drink of water is the definition of active rest; you are resting for a reason. Speaking of this, staying hydrated is essential for an athlete's body to perform well under the stress of training. When training my athletes, my habit has been to take a quick water break after every ten or fifteen minutes of intense training and make sure that everyone on the mat gets some water (whether they say they need it or not). These short water breaks serve as both hydration breaks and as active rest breaks.

Uchikomi Is a Training Drill

Uchikomi is repetition training. For training on throwing techniques, uchikomi (repetitive practice) is practicing all aspects of the technique up to the point of kake (executing the throw). This includes the movement necessary to apply kuzushi (breaking and controlling the training partner's posture and balance) as well as tsukuri (building or forming the technique as a natural and fluid movement from the kuzushi phase). For training on groundfighting techniques, uchikomi is the repeated practice of a technique or movement with cooperation from the training partner.

To get the most out of uchikomi, it's best to look at it as you would any other drill. There are many ways to do uchikomi training. The purpose may be to teach novices how to fit their bodies into the best position when learning a new throwing technique or it may be to create a situation where elite-level athletes want to reinforce a tactical application of a technique or series of techniques. Uchikomi is useful for both throwing and groundfighting techniques.

Uchikomi: This shows an example of uchikomi training. Tori (the attacker) uses a full-body rotation with his hips, shoulders, torso, and head. He fits his body into position for the throwing technique as precisely as possible and does everything in the technique up to the point of throwing his partner. Uchikomi focuses on precise body placement.

Butsukari: Here's a variation of an uchikomi called butsukari. Many people do butsukari and call it an uchikomi, but a butsukari is done for different reasons than an uchikomi. In a butsukari, tori places emphasis on foot placement and foot speed. Tori also emphasizes the lifting-pulling action with his hands and arms when doing butsukari. His body doesn't make a full rotation into the throw (as is done in uchikomi). Butsukari focuses on foot speed and the lifting-pulling action. Both uchikomi and butsukari should be used in training for a total development of throwing techniques.

Uchikomi: A Skill Becomes a Habit

The reason judo athletes practice uchikomi is the same reason they perform every other type of drill training: to develop functional habits in a specific technical skill so that it becomes a habit. A habit is an acquired behavior pattern that is regularly followed so that it has become an automatic response. People can develop bad habits just as easily as developing good habits. For our purposes in training for competitive judo, a "good" habit is a biomechanically sound and efficient way of applying a specific technique. Often, it's during uchikomi training that a judo athlete learns to most efficiently (and effectively) adapt a particular movement or technique so that it has a high rate of success. For this reason, it's a good idea for judo athletes to use a variety of uchikomi drills and not simply perform hundreds of static (non-moving) uchikomi. Using both non-moving (static) and moving (dynamic) uchikomi develops a well-rounded set of skills that provides a judo athlete more realistic training that transfers to practical application in a judo match.

As with other training drills, a judoka can combine uchikomi training with other drills. An example is combining uchikomi (repetitive practice) with nagekomi (throwing practice). A common drill is for one judoka to perform ten uchikomi followed by a full throw. For instance, the judoka does ten uchikomi for tsuri goshi (lifting hip throw), followed immediately by throwing the training partner with the tsuri goshi.

For the most effective results when doing uchikomi training, it's advised to rarely do more than ten repetitions in a set. Much like training in a weight room, performing (for instance) five sets of ten repetitions provides better training than trying to do fifty repetitions of a bench press. It's often difficult for a judoka to maintain functionally optimal form when doing a large number of repetitions. And remember, the goal is to develop good habits in the application of a technique, so it's important to maintain correct technical form when doing uchikomi. Simply doing a large number of uchikomi for the sake of doing a large number of uchikomi is not an effective use of the drill or an effective use of the time when doing the drill. Each and every repetition during uchikomi should be as precise as possible.

In order to get the most effective use of training time and to prevent the training time from becoming boring and stale, use a variety of uchikomi drills. We only have a limited time for training and a limited number of people with whom we can train (even in large clubs), so getting the most efficient use out of the time you have on the mat is essential for success. As an example of what not to do, here's what we often did years ago for uchikomi training. As a young judo athlete in the 1960s and 1970s, I remember the "uchikomi line" where every judoka lined up and the first person in line did ten uchikomi on each partner as he moved down the line. This meant that only one judoka was actually doing uchikomi training at any given time while everyone waited in the line. This wasn't an efficient use of training time. Not only that, doing hundreds of static uchikomi in an uchikomi line is not only boring, it leads to the judo athletes performing ineffective repetitions that ultimately develop bad habits. What started out as crisp, precise uchikomi for the first few people in line turned into sloppy and imprecise uchikomi the farther down the line a judo got. The point of this example is that uchikomi, like any drill, must be performed so that the most efficient and effective use of training time takes place. That said, here are a few effective uchikomi drills.

1. Static Uchikomi/Throw Drill: Judoka A does ten non-moving uchikomi on Judoka B followed by a full throw. Judoka B will do the same. Both judo athletes should do five sets of ten uchikomi/throws.

2. Moving Uchikomi: Judoka A and judoka B move in a specific movement pattern with Judoka A performing ten uchikomi followed by a full throw. Judoka B will do the same. Do this for five sets of ten repetitions so that fifty uchikomi are done.
3. Ugoki Renshu: Judoka A and Judoka B move about the mat in a random movement pattern with Judoka A performing ten uchikomi. Judoka B will do the same. Do this for five sets of ten repetitions so that fifty uchikomi are done. (Ugoki renshu translates to "random movement drill.")
4. Static Uchikomi/Crash Pad Throwing: Judoka A performs one uchikomi on Judoka B and immediately follows it with a full throw on the crash pad (using the same throw). Judoka B will then take his turn doing the same thing. Do this for a specified number of repetitions.
5. Moving Uchikomi/Crash Pad Throwing: This is the same as the uchikomi/throwing drill on #2 listed above, only using a crash pad so that a harder throw can be performed. Judoka A moves Judoka B in a specific movement pattern down the length of the mat performing an uchikomi on every other step and moving toward the crash pad. When Judoka A gets to the crash pad, he will throw Judoka B onto the crash pad. Judoka B will then take his turn. Do this for a specified number of sets (usually five sets are enough).

Matwork Uchikomi

Uchikomi training shouldn't be limited to only throwing techniques; it's effective for developing skill in groundfighting as well. What is called "mat-work uchikomi" is the same as when using uchikomi to develop throwing skills: repeated practice of technical skills so that they become automatic reflexive responses. A good example of a drill to teach and reinforce the skill of rolling an opponent into a strangling technique is as follows. Let's say we are working on a rolling application of kata ha jime (single wing choke): Judoka A's job in this drill is to perform a rolling kata ha jime on Judoka B, first on the right side and then on the left side. This completes his first set. Judoka B then takes his turn doing the same thing. Each judoka will perform ten sets of rolling kata ha jime. This drill is done with total cooperation from both athletes (no resistance). Another way to perform this drill is for the coach to assign a specific period of time for each judo athlete to perform the rolling kata ha jime. For instance, the coach will assign Judoka A one minute to perform as many good (emphasis on good) repetitions as possible on Judoka B. Judoka B offers no resistance. The coach can stipulate that both right-side and left-side techniques must be performed or permit the judoka his choice if he wants to practice the roll from only one side. The emphasis when doing a timed drill like this is for the judo athletes to perform good, skillful techniques and not simply rush through to get as many repetitions as possible. After Judoka A does his drill for a minute, Judoka B will get his turn.

Matwork uchikomi can be done with total cooperation by both judo athletes or by using a varying level of resistance. Total (100 percent) resistance is not recommended during any training drill, including uchikomi. During practice, the defender knows what to expect, and if he gives total resistance in training, it's actually unrealistic. A technique is effective in a judo match because the defender doesn't expect it. Training with matwork uchikomi permits judo athletes to perform multiple numbers of skillful techniques at every training session. Rather than simply waiting until randori to try out a groundfighting technique, a judoka can develop and refine skills so they are more efficiently applied and effectively used in an actual judo match.

Solo Uchikomi Training

One of the advantages of doing uchikomi is that you don't always need a training partner. Ask any judoka who's been around for any length of time and he will tell you how he tied his judo belt to a pole in his garage in order to do some uchikomi training when he wasn't on the mat. In judo, we have two primary types of training: sotai renshu (partner practice) and tandoku renshu (solo practice). Uchikomi can be done with a partner and can be done alone. Anything can be used, including a judo belt, rubber tubing or bands, an old judo jacket, or whatever an enterprising judoka can think of. When going to the gym to lift weights, bring along a judo belt or rubber tubing and do several sets of uchikomi as a warm-up before lifting. When going out for a run, take along your judo belt or rubber tubing and stop every so often to tie the belt around a post or tree and knock off several sets of uchikomi before resuming your run. When you go to judo practice, get there early and tie your judo belt to a pole or onto something on the wall and get in several minutes of uchikomi training before your training partners arrive.

Nagekomi: Throwing Practice

Nagekomi is throwing practice. It's the repeated and structured practice of throwing partners in training. Nage translates to "throwing" and "komi" translates to "applying" and specifically applying something in a practical way.

Nagekomi can be practiced in a static or non-moving situation where the training partners simply stand there and take turns throwing each other. This static nagekomi drill is useful when teaching beginners how to do a throwing technique, but it's also useful for more advanced judo athletes who want to focus on a specific area of improvement on a throw. Nagekomi is often practiced in a dynamic or moving situation where Judoka A will move his partner, Judoka B, in a specific movement pattern in order to set him up for a throw. The throwing pattern is very much part of the overall skill in the throwing technique and this type of moving nagekomi training is effective in developing the "feel" or muscle memory necessary for optimal success in a specific throw.

Nagekomi can be practiced using the judo tatami (mat) only or using a crash pad. Using crash pads for safety in throwing practice has been discussed earlier in this book.

The advantage of doing nagekomi on the tatami is that tori (the thrower) has freedom of movement and can perform a lot of throwing techniques on uke (his partner) in a realistic moving situation. The disadvantage is that if tori throws his training partners with full force repeatedly, he will soon run out of training partners. No one wants to take a lot of hard falls on the mat.

The advantage of doing nagekomi on a crash pad is that tori can throw his training partners full force every time. Doing this develops the explosive power necessary for the best development of the skill necessary for throwing opponents for ippon (full point) in an actual judo match. A judo athlete can do more full throws using full force safely when using crash pads, increasing both the volume and intensity of training. The disadvantage of doing nagekomi on crash pads is that it limits the freedom of movement when practicing throws. The crash pad doesn't usually move so the athletes must make sure that when throwing partners in practice, they take care that the partner being thrown is actually thrown onto the crash pad. There are drills where tori can throw uke onto the crash pad after some movement, but the crash pads do often inhibit a free-moving flow of action during throwing practice.

Most often, a judo athlete will use both uchikomi and nagekomi on a regular basis at practice. These training methods should balance each other out so they work together to develop effective and functional skill in throwing technique. One effective drill is for Judoka A to perform a specific number of uchikomi (for instance, a set of ten repetitions) on Judoka B, and on the eleventh time, do a full throw onto the crash pad.

Solo Nagekomi Practice and Throwing Dummies

Commercial throwing dummies are popular for throwing practice. A nice thing about a throwing dummy is that you don't need a mat. Throwing dummies don't complain about taking hard falls either, so you can slam your throwing dummy as hard as you want and as often as you want. It's a good idea to have a throwing dummy in the dojo as well. Throwing dummies are also effective for training in groundfighting for practicing submission techniques as well as turnovers and other matwork skills.

When there are a limited number of training partners or if no one shows up for practice, a throwing dummy is an ideal training partner who never complains about the abuse you give him. And while a throwing dummy is a good piece of training equipment to have, nothing replaces another human being for practicing throws or groundfighting.

Feedback from Training Partners

Communication is essential during training. Ask for feedback from your training partners and coaches. The best training partner you can have is one who honestly tells you if something is working in the right way or not. Your training partner will observe things you may not see. As you apply a technique, he can experience and feel it firsthand, giving you instant feedback so you can correct a mistake if necessary.

Training Videos

It's not only a good idea to video your matches during a tournament for later review and study; using video during your training sessions to scout upcoming opponents is helpful as well. You can replay the video in your camera on the spot during a workout for an instant review and study the video later for deeper analysis.

Attend Training Camps and Clinics

Go to as many training camps as possible. Training camps offer you a chance to become part of the larger world of judo and are a great place to meet and work out with others.

Meeting people at training camps opens the door for you to advance your career. If you show up to a training camp and are earnest in your efforts, the coaches conducting the camp will take notice and often give more encouragement and technical advice to you. Likewise, attending seminars and clinics by leading coaches or athletes provide you an opportunity to learn new technical skills and information that may improve your training. Judo is a group activity; we need other people on the mat to get the best possible results in learning and training. Attending training camps is a good way to broaden your knowledge and appreciation of judo.

Training Off the Mat

While judo is an excellent method of physical education and increasing physical fitness, judo as a competitive sport requires a good amount of additional training both on and off the mat. A major consideration that must be considered is time. When training off the mat, in the same way as when training on the mat, a judoka has only so much time to devote to training. Unless a judo athlete is a full-time athlete with a sponsor, training time is precious. This is why it's important that a judo athlete knows as much about fitness training as possible.

During the course of a judo match, there are many intense bursts of activity. A judo athlete isn't like a runner who has to run fast for a specified distance that places emphasis on aerobic fitness, or like a weightlifter who has to lift a heavy weight, which places emphasis on anaerobic fitness. There are a lot of "starts and stops" in judo that are explosive episodes of energy followed by short periods of non-explosive activity.

The "Big Three" of Training

In every training session, there are three elements necessary for successful results. They are:

1. Intensity. This is the measure of how difficult the training session is for the athlete.
2. Duration. This is the measure of how long a training session lasts and how long it takes for the athlete to complete the workout.
3. Frequency. This is the measure of how often during the week that the training sessions takes place—how many days during the week that training is performed.

Every aspect of training has its roots in the three elements just listed. These three elements build on and are dependent on each other. If an athlete is hit-and-miss in his training, there will be a big hole in the frequency of his training. On the other hand, if an athlete trains on a regular basis but only goes through the motions and doesn't put in much intensity, an imbalance in training occurs. An athlete might be intense in his efforts but fail to complete his workouts, and then the duration of the training session is cut short and is ineffective. So, when looking at your training, make sure you meet the criteria of the "big three" of training: intensity, duration, and frequency.

Aerobic and Anaerobic Fitness

For our purposes, there are two basic aspects of fitness based on specific and different systems of using energy that are essential for success in judo: aerobic fitness and anaerobic fitness.

Aerobic Fitness: Aerobic means "with oxygen," and this aspect of training involves the respiratory, cardiovascular, and hormone systems. This phase of training enhances the body's ability to use energy most efficiently. The foundation of your fitness training should be aerobic or cardio-vascular training. Strength and anaerobic fitness are essential, but even a powerful engine needs gas in the tank. Commonly called "cardio training" aerobic training means that when you train, aerobically, your heart rate is somewhere between 60 percent to 85 percent of your maximum and for our purposes (when training) is kept somewhere in this target zone of 60 to 85 percent for fifteen to sixty minutes. The energy you expend comes from the oxidation of carbohydrates and fats in your system.

Aerobic fitness is the ability of the body to take in and use oxygen as well as the ability to store and efficiently use oxygen. Aerobic training also toughens the connective tissue (ligaments and tendons), reducing the risk of injury. The more efficient oxygen can be transported and used by the muscles, the stronger a judo athlete will be. A judo match is a series of anaerobic events (sequences of attack-defend counterattack), and the muscles need a constant and efficient stream of oxygen to feed the muscle cells doing the work. The better a judo athlete's ability to transport and use oxygen in the blood system to create energy, the better he will perform. Aerobic fitness also helps a judo athlete recover faster during matches. A judo tournament is usually a day-long affair, and the more energy a judoka has and the better he can recover after a match, the better he can prepare for the next match.

From a psychological standpoint, the words of Coach Vince Lombardi are true: "Fatigue makes cowards of us all." What is meant by this is that the will to win fades as fatigue sets in and a desire to survive takes over. A fit athlete who has the physical ability to withstand the rigors of the physical confrontation in a competition is more confident and has the physical, mental, and emotional ability to apply his technical skills effectively.

Effective aerobic training involves, first, low intensity and long duration training such as running or cycling for long distances; second, medium distance training that include occasional periods of increased intensity (an example is to stop at a point in a run and do some short wind sprints or stop and do several sets of uchikomi); and third, higher intensity aerobic training such as running stairs or hills.

Marathon running is the ultimate example of an aerobic sport. Remember, though, training for a marathon is very different than training for a judo tournament. A judo athlete needs a strong aerobic base in order to recover quickly between intense judo matches that can last for an entire day in a tournament. Because of the unique demands of competitive judo, we have to understand that there is a point of diminishing return at which more aerobic training detracts from the development of explosive power and strength. A judo match lasting four or five minutes is largely anaerobic in nature. This is true even for the matches that go into overtime for another four or five minutes. Judo matches consist of short bursts of explosive and intense activity followed by periods of less intense activity. To meet the physical demands of this type of activity, a judo athlete's training must be well-rounded.

Anaerobic Fitness: Anaerobic means "without oxygen," and this aspect of training involves muscular strength, flexibility, power, and speed. The neuromuscular training that includes the nervous system and training for skill are also included in this aspect of fitness training. While brute strength doesn't help in the development of mechanical skill in a technique, efficient anaerobic training does. The efficient use of strength plays a large role in the development of technical skill. This link of physical strength and technical skill is important because a judo technique isn't done in a vacuum or in an isolated state. A technique relies on the use of force applied in the most effective way. You're not going to control or break an opponent's balance by a slight tug or a flick of the wrist; in order to move a resisting, fit, and skilled opponent, you must force him to move in the direction you want him to go. To generate that force, strength is required, and this is why time in the weight room is a necessary part of a successful judo athlete's training.

When training anaerobically, an athlete builds up an oxygen debt, and in the same way someone my run up too much credit card debt, it needs to be paid off. A product called lactic acid accumulates in your muscles when you work them hard, and if you don't ease up, your muscles will cramp and shut down. When training at high intensity anaerobically, your body is unable to get enough oxygen to your muscles and gets some of the energy necessary for the muscles to work from carbohydrates stored as glycogen in the muscles. When doing anaerobic training, two things are accomplished. First, you train your body to recover a lower heart rate more quickly between periods of intense exercise, such as in between intense flurries of attacks in a judo match. Second, by training anaerobically, you train your muscles to tolerate lactic acid (and other wastes) for longer periods of intense effort before shutting down. It also trains your heart to bring in fresh oxygen-rich blood more efficiently. Anaerobic training enables an athlete to make stronger and more frequent attacks throughout a judo match. One of the best ways to train for anaerobic endurance is interval training.

Interval Training: Interval training is an intense period of exercise followed by an equal period of time for rest. Usually done in sets, interval training develops high levels of fitness.

An athlete can't sustain a near maximum heart rate for very long. Doing so is dangerous and lactic acid will eventually shut down the muscles. In order to keep the quality (intensity) of your work at a high level, you should perform repeated high intensity bouts of some activity that elevates your heart rate, followed by a rest interval or period. Let's call this your "training ratio." For example, if you run a short sprint in fifteen seconds and then rest forty-five seconds before running another sprint, you will have a 1:3 work/rest ratio. The idea here is to allow your heart to return to about 120 beats per minute before doing another bout of exercise. This allows you to put out repeated high-intensity effort. As your anaerobic fitness improves, you will probably be able to reduce your work/rest ratio to 1:2 and eventually to 1:1.

Examples of exercises you can use when doing interval training are running, cycling, or swimming, but an even more efficient way to do interval training is to use some element of judo in your training. Here's an example of how to do this: perform a drill as hard as possible for a specific period of time or repetitions, followed by a timed rest interval. Here's a drill using interval training that both you and your training partner can use.

Judoka A does twenty seconds of uchikomi (doing as many as possible with good form).

Judoka B does twenty seconds of uchikomi (doing as many as possible with good form.)

Allow for twenty seconds of rest before repeating the sequence.

Repeat this drill for three to ten sets depending on the fitness level of the athletes. After doing this twenty-second drill, move to a more intense ten-second drill.

Judoka A does ten seconds of uchikomi (doing as many as possible with good form).

Judoka B does ten seconds of uchikomi (doing as many as possible with good form).

Allow for ten seconds of rest before repeating the sequence. Repeat this drill for three to ten sets depending on the fitness level of the athletes.

This drill gives you a 1:2 work/rest ratio. You will rest twice as much as you work, and your fitness level will improve. As your fitness level improves, you will eliminate the rest period and just get your rest as your partner does his uchikomi, giving you a 1:1 work/rest ratio. When you get to this point, you probably will be grinding opponents into the mat.

Interval Training Using Groundfighting (Newaza) Randori: An explanation of groundfighting randori is doing randori focusing exclusively on newaza or matwork skills. This training is often called newaza randori. Training in groundfighting randori is an effective way to increase fitness levels, both aerobically and anaerobically. It also allows for an athlete to focus entirely on technical skills in groundfighting.

A recommendation for using newaza randori for interval training is to have one practice on the average of once per month of doing nothing but groundfighting randori. Go ten rounds of two to four minutes of newaza randori with a two-minute rest between each round. The level of intensity in these rounds should be light to moderate. When engaged in a training cycle for a specific tournament, the intensity of the training should be increased, both in terms of how many rounds to go as well as the time of each round of newaza randori. As with any form of interval training, the athletes engaging in newaza randori should gradually increase the workload for both the volume and intensity and work to a point where the following training session can be achieved. This training session should be five to ten rounds of four to five minutes of newaza randori with one-minute of rest between rounds depending on when it takes place in the training cycle. The closer this takes place to the actual event being trained for, the fewer number of rounds the athletes should do. It's physically and mentally difficult to sustain this type of pace in training, and this is why it is recommended for use during a training cycle. While this type of interval training doesn't specifically fit the formula for interval training in general, it's still considered interval-type training where the athlete engages in intense training followed by a rest period for a predetermined number of rounds.

"No Gi" Groundfighting Randori: Occasionally, training in newaza randori without a jacket or belt provides a good workout and is a change of pace. Not using a jacket and a belt forces a judo athlete to follow Rene Pommerelle's advice that "everything is a handle."

Usually, if a judo athlete can control training partners not wearing a jacket or belt, he can control training partners or opponents who do.

A Fighter's Physique

When training in the weight room, train to have a "fighter's physique." A judo athlete isn't a bodybuilder, long-distance runner, or cyclist—he's all of that and more in terms of physical capability. The focus of training must be on functional strength and not physical appearance. There certainly will be an increase in muscle size, but more importantly, there will also be an increase in bone density, strength development in tendons, and an increase in strength.

The scope of this book doesn't cover specific exercises used for training in the weight room. The best advice is to find a certified strength and conditioning trainer and develop a training routine focused on your specific needs.

Training Efficiency

What is sometimes called an athlete's "training ethic" is another way of saying "work ethic." A judo athlete's success lies in direct relation to how hard he or she works. Another thing to add to this is how "smart" an athlete works, both off and on the mat. Focus on the training methods that work best for you and do them with intensity. By training smarter, you also train harder. This combination of training hard and training smart is called training efficiency. Training in a systematic, structured way makes you work harder and yields greater rewards for your efforts. Lazy athletes may get by on natural talent for a while, but eventually the athlete who has a better work ethic will surpass the one who doesn't.

Overtraining

Sometimes, and it happens to all of us, we get stale and burn out from training. One of the basic concepts of training is that you want to overload your body so that it responds by an increase in strength, muscular endurance, and an efficient cardiovascular capacity. An athlete progressively increases his workload, and because of this, he runs the risk of "overtraining." Most of us in judo are "type A" personalities and because of this, we are susceptible to demanding too much from our bodies from time to time. Overtraining is the result of physical, mental, and emotional factors that lead to staleness. This not only includes the stress that an athlete places on his body, mind, and emotions during training, it includes the stress of daily living. How effectively an athlete manages his job, home life, and the rigors of training can determine his success, both in the dojo and in his life in general. Sometimes, a judo athlete will have to reassess his priorities and make adjustments to prevent becoming stale and overtrained.

Along with training hard, make sure you balance it out with sufficient rest and recovery as well as sufficient nutrition. Sleep and "down time" from training as well as a healthy diet are vital to your success. A good way to avoid staleness in training is to have some variety. Remember, the more intense your workouts are, the more intense the after-effects from those workouts will be. This is why it's vital that you actively make the effort to rest and recover as well as have good nutritional habits.

When training is no longer enjoyable, or if you have difficulty in concentrating, experience mood swings, or have a general sense of malaise and fatigue, you are overtrained and need to take a break for a while. Here are some signs of overtraining: 1. Irritability and mood swings; generally, "not being yourself." 2. Frequent head colds or getting sick and an increase in aches and pains. 3. Your sleep patterns change and you wake up tired. 4. You lack motivation to work out and you lose interest in judo. 5. Your performance lessens, not only on the mat, but in every aspect of life. 6. You get sore and tired from what used to be light to moderate workouts. 7. Your reflexes, strength, skill, speed, and cardiovascular endurance is lessened. 8. You stay tired for days after a workout. 9. You look for reasons to avoid training.

Tips on Avoiding Overtraining: A good way to avoid overtraining or to lessen its effects is to talk to your coach or teammates and develop realistic training goals. Use training cycles or periodization when training for a major tournament. Use a workout journal to record both your off-mat training as well as your on-mat training and to assess your training so you can better judge when it's a good time to take a break from training.

Here are some tips that you might find useful to avoid overtraining: 1. Balance periods of work and rest. This means rest, recovery, and nutrition between training sessions as well as alternating rest and recovery during your actual workout. Doing this helps you adapt to the training load that you are placing on yourself. 2. Don't make huge jumps in the level of intensity in your training. Gradually increase how hard you push yourself. 3. You need rest, recovery, and nutrition to help avoid overtraining. Getting enough good sleep and food as well as getting enough time away from the grind of training are helpful in avoiding overtraining. 4. Consider your age. Older athletes require more recuperation than younger athletes. 5. Female athletes recover at a slower pace than male athletes because of differences in the endocrine system. 6. Consider the altitude, climate, and weather conditions where you are training. Training at high altitude places more stress on the body than training in lower altitudes. 7. Generally, experienced judo athletes require less time to recover than those with less experience. This is due mostly to the fact that experienced judo athletes have faster and more efficient physiological adaption to intense training. In other words, if you are new to this type of training, take your time and make gradual increases in intensity. This ties in directly with #2 listed above. 8. Vary your workouts. Change your training routine. Doing this really does make a difference in avoiding boredom and staleness in training.

Injuries

Donn Draeger once said, "Judo is the great crippler." He, like every other judoka, knew that there is a 100-percent injury rate in the sport of judo. Judo is a physically demanding and tough sport, and injuries take place.

One of the best ways to avoid injuries, or at least to lessen their severity, is to stay in the best shape possible during the entire year. Not only will you have a better ability to withstand abuse and injury, your body will physically compensate more efficiently when you are in good physical condition. By staying in good condition year round, you will be better able to begin the stressful rigors of a training cycle when preparing for a major judo tournament.

Something else to consider is that when an injury occurs, deal with it analytically and intelligently. Ignoring what happened or trying to work through the injury won't make you uninjured, so deal with it and get on with what it takes to get you back on the mat again. Be realistic about the injury and take the necessary time off in order to heal, rehabilitate, and recover. Training or competing with a serious injury will do you more harm than good.

Just about everyone who competes in judo often has some kind of "ding" or small injury that must be dealt with. Make sure you receive proper, professional medical and therapeutic care. It's always a good idea to know who some good sports orthopedic doctors are in your area. There is a difference between pain and soreness, as well as being genuinely injured or just dinged up. When recovering from an injury, follow your physical therapy plan strictly and consider this as part of your training. Don't reinjure yourself by "testing" yourself or the injured body part. Let your body heal. When you come back from an injury, get back into the swing of things gradually. Also, don't gain too much weight when recovering from an injury. Conversely, don't use this recovery time as a time to cut or lose weight. Good nutrition is part of the healing process. Learn from your mistake, or at least learn from how or why you were injured and plan on not letting that happen again.

Diet, Nutrition, and Hydration

What you ingest is the fuel that provides energy to your body for growth and recovery from training. Eat plenty of fresh vegetables, fruits, and juices. While that may seem obvious, many athletes don't do it. Vitamin or nutritional supplements are just that: supplements. They don't replace a well-balanced diet of heathy food. When shopping, keep in mind that the food you put in your cart is the food that fuels your body. Salty chips, carbonated beverages, and fatty foods provide sludge and not the high-octane energy you need to fuel your engine. If you can afford it, get a good juicer and use it. It's a good idea to reduce or eliminate hydrogenated oil from your diet. You need fat in your diet, but use olive oil or flaxseed oil rather than what's often convenient to buy commercially. Foods with sugar or corn syrup as well as foods containing a lot of sodium are full of empty calories, so it's best to avoid them.

Drink plenty of water. As an athlete, you place a great amount of stress on your body and need adequate hydration. Using commercially available sports drinks is okay, but nothing beats water for providing good hydration. When going to the gym, the dojo, or outside for a run, make it a point to take along a water bottle and drink it as needed. Your body requires regular rehydration during serious training. This includes taking water breaks on a regular basis. Avoid carbonated, sweetened, or flavored drinks; there is no substitute for water.

Use supplements wisely. While vitamins and supplements are helpful, there is no magic potion or super food that will give you an edge. Supplements are not replacements for the good nutrition that you get from a well-balanced diet. Other types of supplements that should be avoided are performance enhancing drugs or anabolic steroids. Abuse of these drugs is a matter of life and death. Both the physical and psychological effects of performance enhancing drugs have ruined lives—not only the lives of the athletes using them, but also the lives of their family, friends, and training partners. No medal is worth it.

Pre-tournament Meal and Tournament Nutrition: Eat a meal high in complex carbohydrates before a tournament. Carbohydrates are digested easily and provide for a normal level of blood glucose and glycogen before your matches. This is especially important if you've been cutting weight and need to get your blood sugar levels back to normal. Avoid high-protein foods such as steak as a pre-tournament meal as it takes too much energy to digest the steak and you need all the energy you can get for the tournament. Digesting all that protein also dehydrates your body because the process takes a lot of water. Not only that, it's important to have a clean colon as possible when you walk onto the mat and that's where adequate hydration is necessary. A meal based on carbohydrates the evening before you compete not only supplies you with the necessary nutrition, the fecal matter from the meal is eliminated more easily than a meal based on protein.

When at the tournament, have a supply of carbohydrate snacks and plenty of water. Avoid using commercially available sports drinks or energy drinks. One reason is that if you are competing in a tournament where drug testing is performed, the energy drink or supplement may have banned substances. Some of these energy drinks and supplements provide a quick burst of energy but then cause your system to "crash." That "sugar high" or "caffeine high" is always followed by a serious reverse rebound and results in a dull performance.

Everything is a handle.

—Rene Pommerelle

CHAPTER 5

Gripping and Movement

Your first contact with your opponent is with your hands. How you grab or grip your opponent plays a vital role in your success. The purpose of gripping is to control your opponent's body and how, where, and when he moves it. The better that a judo athlete controls the grip, the better he will control how his opponent moves. Gripping and movement combine to control an opponent's body. This section of the book concentrates on how the effective use of gripping and holding onto an opponent often determines how and where that opponent moves. The first part of this section focuses on gripping and grip fighting, and the second part of this section focuses on movement in judo and how movement is determined by gripping.

Gripping in Judo

How you grab onto your opponent directly determines how, where, and when he moves. Likewise, how your opponent grabs onto you determines how, where, and when you move. The judo athlete who controls the grip will control the movement. Gripping and movement are linked together in the same way a train engine pulls the freight cars. The grip is the engine and determines how, where, and when the freight cars move. Let's now examine gripping and grip fighting.

Everything Is a Handle

Any grip that works for you with a high rate of success is a good grip. In most cases, the throw you choose is designed from the grip that you control your opponent with or counter with. Knowing the many ways to grip, grab, and manipulate your opponent to control him is an essential skill in judo. It's best to think that every part of your opponent's body and uniform (and every part of your body and uniform) are handles. Everything is a handle when it comes to gripping. Using your hands to grab your opponent is the primary way of connecting your body to his, but you should learn how to use your arms, elbows, shoulders, hips, and any part of your body possible to control him. Generally, if you are a right-handed thrower, your right hand/arm is the "steering hand/arm" and your left hand/arm is the "leading hand/arm." The Japanese consider the right hand the "tsurite" or "lifting hand" and the left hand the "hikite" or the "pulling hand."

Tying Your Opponent Up with the Grip

If you think of your grip on your opponent's jacket in the same way you would think of wrapping a belt or rope around him, you have a good concept of how to control your opponent with your grip. If you successfully control your opponent's grip, you are "tying him up" with the grip, controlling and breaking his posture, controlling his body movement, controlling the tempo of the action, and ultimately controlling how you throw him to the mat. Your grip is the first link in how you throw your opponent. Your posture and your opponent's posture are part of how you grip with him and dictate the type of throw you will choose to attack or counter with. The space between your hips and your opponent's hips dictates the posture and often dictates how you will choose to grip fight with him.

Take Control: Tactical Purpose of Gripping

Don't just show up on the mat and "see what happens"; take control from the start of the match. To accomplish this, you must have a plan and the plan you have is made up of the tactics you employ. This starts with how your grip your opponent. There are two primary purposes in grip fighting. They are: 1. Control your opponent in order to give yourself more mobility and freedom of movement. In doing this, control the space between your body and your opponent's body. By doing this, you must also control how slow or fast you and your opponent move about the mat (the tempo or pace). 2. Control your opponent to limit his ability to attack you. Do everything allowed within the rules to shut your opponent down and prevent him from launching an attack.

In every throwing technique, how you grab your opponent dictates the success of the action. The better you control your opponent with your grip, the better you will throw him. An important point to remember is that if you don't grip or tie up your opponent well, you most likely won't throw him very well either. It can't be stressed enough that before you can control your opponent's posture, movement, or other aspects of throwing him, you must have a grip that works for you. Your throw often flows directly from your grip, and this is why it's vital you have good gripping skills if you want to be able to throw opponents with a high rate of success.

Each of your hands and arms as well as shoulders and hips work independently of each other in that they each have specific jobs to perform in the overall scheme of things. An example of this is when one hand grips the opponent in a certain way to isolate his arm or shoulder and pull it down while the other hand and arm reaches over his shoulder to secure a back grip. The objective is to get the back grip, but one hand has to control the posture and movement of the opponent so that the other hand can get the desired grip.

Your posture is vital to good gripping. Your body must be close enough to attack and defend at will, and your body must be in a position to move as freely as possible. As stated throughout this entire book, leading with your hips is important in attacking, defending, and moving freely. Your hips should be close to your opponent so you can immediately attack him and be close enough so you can disrupt the momentum of his attack in defense. With this in mind, gripping is a tool that allows you to be in a position to attack and defend in a fluid, constantly moving situation. I call this "grips and hips," and it's a good way to remember that grip fighting and fluid hip action are interconnected and rely on each other for success in throwing and defending against throws or takedowns.

Goals of Gripping and Grip Fighting

Decide what you want to accomplish with your grip. What's the purpose of grabbing your opponent in the way you are grabbing him? Using the grip or tie-up is fundamentally important tactically in a judo match. The bottom line is this: why are you gripping your opponent the way you are gripping him? What's its purpose? Here are some goals to consider when grip fighting.

1. Limit your opponent's movement; shut him down.
2. Use your grip to set up your favorite throwing attack.
3. Control your opponent's posture.
4. Force your opponent to move in a specific direction.
5. Control the tempo or pace of the match.
6. Engage your opponent in grip fighting to kill time on the clock if you are ahead in the score.
7. Neutralize your opponent's strong (power or steering) hand.
8. Neutralize your opponent's pulling hand.
9. Control the space between you and your opponent.
10. "Kill" or control your opponent's forward shoulder so that it's not stable or useable.

Kumi Kata

The kumi kata is the standard and neutral grip used in the learning and practice of judo. This is considered the basic grip. For example, a right-handed judoka will use his right hand to grasp his partner's left lapel and use his left hand to grasp his partner's right sleeve. The phrase "kumi kata" is made up of two words; "kumi" implies grappling or engaging with another person in a contest, and "kata" translates to form. So, kumi kata is a general description of the form of holding onto another person to engage in grappling. During the course of judo's history, kumi kata has come to describe all gripping and grip fighting used in judo.

Jigoro Kano initially developed the neutral grip or "kumi kata," also often called the normal grip or natural grip. After Professor Kano designed the judogi (judo suit or uniform) about 1907, he saw the necessity to develop a standard and neutral method for his students to grab onto each other in order to better learn and practice throwing techniques. Prior to this, there was no standard judo uniform and there was no standard way of holding the uniform in order to practice judo. The kumi kata allowed for the free movement and practice of throwing techniques and revolutionized the entire way of practicing jujutsu and Kodokan judo. It was now possible to have a common way of gripping or holding a training partner to learn fundamental throwing techniques. This method of gripping, the kumi kata, was so effective that it has stood the test of time and continues to be used today in the teaching and learning of throwing techniques. There are three primary gripping situations.

Neutral Grip

This is a situation where neither you nor your opponent have an advantageous grip. You're fighting on even terms, all the while attempting to gain a dominant grip and control the action of the match. What usually takes place is that you and your opponent are holding with a lapel/sleeve grip. This grip is the usually kumi kata and is taught to beginners so they have freedom of movement and can work on equal terms when learning new throwing skills. That doesn't make it bad. A lot of great judo athletes have used the kumi kata with amazing success. This is a neutral grip and gives neither fighter the advantage, unless of course one athlete can use it with a higher degree of skill than his opponent. Learning the basic, core throws from the neutral (kumi kata) grip initially offers novices the best opportunity to learn skills. However, after having learned the fundamental mechanical skills of the throw, it's best to transition the grip to one that will work best for the throwing technique being used in the given situation. In other words, match the grip to the throw for the best results in achieving a high rate of success in actual competition.

Dominant Grip

Make every attempt to dominate the grip. When fighting an opponent, your goal should be to dominate the gripping situation and control his movements as much as possible. You can assert yourself as well as nullify your opponent's body movement (and any attack he may attempt) with an aggressive, dominant grip. You want to fight him on your terms, not his. This is the grip that you want to impose on your opponent so you can set him up for your throw. You may work the same throw from different grips, but each of these grips works well for you on the same throw from a different situation. In every judo contest, there is an ebb and flow of who dominates the grip at any given time, so don't expect to dominate in every situation, but it's important that you do. You should experiment with your grips during your workouts to find the grip(s) that work best for you in realistic situations.

Defensive/Counter Grip

If your opponent has managed to dominate or control the grip or how you grab each other, you must work to defend yourself and counter with your own grip. Do everything you can to avoid fighting on his terms. Your defensive grip can buy you some time or space to survive your opponent's attack and neutralize the action. Your defensive grip can also be used as a counter grip to attack your opponent and make him pay for attacking you. In practice, use a variety of grip-fighting drills with a variety of training partners so you can adapt to as many grips as possible and learn how to counter them with your own grip and body movement.

Tactical Considerations: Grip Distance, the Anchor Hand, and Transition Grip

The distance between the two bodies of the contestants is a part of judo that is important to understand, both in terms of technical application and tactical application. Usually, how the two contestants grip each other determines this body distance.

Short Grips and Long Grips: There are two types of grip that should be considered from a tactical standpoint in terms of the distance between the two contestants. The first is the "short" grip and the second is the "long" grip. These gripping distances are measured primarily from the shoulders and to a lesser degree measured from the distances of the hips of the contestants. In a practical sense, a short grip is one where an athlete's primary control point is his opponent's shoulders. A long grip is where an athlete's primary control point is his opponent's arms. In most cases, a short grip leads to less distance between the two athletes and may produce a slower tempo when the athlete moves about the mat. A long grip tends to lead to more space between the opponents and makes for a faster tempo when the athletes move about the mat.

The Anchor Hand: It's rare that a judoka will grip his opponent with both hands at the same time. Usually, an athlete will use one of his hands to establish initial control. This hand is called the "anchor hand." The anchor hand may not always be the hand that takes the initial grip, but often is. An example is when a judoka initially uses his left hand to grip low on his opponent's sleeve to make initial contact but quickly grips with his right hand to control his opponent's shoulder at the lapel. This now becomes the anchor hand that can be used to hold onto the opponent as the match progresses. It's the hand used to control the opponent long enough to allow the attacker the opportunity to establish his position and stance.

Transition Grip: This is a grip that the attacker uses temporarily to secure the grip he really wants. A transition grip is exactly that: a grip that transitions to another grip. A transition grip isn't used as the primary grip to launch an attack from. Transition grips are also useful for breaking an opponent's posture before moving the opponent in the direction the attacker wishes. Transition grips are an essential way of connecting one grip to another in grip fighting.

The Use of the Limbs in Gripping

Each of your hands and arms has a specific job in controlling an opponent. They work independently of each other, but all the while they are interdependent on each other for achieving the most effective way of controlling an opponent. For this reason, it's important to know what each limb's primary job is and how each limb does what it does.

It's helpful to remember that the hands are connected to the arms and the arms are connected to the shoulders, and the shoulders are in a direct line positioned above the hips. The hips are connected to the legs and feet. Think of this as a chain and each body part as a link in the chain. When one link is moved, it affects all the other links connected to it. So, when gripping an opponent, you are starting this chain reaction of events that move and control his entire body.

Hikite: This is the pulling hand. In a kumi kata, it's the hand that holds the opponent's sleeve, but the hikite is not limited to only holding onto the sleeve. The hikite starts the action of breaking and controlling an opponent's posture and balance. The hikite is important because of this. Ideally, the best area to grip using the hikite is the opponent's upper arm at the triceps area on the back of his sleeve. As the attacker initiates his attack with his pulling action, he will rotate his wrist and hand as if he were looking at his wristwatch. This initial pull should be done with a snapping action. The rotation of the attacker's pulling hand traps the defender's upper arm as the attacker's hand grips the defender's sleeve and tightens the grip on the sleeve in a sharp, jerking movement. This is the start of the pulling movement necessary for generating control and power with the hikite.

When using the hikite (pulling hand), the attacker doesn't only use his hand to pull, he uses his elbow as well. The direction of the attacker's elbow is important because it creates a line of pull (or line of force) with the attacker's body turning into the direction of the throw. Because of the way the hand, arm, and shoulder are connected to each other, the attacker must always pull with his hikite (pulling hand) in the same direction his elbow goes. In pulling, the hand follows the elbow. Conversely, when pushing, the movement of the elbow follows the movement of the hand. Sometimes, the attacker uses his hikite to pull upward and forward. Sometimes the attacker uses his hikite to pull his opponent's elbow and arm into the attacker's body in a rotational pulling action. In this situation, the attacker does not use his hikite to pull up and forward but instead uses it to pull his opponent downward and close to the attacker's torso. Sometimes, the attacker pulls downward (to the mat) with his hikite.

The action of the hikite puts the attacker's entire body into motion in order to control and break the opponent's posture and balance. The attacker's arms are not the only things that start the pulling action in a throwing technique. The attacker's pulling action also involves his entire upper body. The rapid turning of the attacker's body is generated from the turning of his hips as he uses his hand and arm to pull his opponent. During this initial pulling action, the attacker usually lifts (but sometimes also pulls down, depending on the situation) in a straight line. This action of pulling and steering with the elbow greatly helps the attacker in the pulling and steering action of the hand that holds onto the opponent's sleeve.

Here are three of the most common and effective methods of using the hikite: the standard line of pull, the rotational line of pull, and the downward line of pull.

Standard Application of Hikite: Many throwing techniques in judo use this type of hikite where the thrower pulls forward and slightly upward in a straight line of pull into the direction of the throw.

Rotational Application of Hikite: Another common use of the hikite is for the thrower to pull the defender's arm forward and then quickly pull the arm down to the thrower's far hip. This creates a rotational pulling action.

Pulling-Down Application of Hikite: Another common use of the hikite is for the thrower to pull the defender's elbow downward to the mat as shown here.

Tsurite: This word translates to "lifting hand," and generally that is an adequate description. But the tsurite does much more than lift. The tsurite is also called the "power hand," "steering hand," and "direction hand" because the tsurite does all of these things. The tsurite has two basic jobs. Its first purpose is to lift the opponent's body sufficiently up forward, backward, or to the side to allow the attacker's body the necessary space to start its entry (by turning) into the throw. In other words, the tsurite "steers" the opponent's body along in the same direction that the attacker's hikite (pulling hand) is pulling it. The second job of the tsurite is to control the opponent's body as it is being thrown. Just like a rocket ship has a trajectory or flight path when in the air, the human body has a flight path once it's been lifted up and put in the air.

The tsurite is the hand that not only lifts but also traps, hooks, and manipulates the defender. An example is ippon seoi nage (one-arm shoulder throw) where the attacker uses his tsurite to trap his opponent's arm and then lift it in order to steer the opponent into the direction of the throw.

This shows the tsurite in a standard application where the attacker uses his right hand to grip his opponent's jacket and lift it upward and forward. In this photo, the attacker's right hand grips the defender's lapel with the attacker's hand pointed upward. The attacker's right forearm is placed along the outside of the defender's pectoral area with the attacker's right elbow pointing downward. Many basic applications of judo's throwing techniques make use of the tsurite in this way.

This shows using the tsurite to trap opponent's arm. The attacker's right arm hooks and traps his opponent's right arm, using it to better control him. In many throws such as ippon seoi nage (one-arm back carry throw) morote seoi nage (both-hands back carry throw), the opponent's arm is trapped in this way. The arm isn't the only thing that can be trapped. In throws such as koshi guruma (hip wheel), the attacker will use his arm to trap his opponent's neck and head.

This shows the attacker using the tsurite in a back grip to steer and control his opponent. There are several effective back grips, and this photo shows how the attacker is using his tsurite to grip and control his opponent's back and "kill" the opponent's shoulder by pulling it downward to the mat.

This shows the attacker using the tsurite to "tightwaist" an opponent and throw him with ogoshi (major hip throw). The attacker uses his hand and arm to reach around his opponent's waist or hip area and grab it tightly (thus, the name "tightwaist").

This shows the judo athlete on the left using his right arm and hand as the tsurite to make space between himself and his opponent.

Your head is the "third arm." The old saying, "Where your head goes, your body follows" is true. Rene Pommerelle called the head the "third arm," and it's a good description of how we use the head in judo. Your head provides directional control and applies force in the application of a technique, both for throwing and groundfighting techniques. Usually, the rotation of the attacker's head is aligned with the turning or rotation of his body in a throwing technique. This head rotation generates force working in unison with the force created by the turning of the attacker's body as the throw is started. The head is connected to the shoulders, the shoulders are connected to the hips, and the hips are connected to the legs and feet. Everything works in unison for the attacker to effectively fit into position to throw his opponent. The synchronized power chain that emanates from the attacker's feet and up through his legs to his hips and torso, to his shoulders, and then to his head is what makes a throwing technique work efficiently (and effectively).

Some General Observations on Grip Fighting

Any grip that works for you with a good rate of rate of success is a good grip. The throw you choose to use is almost always originated from the grip with which you control or counter your opponent. Knowing the many ways to grip, grab, manipulate, and control your opponent's jacket, belt, pants, shorts, head, shoulders, arms, hands, legs, or any body part or any part of his clothing is essential to knowing how to apply an effective throw. Everything is a handle used to grab and control your opponent.

Connecting to Your Opponent: Using your hands to grab your opponent is the primary way of connecting your body to his, but you should learn how to use your arms, elbows, shoulders, hips, and any part of your body possible to control him. Generally, if you are a right-handed thrower, your right hand/arm is the "steering hand/arm" and your left hand/arm is the "leading hand/arm." The Japanese consider the right hand the tsurite or "lifting hand" and the left hand the hikite or the "pulling hand." As mentioned above, if you think of your grip on your opponent's jacket in the same way you would think of wrapping a belt or rope around him, you have a good concept of how to control your opponent with your grip. If you successfully control your opponent's grip, you are "tying him up" with the grip, controlling and breaking his posture, controlling his body movement, controlling the tempo of the action, and ultimately, controlling how you throw him to the mat. Your grip is the first link in how you throw your opponent. Posture, both yours and your opponent's, is part of how you grip with him and dictates the type of throw you will choose to attack or counter with. The space between your hips and your opponent's hips dictates the posture and often whom you will choose to grip fight with.

Guidelines for Grip Fighting

Here are some practical guidelines to know and apply every time you engage with an opponent. The whole idea is to control your opponent, so it's important to try to achieve the dominant grip as often as possible. However, that doesn't always happen in a judo match, so if you've been placed in a defensive situation, it's also vital to know how to neutralize and counter your opponent's grip, and then go on to gain the dominant grip.

Remember, the end result in getting the grip is to throw your opponent and win the match. Grip fighting is simply a means to an end and is a set of necessary (and important) tools for you to achieve your ultimate goal of throwing your opponent.

1. Immediately after you start the fight or match, or after any break in the action after which you start again, hold your hands up at chest level with your palms facing your opponent, as if pretending you are looking at your opponent through a television screen or picture frame. This is a good ready posture.
2. Always try to get your hands on your opponent first and get the dominant grip. Don't fight on his terms and don't let him attain the better grip or tie-up. Be aggressive in getting your grip. How you grip fight or fight for the tie-up not only puts you in a position to attack him better, but it lets your opponent know you mean business. Your initial contact with your opponent is that grip. Be the one who takes control and dictates the terms of the fight.
3. If you can't get the dominant grip, try to break his grip and counter with your own grip or tie-up. If you can't counter and get the dominant grip, at least get a neutral grip.
4. If you have to initially be in a neutral grip or tie-up situation with your opponent, work hard to dominate the grip. You want all the odds in your favor, and a neutral grip gives him as good of a chance to throw you as you have of throwing him, so do everything you can to get the dominant grip.
5. Your grip should lead to something. Use your grip or tie-up to set your opponent up for your throw or takedown. Your throw flows naturally from your grip. Make sure the grip you use works best for the throw you want to use.
6. Try not to let your opponent get both hands on you. If he's a one-handed fighter, he can't control you as well as he could if he had both hands on you.

7. Never, ever grab with the same hand as your lead leg. In other words, if you lead with your left leg, don't grab your opponent initially with your left hand. Instead, if your lead (sugar) foot or leg is the left one, reach with your right hand to get your initial grip. This way, you're not off balance and allowing your opponent to foot sweep you or attack you with another throw or takedown.
8. Use your steering hand as "radar." If you are a right-handed fighter, try to use your right hand to feel your opponent's movements, whether your right hand is on his lapel in the middle of his chest, on his back or shoulder—really anywhere that you can feel his movement. I used to train with a guy who was a left-handed fighter who liked to keep his left hand planted on his opponent's chest, right in the middle if he could. He told me that this was his "radar" and he could feel if his opponent turned, even slightly.
9. Neutralize your opponent's steering hand. If he's a right-handed judoka and wants to get his right hand on you, grip it first and keep it pushed down and away from you so he can't get his hand on you. This ties in with making him a one-handed fighter.
10. Emphasize your steering hand. If you are a right-handed fighter, this is your right hand. This is called the tsurite (lifting hand). However, this hand does more than simply lift your opponent; you use it to steer and control your opponent. Your left hand would then assist in getting the grip, pulling him, fending off his hand, or any variety of uses. The steering hand is also called the "power" hand and this is a good description as well, but remember that the purpose of this hand is to steer your opponent.
11. Getting the thumb caught in the opponent's lapel when grabbing it is a weak grip. This often leads to a "floating elbow," the malady that happens when a judoka attacks with a right-sided throw and his right elbow goes up in the air, often with the right wrist bent and ineffective. By getting your thumb stuck in your opponent's collar at his neck, you are limiting yourself in how you attack and defend.
12. Your posture is important. Make sure your shoulders are directly over your hips and lower your stance with your legs, keeping your back straight and maintaining good posture. Don't bend forward with your buttocks sticking out and your shoulders leaning forward (this puts your body off-balance forward). If you must get lower than your opponent or like to fight from this position, lower your level with your legs and don't bend forward at the waist.

13. Your weight distribution should be 50/50 (50 percent of your weight is placed on one leg and 50 percent of your weight is on the other) most of the time. Try to have your weight distributed evenly and don't place too much weight in your heels. Don't be "heavy footed" and try to stay on the balls of your feet. Be graceful and don't plod.
14. Here's an old rule, but one that still works: don't cross your feet. You're asking to get thrown or taken to the mat. Not only that, you are off balance when you cross your legs or feet and you can't attack or defend quickly.
15. Once you have a grip on your opponent, stay attached to him so you can achieve a throw or takedown. If you need to change your grip, don't let go unless he's beaten you to the grip and is controlling you and you are forced to break free and regrip.
16. Always use two hands to control or attack your opponent's one hand. In other words, if your opponent comes in to grip with you and leads with his one hand, it's easier to deflect his one hand with your two. You can counter-grip more effectively using both hands when possible. A good example is for you to "kill" (or neutralize) your opponent's right-hand lead. You grab his hand with both of yours, then when you pull it down to neutralize it, you can adjust your counter-grip and get the grip useful to you.
17. Avoid moving directly backward or running forward directly to your opponent. Moving directly back or forward is too easy for your opponent to throw you. By moving back or backing away from your opponent in a straight line, you appear to be passive and the referee may penalize you for it. Don't back up; instead, try to move in angles, and if you have to move to avoid him, try to move laterally.
18. If you break your opponent's grip or tie-up, don't back up or back away. This is perfect time to regrip or counter-grip and take the offensive. If you back away as you and you and your opponent lose grip of each other, it appears passive to a referee.
19. Use your head as a wedge to break the grip if necessary. Sometimes, you may have to bury your head on your opponent's chest, shoulder, or even his arm and use it as a wedge to open up the distance between your bodies. You may even use your head to shuck your opponent's grip on your collar or lapel, or use your head to duck under your opponent's arm or shoulder to get to the outside. You can even wedge your head on your opponent's head or neck to gain an advantage. As mentioned earlier, Rene Pommerelle used to call the head, when used in this way, the "third arm."

20. Don't get locked into the thought that you can only grip with a neutral grip (or the head and arm, or collar tie-up). While this is the basic grip used to learn new throwing skills, remember that it's only one of the many ways you can grip or tie up an opponent. Don't fall in love with a grip for any reason other than that it works and is the best to use to throw an opponent. Be willing and prepared to change grips to suit the situation.
21. Control his shoulders. You can "steer" him by controlling his shoulders to manipulate his body better. Also, "kill his shoulder" by forcing his near shoulder down low. Doing this makes him weaker and unable to mount an attack or defense.
22. Don't only use your hands to control your opponent. Your hands grab him, but your elbows, arms, shoulders, and head all help in steering your opponent and controlling his movement.
23. Use your grip like a radar. You can feel the direction your opponent is moving with your hands that are gripping onto your opponent's jacket. Often, your grip on your opponent's lapel will give you enough "feel" as to where he will move his body.
24. This is the most important rule of grip fighting: any grip that works for you (and is allowed by the rules of your sport) is good.

Commonly Used Grips

What follows are some common grips and situations involving gripping used in judo. Not all grips used in competition are shown here. It seems there's always something new that someone uses to outgrip his opposition. But, for the most part, these are the most frequently used grips. How effectively you grab or grip your opponent often dictates what throw you will use, so practice gripping drills and grip fighting so you are confident and skilled in grips that offer you the best opportunities to throw your opponents.

Think of the grip as the first link in any throwing action. Don't hurry in and attack your opponent with a throw before getting a good grip or hold on him first. One of the best ways of making a particular technique work for you is to find an optimal grip that works best and work your throw in from that grip. Or you can take another approach: decide on your favorite throw and develop a grip that works well with that throw. Some grips don't suit some throws, so you'll have to experiment about what grip works best for you and for your throw. For the most part, how you grip your opponent dictates how you move your opponent. The grip also determines the space between your bodies and other factors in making any throw a success.

There are many ways to grip with your opponent—using the jacket, your opponent's body, or anything else permitted in the contest rules. Don't hesitate to experiment with your grips during practice and find out for yourself what works best for you.

All of the grips can and should be used in combination with other grips. Establish an "anchor" with a grip to establish initial control, and from this anchor move on to another grip to gain more control over the situation. This initial anchor is called the "anchor hand," and it is the first link in the chain of events for controlling an opponent's movement and setting him up for an attack. An example is when one athlete uses his right hand to secure a grip over his opponent's left shoulder and onto his back and then uses his left hand to grip his opponent's right sleeve slightly above the elbow.

Ready Posture with Hands Up: Always have your hands up and be ready to grab or deflect your opponent's hands, arms, shoulders, or chest. In the same way a boxer keeps his guard up so he can hit his opponent and block his opponent's punches, judo athletes have their hands up. Have your hands up near shoulder level with them open as shown in this photo and pretend you are looking through a television screen. Keeping your hands up will enable you to use them freely to attack and defend.

Kumi Kata (Lapel and Sleeve Grip): The neutral grip, called "kumi kata" in judo, is a standard grip and excellent for learning the basic skills of most throwing techniques. This grip (initially developed by judo's founder, Professor Jigoro Kano) allows both people to attack and defend freely, giving neither an advantage. He designed the grip to allow this free exchange of techniques. In a right-handed situation, both judo athletes use their right hand to grab the patterner's left lapel just below his collarbone area and their left hand to grab the partner's right sleeve just above the elbow. Many athletes use this neutral grip as part of their grip-fighting set of skills as it can accommodate many types of throwing attacks.

Collar Grip: The athlete on the left is using his right hand to grab his opponent's collar or lapel toward the side or back of his opponent's neck. This is a variation of the kumi kata or neutral grip and is also similar to a shoulder or back grip. This grip is effective for a variety of throws and is one of the most popular grips in judo or any form of jacket wrestling.

Get the Inside Grip: The athlete on the left has used his right hand to get the grip inside his opponent's left arm and has grabbed his left lapel. Doing this gives the athlete on the left a good steering hand that he can use as "radar" to feel his opponent's movement and steer him as well.

Neutralize Opponent's Grip: In the same photo, the athlete on the right has managed to wedge his left hand over his opponent's right arm and grab his left lapel to neutralize it and keep his opponent from controlling him with the inside gripping hand. Grip fighting is a series of movements where each athlete attempts to dominate his opponent by means of grabbing his jacket, belt, or most any part of his opponent's body.

Back Grip and "Killing" Opponent's Posture: The athlete on the right is using his left hand and arm to reach over his opponent's left shoulder and grip his back. He is bending his opponent over in an attempt to control his movement and tempo. This is a very effective grip for almost every throw and gained wide popularity when Soviet sambo wrestlers introduced it in the 1960s.

Using Elbows in Grip Fighting: You are not limited to only using your hands. Use your elbows, shoulders, and head to manipulate your opponent.

Near Shoulder Back/Belt Grip ("Georgian" Grip): The athlete on the left is using his left hand and arm to reach over his opponent's left shoulder. In this photo, he is grabbing the belt but could also have grabbed any part of his opponent's jacket. As shown in the previous photo, this grip is ideal for pulling and "steering" an opponent into a throw. You can see how this grip effectively closes the space between the athletes' bodies and for all intents and purposes makes the thrower and defender one body connected together.

Under-Arm Grip and Over-Hook Transition Grips: The athlete on the right is using his right hand to reach under his opponent's left arm, but his opponent is countering with his own grip by using his left hand to hook over his opponent's right arm. Both grips are effective, and this constant battle to see who gets the dominant grip is part of the art and science of standing judo. Both of these grips are "transition grips." More likely than not, these grips will be held long enough to control the opponent and then each athlete will work for a more secure grip. This isn't always the case, and this is why grip fighting is such a fluid, aggressive activity. Look at how these athletes are both attempting to bend the other overusing his specific grip.

Shoulder Grip: The attacker (left) is using his left hand to grab over his opponent's right shoulder at the judogi. The attacker is using his left arm to press down hard on his opponent's left shoulder to steer him effectively. If done right, pulling down on the opponent's shoulder "kills" the shoulder, making it almost useless for the opponent. This is a common and effective grip and adaptable to many throwing attacks.

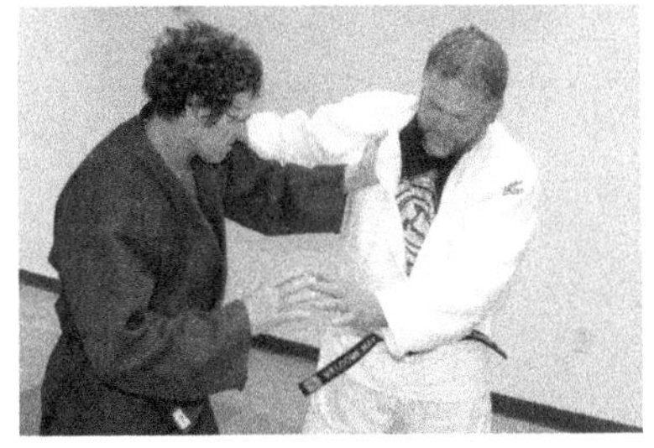

Anchor Hand/Radar Hand: The judoka on the left is using his left hand to grip his opponent's right lapel and using it as an "anchor" to control and feel his opponent's movement. This anchor hand can also serve as a form of radar to detect the change in movement of his opponent.

Low Sleeve and Pistol Grip: By grabbing low on an opponent's sleeve (near his wrist), you can effectively keep him at a safe distance from you. This is a good grip when ahead in the score and you want to keep your opponent from grabbing you to mount an attack and is also useful when you want to keep your opponent from gripping you with his strong (steering) hand. If you look closely, you will see that the athlete on the right is using his left hand to "pistol grip" his opponent. Grab the end of the sleeve in the same way you would grab a pistol. This tightens the sleeve onto the wrist and gives the athlete using it good control of his opponent's arm and hand movement. Pistol grips are allowed in freestyle judo rules.

Lapel Grip: An effective way of controlling an opponent's shoulder or shoulders is to use a lapel grip. Both athletes are using this grip in this photo. By gripping onto the lapel, you close the space between you and your opponent and "shorten" the throw. In other words, you will close the space between you and your opponent better than if you were to grab his sleeve. Grabbing the sleeve controls the arm, but it's harder to control the shoulder. Using a lapel grip is an effective way of "steering" and controlling an opponent's shoulders simply because you are grabbing so close to the shoulder. The athlete on the left eventually attacked with a knee-drop seoi nage (back carry or "shoulder" throw). Look at how the athlete on the left is using his left hand and forearm to block his opponent's right arm. Doing this controls the right arm and nullifies it effectiveness.

Double Lapel Grip: This is a useful grip that does a good job of steering or controlling an opponent's shoulders and is a classic example of what is called a "short grip." A short grip is when there is little body space between the attacker and defender, usually measured at the area of the shoulders. This double lapel grip gives the attacker better control in moving the defender's shoulders much like a person would when riding a bicycle and using the handlebars to steer.

Steering Hand: What is known as tsurite or the "lifting hand" is the hand that "steers" an opponent into the action of a throw. In this photo, the attacker is on the right and is using his right hand to drive his opponent's head into the action of the throw. This is often called "head control" in judo. Driving your hand into the side of your opponent's head certainly does control his head.

The steering hand doesn't only control the head. This photo shows how the attacker's right hand is gripping his opponent's upper back and low shoulder and his right elbow clamps down tightly on the defender's left arm. The attacker is using a ko soto gake (minor outer hook) and his right arm and hand are steering his opponent to the opponent's back side.

Pulling Hand Switches to Steering Hand: What may have started out as the steering hand may quickly change to be the pulling hand and vice versa. What may have started out to be the pulling hand may have to adapt to steering an opponent over. The attacker initially set his opponent up with a forward throw, using his right hand as the steering hand. He quickly changed direction and threw his opponent with a sasae tsurikomi ashi (propping lifting pulling ankle throw) and switched the roles of his hands. His right hand quickly became the pulling hand and his left hand quickly became the steering hand to drive his opponent over.

Pulling Hand on Sleeve Grip: This is the classic definition of "tsurite" or pulling hand in judo; using your hand to "screw up" your opponent's sleeve gives you more control of his arm. The better control of his arm, the better you pull him. The athlete on the left in this photo is using his right hand to grab between his opponent's elbow and shoulder at the triceps area. Gripping in this area affords you excellent control of his entire arm and shortens the distance between the attacker and the defender. Gripping the sleeve as close to the opponent's shoulder as possible shortens the distance between the two bodies and controls the opponent's shoulders effectively. The lower down the sleeve the attacker grips, the longer the lever and the more space he has between the two bodies.

Pulling Hand with Low-Sleeve Grip: This photo shows the attacker on the right using his left hand to grab low on his opponent's right sleeve and pull as he attacks. Continuing from the above description of the sleeve grip, this lower sleeve grip is a "long" grip and as shown in this photo, requires more movement of the attacker's body to get close to his opponent. This is an effective grip, especially in fast-paced matches where there is a lot of space between the athletes and a lot of fast movement.

Double Sleeve Grip: This is a useful grip when the attacker wants to make space between her and his opponent. This grip is also a useful set up for numerous throws where the attacker uses a fast tempo to throw her opponent such as knee-drop attacks, foot sweeps, and other throws. The double sleeve grip is also used tactically by one judoka against her opponent in order to create space between the judo athletes to waste time on the clock.

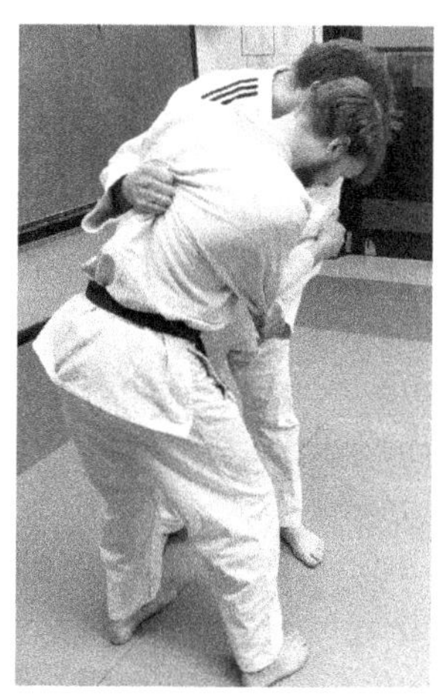

Loop Grip: Imagine looping or wrapping a belt or rope around your opponent's body and you can see how much control you have with this grip. This grip is useful for almost every throw using in judo and is a grip commonly used in "short grip" situations where there is close body space between the shoulders of the opposing judo athletes.

Cross Grip: Getting Both Your Hands on Opponent's Sleeve: What's called a "cross grip" is basically when the attacker controls his opponent's arm and generally pulls it across to his opposite hip. The attacker will use this grip to attack, set up the opponent for another grip, or use it as a defensive grip. This series of photos shows the athlete on the left using his right hand to grab low on his opponent's right sleeve. As he does this, the attacker immediately uses his left hand to grab the top of his opponent's right sleeve. Doing this isolates the opponent's right extended arm. The attacker on the left uses both hands to clamp tightly on his opponent's right lower sleeve. The attacker begins to pull his opponent's right arm forward and toward his right hip.

Cross Grip: Pulling Opponent's Hand to Your Hip: The attacker starts to close the space between the two bodies as he continues to pull his opponent's extended right arm and hand toward the attacker's right hip as shown. Notice that the attacker moves in closer to his opponent to close the space even more. You can also see how the attacker is using his left shoulder to drive downward onto his opponent's right shoulder, "killing" it or controlling it.

Cross Grip: Closing the Gap: The attacker on the left uses his right hand to clamp his opponent's right arm tightly to his waist as he uses his left arm to reach over his opponent's shoulder and back as shown. This "closes the gap" or closes the space between the bodies of the two athletes. The attacker has now controlled his opponent's posture and managed to get his hips in close to his opponent to launch an attack. From this grip, the attacker (on the left) can attack his opponent in any direction.

Transition Grip Using a Two-on-One Arm Grip: This grip is useful as a transition grip or it can be used to break an opponent's posture. The attacker on the right has successfully gained his cross grip and is using his right front shoulder to drive down on his opponent's left rear shoulder. Doing this "kills" the opponent's left shoulder and enables the attacker to control his opponent more effectively. From here the attacker will immediately move to another grip that he intends to use in order to launch his attack.

Movement in Judo

Judo is movement. What this means is that everything that takes place when doing judo relies on the movement of the human body. Movement is controlled motion in a specific direction. Motion takes place when a human body changes or shifts its position. Every physical aspect of judo is determined by movement. The task of a judoka is to control how, where, and when his opponent moves.

In order for a judo athlete to be able to control his opponent's movement, he must make physical contact with him first. Making this physical contact is called gripping and was examined previously in this section of the book. To understand movement in judo and how to control it, it's important to understand that the judo athlete uses his grip to control movement. He uses the grip in two primary ways, first as a steering mechanism and second as a way of generating momentum and force. Momentum is the speed of a body in movement, and this momentum creates force. This combination of steering and generating force controls how, where, and when an opponent moves. In other words, if you control the grip, you control the movement. This is true in both standing judo situations and situations in groundfighting.

When a judo athlete starts a throwing attack, he wants to create enough movement to overcome his opponent's initial resistance. This is how kuzushi (breaking posture and balance) works. The judo athlete then continues his attacking movement in order to accelerate or speed up the momentum of the attack to form his technique. Forming the technique is called tsukuri. When the judo athlete gets his opponent moving, he must keep the opponent moving in the direction he wants him to go. Now that the attacker has formed his technique and both he and his opponent are connected together (called coupling), the movement accelerates and builds momentum until the termination of the throw (with the defender being thrown to the mat). This action of controlled momentum with the attacker and defender coupled together resulting in the culmination of the technique is called kake.

Movement Requires Stability: Stability is produced by the even distribution of weight on each side of the body. The distribution of weight and distance between your feet are important for optimal stability and balance. When standing, your two feet are connected to the mat and form a base of stability for your body. As mentioned elsewhere in this book, the optimal distance between your feet should be so that each foot is reasonably in a direct line under your hips. Don't allow your feet to get too far apart or too close together. When the feet are positioned correctly, the judoka will be better able to distribute his body weight efficiently.

Using Your Feet: We don't simply stand on our feet; we use our feet to grip and connect us to the mat in the same way we use our hands to grip and connect to an opponent. Our feet are used for stability and to generate force. Use every part of each of your feet to connect to the mat, including your toes. Learning to use your toes to help stabilize, balance, and generate force takes some experience, but if you understand this, you will learn how to use your feet more efficiently.

Slide Your Feet—Don't Have "Heavy Feet": The most efficient way to move about the mat so that you are well-balanced and able to move your feet efficiently is to use suri ashi ("sliding feet"). Stay light on your feet so that when you move about the mat, there is a "swishing" sound made by your foot as it slides across the surface of the mat. Do not put excessive weight in your heels, and slide your feet across the mat instead of lifting one foot up and then putting it down as in normal walking. Do this even when using the ayumi ashi (normal step) footwork pattern. A good analogy is what the heavyweight boxing champion Muhammad Ali said: "Move like a butterfly and sting like a bee." This is the opposite of "heavy feet" where a person places too much weight on the feet, plodding along. Often, judo athletes who wrestled extensively before starting judo have heavy feet.

In wrestling, this is an attribute while in judo it is not. When attempting a takedown, a wrestler "shoots" into the move such as a double-leg takedown with his weight on his feet to get a firm base in order to lift his opponent or take him to the mat. A judo throw is different than a wrestling takedown and how a judoka moves his feet dictates the efficiency of his general movement.

Feet Directly Under Hips: In every movement pattern it's important that the attacker does not extend his foot and leg out too far in front or to the side of his body. The attacker must always strive to keep his feet under his hips. Don't step out too far or have your feet too close to each other. The movement starts with the hips, and the leg and foot should always be in a direct line under the hip when moving.

Change of Direction: The direction of movement in a judo match can change in an instant. To an untrained eye, the movement that takes place in judo match may look random, but the reality is that each judo athlete is working on establishing the movement pattern and direction he wants, and his opponent is doing the same thing. For one judoka to have an advantage over his opponent, he must control the speed and direction of how the opponent moves. Directional change is often used in combination techniques where one judo athlete focuses his initial attack in one direction and quickly changes direction and uses another technique to finish with the throw.

Generating Force with Feet: The action of the judo athlete's feet pushing off the mat creates force. He will push off the mat using both feet or one foot, depending on the throw. In the application of a technique, the attacker starts his movement by driving off one or both feet in the direction of the attack. As the attacker drives off his feet to generate power, he will also use his feet to control the direction of the movement of his body. This is the force necessary for completion of the throw.

The Movement Patterns in Judo

Since every aspect of judo is based on movement, the more efficient the movement is, the more effective the outcome of that movement (a technique) will be. For practical purposes, there are three distinct body movement patterns used in judo. Let's now examine them.

Each of the three primary movement has multiple applications and variations. These three patterns are: 1. ayumi ashi ("walking step"), 2. taisabaki (moving the opponent in a circular direction), and 3. tsugi ashi ("follow foot"). The generic name for these movement patterns in judo are called shintai (this word translates specifically to moving forward and backward but is also used to describe all movement patterns in general).

How Ayumi Ashi Works

Ayumi ashi, as mentioned above, translates to "walking step" and refers to moving an opponent directly forward or backward. Even though this pattern is called "walking" it's important to use a sliding step (suri ashi) and not lift your feet up off the mat too far (see the previous section on suri ashi). Ayumi ashi is a common footwork pattern used in just about every throwing technique. It's often the first movement pattern used by coaches to teach beginners how to move a training partner into position in order to apply a throw. It's important that your body is relaxed and not stiff or rigid. Move naturally. Too often, beginners are taught to move like a robot using exaggerated body movement and footwork.

Ayumi Ashi: This movement pattern is the "normal step" in judo. Ayumi ashi is a forward and backward movement pattern in a straight line. This movement pattern is ideal for just about every throwing technique in judo and is often used as the first movement pattern taught to beginners.

This photo offers a different view of ayumi ashi. The judo athletes use a suri ashi (sliding foot) way of moving rather than lifting their feet up off the mat.

How Taisabaki Works

Taisabaki translates to "body management" and refers to moving an opponent in a circular direction or pattern, leading to a specific attack or technique. There are two primary directions when moving an opponent with taisabaki: 1. steer the opponent to your tsurite (lifting hand) side, or 2. steer the opponent to your hikite (pulling hand) side. Anytime you move your opponent in a circular direction, you're using taisabaki. One feature of taisabaki is that it really does help increase the velocity of your opponent's body for setting him up for a throw. When using taisabaki, think of yourself as the hub or center of a wheel and your opponent as the outside edge of the wheel at the tire. In the same way the hub of the wheel doesn't move and makes the outer edge of the wheel move in a circle, your body does the same thing when you move an opponent using taisabaki. You don't have to move much at all in order to make your opponent move around you. There are many throwing techniques that work more effectively because a judoka uses taisabaki as the movement pattern to set up the throw.

Taisabaki: This is a circular movement pattern used often in judo. The attacker has the option to move his partner to his tsurite (lapel hand) or to his hikite (sleeve hand). In this sequence, the attacker will move his partner to his right side and lapel hand.

The attacker starts by sliding his right foot back toward his right side in a circular pattern as he uses his right hand to pull on his partner's left lapel.

The attacker has moved his partner to the attacker's right side in a circular pattern and is now ready to launch his throwing attack.

How Tsugi Ashi Works

Tsugi ashi translates to "follow foot" and is done in two primary directions: lateral or at an angle. The reason this pattern is called "follow foot" is because the attacker (the person initiating the movement) moves so that his rear foot slides up immediately behind his front foot and then the front foot slides forward. The attacker uses his back foot to initiate the movement either laterally or to the front right angle, front left angle, rear right angle, or rear left angle.

When doing okuri ashi barai (send after foot sweep), what we call a lateral or side-moving "tsugi ashi" is more specifically a movement pattern called okuri ashi ("send after foot"). This is a direct lateral movement pattern where the foot in the direction of the movement is moved first. This is why okuri ashi barai is so named. For instance, when moving his opponent to his right, the attacker initiates his direct lateral movement with his right foot and his left foot follows. The reason okuri ashi isn't used at front or rear angles is because a judoka who leads with his front foot followed by his rear foot puts the judoka in jeopardy of having his lead foot swept out from under him. This is how de ashi barai (advancing foot sweep) works.

Tsugi Ashi: This movement pattern is called a "follow foot" pattern where the attacker (back to camera) will slide to his right side laterally. This photo sequence shows a lateral tsugi ashi pattern. Another way of applying tsugi ashi is that the attacker can slide at an angle to his front or rear corner.

The attacker moves to his left side, making sure he does not make long strides with his feet positioned too far apart. The attacker does not extend his feet too much past the line of his hips as shown here.

The attacker has moved laterally to his right and is now ready to launch his throwing attack. Using a lateral movement for throwing techniques is effective because the defender often has a difficult time applying a defensive action from this lateral direction.

Some Guidelines for Effective Movement

Stability, both when standing still and when moving, is an essential aspect of efficient and effective movement in judo. There are some fundamental things to consider and put into practice when moving about the mat with an opponent who wants to move you as much as you want to move him.

1. Don't follow your opponent and don't walk into a throw. If a judoka walks directly forward in a straight line, he will often literally walk into an opponent's throw. Don't walk in a straight line to your opponent. All it takes is one step forward for a throw to work.
2. Move in angles. When moving in to take a grip with an opponent, move laterally at an angle to meet him, and move in the direction that best suits the throws you want to use. A smart opponent will see this, so you may have to move laterally to the other side and then double back to keep the opposition guessing. By walking in a straight line either forward or backward, a person is predictable in his movement. I've often said that wrestlers walk in straight lines and forward, and judoka move in angles.
3. Keep your weight evenly distributed. Good balance is essential. Don't lean forward with your head and shoulders where they are closer to your opponent than your hips. Likewise, don't place too much weight in your buttocks or heels.
4. Don't be predictable in how you move. Have more than one way of moving and setting up your favorite attacks. Keep the opposition guessing as much as you can.
5. Pull and don't push. This may seem to be out of place when discussing movement, but it's not. In judo, we pull more often than we push. This is because a judoka wants to draw or pull his opponent in closer to his body in order to control and break his opponent's posture and balance. If a judoka pushes, the push is aimed directly forward so that the person pushing is moving in a straight line to his opponent. The opponent will more easily throw someone who pushes.

6. Lead with your hip. This has been examined in other parts of this book but is worth repeating here. Your hip is the center of your body. In your lower body, your hip and your feet are connected to your legs. In your upper body, your hip is connected to your spine and your spine is connected to your shoulders, which are connected to your arms and hands. Your head is connected to your spine. Everything is connected in a big chain that takes its cues on how to move from your hip. Your hips direct where your body moves. By leading with your hip with a good upright posture, you are better able to attack and defend more freely.
7. A straight (not rigid) upright posture gives a judo athlete more freedom of movement. If a judoka is bent over at the waist with his hips far away from his opponent, he limits his own movement.
8. Don't be heavy footed. Slide and move gracefully. Do not put too much weight on either or both feet, especially in the heels of your feet. Heavy feet are slow feet.
9. Don't let your legs and feet get too close together and don't let them get too far apart. Keep your legs and feet in a straight line directly under your hips. Also, don't cross your feet or legs. Doing this will simply help your opponent trip you up and throw you.

I'm sure there are more guidelines specific to you and how you move in judo, but these nine guidelines will serve as a good starting point. Now, let's examine some throwing techniques that have been selected for their high rate of success as well as how each demonstrates how gripping and movement work together to throw a resisting, fit, and skilled opponent.

CHAPTER 6

Throws, Transitions, and Defense

No matter what you call it, just call it ippon!

—Don Bunch

This section of the book focuses on three related areas of competitive judo skill: throwing techniques, transitions from standing to the mat, and defensive skills. While there are sixty-seven throwing techniques recognized by the Kodokan, the reality is that there are countless ways of throwing another human being to the mat. The only limiting factors are the imagination of the judo athlete and the mechanics of how the human body works. This section will first examine some throwing techniques that effectively serve as both ways of scoring points and transitioning to groundfighting. This first examination of throwing techniques will blend into an analysis of some transition skills you might find interesting. Finishing up this section will be an analysis of defensive skills in standing judo.

Nage Waza

Nage waza are the throwing techniques of judo. Nage translates to "throw, cast, or fling," and waza translates to "techniques." Competitive judo consists of about 70 percent throwing techniques and about 30 percent groundfighting techniques.

Many Throwing Techniques Merge Together

In many situations, throws used in competitive judo will merge or blend into each other. For instance, a throwing attack starting out as o soto gari (major outer reap) can quickly turn into an ashi guruma (leg/foot wheel) or a harai goshi (sweeping hip). For this reason, when making an analysis of throwing techniques, I will make a grouping of throws that are similar in one or more ways to what takes place in actual competitive judo situations. This is why one of my athletes Don Bunch said, "No matter what you call it, just call it ippon!"

Throws, Takedowns, and Transitions: Their Purpose

There are differences among throws, takedowns, and transitions. Each has its own distinct purpose technically and tactically, and a smart athlete will use each of these skills to his advantage. There is a difference in the purpose of each, and sometimes it's a blurred line that divides them, but it's the intent of the attacker that really determines whether a technique is a throw, takedown, or transition. Realistically, the intent of the attacker is based on the tactical situation in the match in which he is engaged.

Here's a good example of how tactical considerations affect whether to use a throw, takedown, or transition. Some years ago, one of my athletes was competing in the finals of a regional judo tournament against a rugged wrestler who also competed in judo. On scouting the opponent in his earlier matches, we noticed that this athlete had an effective defense against the throws of all of his opponents. Additionally, while he was a strong wrestler, we noticed that he made some mistakes by extending his arms out too far when in groundwork. This opponent looked to be a hard guy to throw, and while my athlete was skillful at throwing techniques, he was even more skillful at doing juji gatame. We knew that our best bet was to get this guy on the mat quickly and work him over with juji gatame. In the final, after some preliminary grip fighting, that's exactly what my athlete did. He used a yoko tomoe nage to transition immediately to juji gatame to get the tap-out and win by ippon. A bit later, the referee of the match told me that my athlete was "lucky to win by a trick armlock since he couldn't throw the other guy." My reply was that my athlete had no intention of throwing his opponent and wanted to get him onto the mat to armlock him. The referee replied with a question, "Why would he want to do that?" I said, "Because he wanted to win, and he did." In this case, the tactically smart thing to do was to use a transition to get the opponent to the mat and apply an armlock.

The lines between throws, takedowns, and transitions can be blurry. Sometimes an attacker uses a takedown that is so hard that it merits an ippon score and wins the match. Sometimes, an attacker has every intention of slamming his opponent flat on his back with a throw but the opponent turns out, and the attacker immediately transition to a pin, choke, or armlock and secures the win. While it may be splitting hairs to some, there is a difference in each of these types of techniques. Each has its own purpose and each is useful to every judoka who uses them; a smart judo athlete will train on all three as often as possible at practice. With that in mind, here are the purposes of each.

A Throw (Purpose: Control and Force): The primary purpose of a throw is to finish the fight. Throw the opponent with force and control, landing him mainly on his back or backside. An ippon score is the ultimate score in judo much like a knockout in boxing or a pin in wrestling. The goal is to throw the opponent to the mat in such a way that groundfighting may not be necessary. Throw him with control and throw him hard. If you throw your opponent so hard that you take the starch out of him, it will soften him up for a good ground move, but more important, it could end the fight or match. Often, the attacker will throw his opponent and land on (or near) him in a position to transition to a pin or submission technique. This transition will be necessary to control the opponent on the mat if he wasn't thrown for ippon.

A Takedown (Purpose: Control): The primary purpose of a takedown is to take the opponent from a standing position to the mat and exert further control over him. A takedown can certainly result in a hard landing for an opponent, but the purpose of a takedown is control, not force. A takedown is well-named: the attacker takes his opponent down to the mat. A takedown is a means of getting the opponent down to the mat from a standing position in order to gain control over him. The attacker may not have a specific technique or move in mind when taking his opponent down. Often, takedowns are tactical moves. When taking an opponent from standing to the mat, the attacker may be ahead in the score and want to use some time in groundfighting to keep his lead, or the attacker knows that he is superior to his opponent in groundfighting and that is where he wants to match to take place.

A Transition (Purpose: Specific Control): The primary purpose of a transition is for the attacker to take the opponent from a standing position to the mat with a predetermined or specific technique in mind to finish off the opponent. A transition is the link or connection between fighting standing up and fighting on the ground or mat. It's fluidly moving from a throw or takedown to a groundwork attack without hesitation. After the attacker throws his opponent, he immediately finishes him off with a groundfighting technique. That immediate, fluid, follow-through after a throw or takedown is the transition in process. The most common transition is when an athlete throws his opponent and, without any hesitation, moves immediately to a pin, choke, or armlock.

Success in Throwing

Not every throw works the same for everybody. There are a lot of throwing techniques; it takes a lot of time and effort to find the throws that work best for you and then mold them to work for you in a variety of situations. Finding the best throw or throws is much like finding a good spouse. Something clicks. This has been discussed earlier in this book. The Japanese have a good saying: "You have to feel your judo." There's that kinesthetic feeling and awareness that go beyond the cognitive thought process. Success in throwing depends on a variety of factors, but generally a successful throw is dependent on an athlete's weight, height, strength (and fitness) levels, flexibility, aptitude, the situation, tactical considerations, and contest rules. That said, don't limit yourself to a particular throw or type of throws simply because of your size. What I mean to say is that some heavyweight athletes get locked into the belief that they have to do "heavyweight throws." Sure, it's true that some throws simply don't work all that well for some people based on body size or type, but don't hesitate to give them a try and, if you believe you have a proclivity for a particular throw, see how it can work best for you. A throw that may not work for you now could be a throw that works for you later in your career or vice versa. We all change, and you may find that with the physical, mental, and emotional changes we undergo as athletes and people, we may find success in a throw or takedown in the future that we never thought possible.

How you grab your opponent, how you move about the mat, and how you stand when fighting an opponent are all linked. These three elements of judo are dependent upon each other much in the same way that things happen in a sequential process. One thing leads to another, and this chain reaction of movement (and who controls it) determines the effectiveness of an attack. The speed at which you and your opponent move about the mat is called tempo (or pace). The overriding premise of this entire section of the book can be condensed into several vital skills and are discussed throughout this whole chapter. These skills are:

1. Grip fighting and knowing how to use the grip to attack with an effective throw.
2. Leading with your hips so that you are close enough to attack and defend freely.

3. Knowing how a fluid offense/defense is vital to success and the importance of an aggressive defense.
4. Follow-through and transition without hesitation from a throw to groundfighting to finish your opponent.

Control and Force

Every successful throw has two major elements: control and force. If either of these elements is missing, the throw will be scored less than ippon (full point). A judoka must control his opponent's body and throw him to the mat with sufficient force to win the match. With good control, the attacker not only dictates how hard the defender lands but where he lands. Much in the same way a quarterback in football throws a pass, a judoka must throw his opponent with precision so the opponent lands mostly on his back or backside with control and sufficient force to end the fight.

Physical Fitness for Throwing

To perform a throw against a resisting, skilled, motivated, and fit opponent, a judoka should be physically able to do it. Your fitness level directly determines your success and ability to perform at your fullest potential. A major aspect of effective throws and takedowns is that you are physically fit enough to attack your opponent or defend yourself and make use of the skills necessary to attack and defend as the need arises. Being physically able to perform a technique is an important part of the skill. Skill is the practical application of technique, and to be able to apply a technique practically (with skill), fitness is vital. If you're physically strong and have developed explosive power in the gym, you have a better chance of excelling in any athletic activity, especially throwing someone.

A Throw Is a Tool

A throw is a tool and utilitarian in nature. Like any tool, the better a judoka knows how to use it, the more effective it will be. The same can be said for any judo technique. Every tool has a purpose, and every judo technique has a purpose. It's up to the judoka (as well as his coach) to first find the best tool to get the job done, and once that is accomplished, find the best way to use that tool to get the job done. "Getting the job done" is successfully using that technique against fit, motivated, and skilled opponents with a high rate of success. Along with this, it's knowing how to use the right technique at the right time. If you think of a technique in this way, you will be better able to find the right technique or series of techniques and mold them so that they are efficient when they need to be, which means that they are effective.

Double Trouble

Throws that score points and transition immediately into a pin or submission techniques are "double trouble" for an opponent. Finishing an opponent on the mat after throwing him will greatly enhance your chance of beating him.

Three Types of Throwing Attacks

From a tactical standpoint, there are three primary situations where an athlete will throw his opponent. When someone throws an opponent to the mat in any level of competition, it comes out of one of these situations.

Direct Attack: The thrower attacks his opponent directly and with every intention of slamming him to the mat. This is a direct, no-nonsense, relentless throwing attack. Hit him with your best shot, and if you did everything right, he'll go down and go down in the way you want him to.

Counterattack: Your opponent has initiated the attack and you counter it. There are two categories of counter throws. 1. You may block his attack and stop his momentum, then counter with your own throw. 2. You use his attacking movement or momentum against him to throw him with your counter technique.

Linked Attack: The basic idea of this type of attack is that the attacker does something to make his opponent move in such a way that he can throw him. The attacker hits in with a movement that elicits a response (usually a predetermined response) on the part of the defender, then throws him. It could be planned by the attacker or take place by happenstance. This is called hando no kuzushi (breaking balance by use of a diversion). There are two specific types of linked attacks: renraku waza (combination techniques) and renzoku waza (continuation techniques); both have four defining features that make them distinctive, yet similar. 1. The attacker might do something as simple as deliberately bumping his opponent with his leg or hip, or simply stepping or moving in such a way to make him move in the direction the attacker wants so he can throw the opponent with the intended throw. 2. Another method is to fake an attack with a throw to make him move into your main attack. 3. A third method is to actually try to throw an opponent with a direct attack and it fails. Then you follow up with another throw to get the score. 4. Linking attacks together usually means that more than one initial attempt or fake has taken place before the throw takes place. An example is attacking with a foot sweep, forcing your opponent to step away from it, then hitting in with an o uchi gari; again, anticipating your opponent's avoidance and then stepping across your opponent's body and attacking with o soto gari (major outer reap), which was your intended throw. The two specific types of linked attacks are:

Renraku Waza: Often called a "combination technique," renraku translates to "connect." The attacker is connecting or linking two or more techniques together when doing a renraku waza. A renraku waza is often defined as attacking in one direction and then changing the direction with a successive technique that throws the defender, but this directional change isn't always needed for an effective renraku waza. Any time two or more techniques are linked together, it's a renraku waza.

Renzoku Waza: Renzoku translates to mean "continue" or for there to be a consecutive series of something. Renzoku waza are often defined as attacking with a technique in one direction and any successive attack used in combination that throws the defender is done in the same direction as the initial attack. It is a continuous series of actions going in the same direction as the initial attack. A renzoku waza is two or more techniques linked together that flow successively together in the same direction.

The Four Stages of a Throw: Kuzushi, Tsukuri, Kake, and Kime

An established part of the theory of Kodokan judo is that kuzushi (breaking the opponent's posture and balance), tsukuri (building and forming the technique) and kake (execution of the technique) are the three phases of a technique. This provides a general biomechanical description of how a technique works, but this theory makes the assumption that in the final phase, kake, the attacker will finish the technique with control. In reality, this doesn't always happen. Adding a fourth phase, kime, provides an "insurance policy" so that the attacker maintains total control from the start to finish of a technique. There will be more on kime a bit later.

Throwing another human being to the mat or ground relies on a number of factors, not the least of which is skill. To achieve the skill of being able to consistently throw a resisting, fit, and skillful opponent, an athlete should completely understand why his throwing technique works. A good way to examine "why" is to break down the process of a throwing technique into its individual parts and see how they fit together to make the whole thing work. Before we start, please keep in mind that all four of these parts or elements listed here work together. They are sequential and rely on each other for a successful result.

It also goes without saying that the largest amount of time spent in learning skills and developing them is in the area of throwing techniques. Newaza, the groundfighting of judo, has a shorter learning curve than nage waza, the throwing techniques. The reason for this is that throws almost always must be done in a moving situation and as a result, take place faster than the pace of action in groundfighting. Also, in standing situations, there is more space between the contestants' bodies, and knowing how to close that space skillfully takes time and practice. These two reasons make the margin of error greater when attempting to throw an opponent, and as a result, an athlete must spend more time working on the exact movement necessary to ensure a high rate of success. In every aspect of judo, small things often make big things happen, and this is very true in standing judo and throwing techniques. An athlete can make his opponent take only one step with a hip fake and then launch him with a powerful throw for the ippon. That little thing, a quick hip fake, is what sets off a chain of events that leads to the big thing, the ippon-scoring throw.

Kime Is the Fourth Phase: An established part of the theory of Kodokan judo is that kuzushi (breaking the opponent's posture and balance), tsukuri (building and forming the technique) and kake (execution of the technique) are the three phases of a technique. This provides a general biomechanical description of how a technique works, but this theory makes the assumption that in the final phase, kake, the attacker will finish the technique with control. In reality, this doesn't always happen. Adding a fourth phase, kime, provides an "insurance policy" so that the attacker maintains total control from the start to finish of a technique. If you are uneasy about calling kime a "fourth phase" then label it the "third-and-one-half phase," but in practical terms, it's an action that finalizes the entire movement that takes place in the technique. More on the kime phase will be explained a bit later.

So, if you understand these four factors, you understand why and how throwing techniques work. They are: 1. Kuzushi, or breaking and controlling an opponent's balance, movement, and body position. 2. Tsuriki, which is the movement where the attacker builds the technique and fits his body into position to throw his opponent. 3. Kake, the actual execution of the throw where the defender is suspended in the air. 4. Kime, the follow-through or finish to the throw. All of these factors are connected and are sequential in nature; they fluidly move from start to finish if done correctly. And to be able to do them correctly, it takes time, effort, and a lot of practice, but first of all, it takes a thorough understanding of how and why they work to make another human being fall to the mat with control and force. There is an obvious action that takes place for these four phases of a technique to be able to work. It's so obvious that we tend to ignore its importance. That obvious thing is that the attacker and defender must be in contact with each other, and that connection of the two bodies is called coupling.

Coupling in Judo: The physical contact of the attacker and defender must take place for a judo technique to work. That may sound obvious, but it's important to understand that every technique in judo happens because the attacker and defender are connected to each other in some way. So in order to understand and appreciate how the four factors of kuzushi, tsukuri, kake, and kime work, it's essential to understand the concept of "coupling" and how it is used in judo. Coupling is the connection of two bodies in such a way that they work together as one unit. Coupling takes place during the kuzushi phase where both the attacker and defender grip onto each other and when the attacker makes his initial action of breaking the defender's posture and balance. The tsukuri phase is when most of the coupling takes place. Tsukuri, the act of constructing or building the technique, is directly related to the process of coupling. As mentioned before, coupling is the connection of two bodies in such a way that they work together as one unit. Tsukuri is the vital middle link in the application of a technique. The velocity (speed and direction) and resulting force of a throwing technique, as well as the control of the directional movement in the technique, is the result of the action of tsukuri. The defender unwittingly adds to the effect of the throwing action by merely being held onto and controlled by the attacker. Coupling fully occurs in the tsukuri phase (but is initiated in the kuzushi phase) where tori forms and builds the technique, connecting his body to the defender's body in the process. The apex of this coupling takes place in the kake phase of the technique that is the "power peak" of the throwing movement where the attacker has full control over the defender's body as it travels through the air and then onto the mat. The kime is the finish of the throwing technique where the attacker follows through to ensure that the defender lands where and how the attacker wants him to land. The entire coupling action is finished in the kime or final phase of the throw where the attacker either follows through to the mat to secure a pin or submission technique or simply finalizes the coupling process by controlling how the defender lands on the mat.

Kuzushi: Breaking Balance and Posture

There's more than one way to break balance, and movement is the most important part of kuzushi. The word "kuzushi" translates to be the action of breaking down the body. You not only break his balance but you also break his posture so that the structure of his body has been broken and is under your control. It's controlling an opponent's body, and the most effective way of doing that is to do it when he is moving. Controlling and breaking your opponent's balance and posture is a combination of a lot of things that happen in a sequence (but in a fast and controlled sequence) of events, and movement is the most important element. When you "break" your opponent's balance, it's because you've controlled the grip or tie-up, the space between your body and your opponent's body, the movement of both your body and his body, the speed of how fast your bodies move about the mat, as well as the direction you want to go and the momentum into the direction of the attack. Sometimes, it can be a subtle movement on your part but just as often the throwing attack is a result of an explosive and continuous body movement on your part resulting in a throw. Kuzushi operates in two phases that are dependent on each other.

1. The attacker physically moves his opponent, even if it's only by making the opponent's body lean to one direction or making the opponent take only one step in the direction that the attacker wants the opponent's body to go.
2. Once the attacker moves his opponent, the attacker controls and breaks the opponent's posture in the same way a building is torn down. This breaking of the posture causes the opponent to be off balance and vulnerable to being thrown.

These two phases of kuzushi are the result of several different ways of putting the kuzushi into action. Shown here are the six most commonly used and effective methods, which I have observed in all levels of competitive judo, of breaking and controlling an opponent's balance and posture.

Using and Controlling Opponent's Force: This is what most people think of when kuzushi is mentioned. Yield to your opponent's force and then guide him in the direction you want to go. Doing this multiplies your force. Pull when your opponent pushes or push when your opponent pulls. Pulling an opponent up and forward onto his toes using a tsurikomi (lifting-pulling entry) is effective and common in all forward direction throwing techniques.

Upper Body/Lower Body Kuzushi: This is a practical way of breaking and controlling an opponent's body and is used in many leg and foot throws. The upper half of the opponent's body will move at a different speed than the lower half of his body. Throws such as o soto gari (major outer reap) where the attacker moves his opponent's upper body at a faster speed than the opponent's lower body use this type of kuzushi. This is also the case for many foot sweeps where the defender's lower body moves at a faster speed than his upper body.

Movement as Kuzushi: One of the most common uses of kuzushi it for the attacker to move his opponent in a specific direction and then attack with a throwing technique. The taisabaki (circular) movement pattern is often used, but moving an opponent in a straight line (either laterally or forward/backward) works well also. Generally, the attacker only needs to take one step in any direction in order to launch his attack. This photo shows the attacker using an uchi mata (inner thigh throw) after using the taisabaki movement pattern to break his opponent's posture and balance.

Blast in Kuzushi: This is an explosive, sudden, direct, and continuous application of force by the attacker. In many cases, when the defender is standing flat-footed, still, and balanced, a sudden blast of an attack by the attacker breaks the balance and posture of the defender. This method of kuzushi is used in some applications of o uchi gari (major inner reap), o soto gari (major outer reap), as well as morote gari (both legs reap) and other throws where the defender is thrown in the direction of his back.

Bodyweight Kuzushi: The attacker using the weight of his body to roll under his opponent in a sutemi waza (sacrifice technique) is a common method of kuzushi. The attacker goes under the defender's center of gravity usually by rolling (but not always: sometime throws such as yoko wakare or side separation throws, where the attacker's body is more linear, has the same effect as rolling).

Tsukuri: Building the Technique

This is the phase during the throwing action when the thrower actually applies the throwing movement and constructs the throw. "Tsuku" means to prepare or build something and "ri" implies doing it to a person. The concept of tsukuri implies "preparing a person" to be thrown. Often, judo people translate it to mean "fitting in," and this is a good translation as well. What this all means is that the thrower moves his body into position to prepare his opponent to be thrown. Kuzushi and tsukuri blend together into a kuzushi/tsukuri movement rather than two separate movements. Tsukuri is dependent upon kuzushi to be effective. It's during this tsukuri phase that the bodies of the attacker and defender are most closely joined together in what is known as coupling, where the two separate bodies form as one and move in unison with the attacker controlling the direction and speed of the attack.

Coupling with Maximum Body Contact: The bodies of the attacker and the defender are coupled together with the attacker controlling the direction and speed of the throwing action. In this type of tsukuri, the attacker's body is the focus of the contact. This takes place in most throwing techniques in a forward direction.

Coupling with Less Than Maximum Contact: In leg reaping throws, the attacker is primarily connected to the defender with a foot or leg, with the foot or leg being the focus of contact, but there is often some body contact as well.

Coupling with Minimum Body Contact: Often, in foot sweeps, foot props, or in many sacrifice throwing techniques, the attacker's foot or leg is the focus or point of the contact, and the attacker and defender are connected only by a foot or leg along with the hands that the attacker uses for control.

Kake: Execution of the Throw

This phase of the throwing attack is the actual execution of the throw. Kake translates to a phrase that implies suspending or hanging an opponent in the air. In other words, the attacker's body and the defender's body are connected together at the instant the attacker applies his technique. The attacker is in control of how both the defender's body and his body get to the ground or mat. Kake, then, has two parts to it that make it work.

1. The initial lifting or throwing of the defender so that he is being projected through the air.
2. The control (or steering) that the attacker exerts over his opponent as he throws him, much like the trajectory of a rocket.

Initial Lifting of the Defender: This is the initial phase of kake where the attacker lifts his opponent up and off the mat and suspends him in the air. The attacker is fully committed to this uchi mata (inner thigh throw) as he elevates his opponent up and off the mat. The attacker has driven off of his base foot and leg to provide the necessary force to lift him.

Steering the Defender: The attacker controls the trajectory or flight path of his opponent through the air and onto the mat with control. The attacker continued to drive off of his right foot and is at the power peak or apex of the throwing action with full control over his opponent.

Kime: Finishing the Throw

This is the "follow through" that enables the thrower to determine how hard (or soft) his opponent lands on the mat as well as where the defender lands (primarily on the back). The concept of kime implies the focus, follow-through, or finish to the technique. The momentum of the attacker's body and the defender's body creates a "follow through" in the exact same way a golfer follows through in his swing after he hits the ball with his club. If the attacker tried to stop the action at the point of kake, he would lose control of his opponent's body, and the effectiveness of the throw would be lost, or certainly diminished. For a throw to be effective, kake blends directly into kime with no stop in the action.

Sometimes, the attacker will finish the throw with control and force and remain standing, usually ready to follow his opponent to the mat to transition to a pin or submission technique.

Sometimes, the attacker will use makikomi (wrapping or winding finish) and land on, or near, his opponent. This makikomi finish often lends easily to a transition to a pin to finish the opponent.

Sometimes, the attacker will throw the defender and finish the technique by landing directly on the defender with a pin.

The Movement Patterns in Judo

As mentioned often in this book, knowing how to move an opponent is essential for success in judo, especially when using throwing techniques. There are specific directions a human body moves when standing, and these are movement patterns. These movement patterns are the directions a human body is capable of moving and how the human body reacts when moved in these patterns. If you, as an athlete, have an understanding and appreciation of the fact that you can move and steer an opponent into a certain direction, you will be better able to learn how to move that opponent and throw him. A successful judo athlete doesn't simply go out on the mat and try one throw after another, blindly hoping something will work. It takes planning. You must move an opponent into position in order to throw him. Much like an army that maneuvers an opposing army into a trap, a judoka can maneuver his opponent into the best position in order to throw him. There are three primary movement patterns used in judo and each has multiple applications and variations.

1. Ayumi Ashi ("walking step").
2. Taisabaki (moving the opponent in a circular direction).
3. Tsugi Ashi ("follow foot").

These movement patterns in judo are called shintai (this word translates specifically to moving forward and backward but is also used to describe all movement patterns in general). Knowing these movement patterns and using them to move an opponent into position in order to throw him is an important part of applying throwing skills with a high rate of success. Spend some time at every practice working and refining the movement patterns that work best for the throwing techniques you intend to use. Much like a boxer does shadow boxing, a judoka must work with a training partner to get the best "feel" for how a throw works and what is the best movement pattern for that throw.

Feet Directly Under Hips: In every movement pattern it's important that the attacker does not extend his foot and leg out too far in front or to the side of his body. The attacker must always strive to keep his feet under his hips. Don't step out too far or have your feet too close to each other. The movement starts with the hips and the leg and foot should always be in a direct line under the hip when moving.

Slide Your Feet: Don't Have "Heavy Feet"

First of all, before examining the primary movement patterns, it's important to examine how to move your feet across the mat. When moving about the mat, slide or glide with your feet, avoiding placing too much weight on the heels of your feet. Always attempt to place an equal amount of weight on each of your feet as you move. This suri ashi (sliding feet) type of movement enables you to move more efficiently.

This is the opposite of "heavy feet" where a person places too much weight on the feet, plodding along. Often, judo athletes who wrestled extensively before starting judo have heavy feet. In wrestling, this is a desirable attribute (while in judo it is not). When attempting a takedown, a wrestler "shoots" into the move such as a double-leg takedown with his weight on his feet to get a firm base in order to lift his opponent or take him to the mat. A judo throw is different than a wrestling takedown, and how a judoka moves his feet dictates the efficiency of his general movement.

How Ayumi Ashi Works

Ayumi ashi translates to "walking step" and refers to moving an opponent directly forward or backward. Even though this pattern is called "walking" it's important to use a sliding step (suri ashi) and not lift your feet up off the mat too far.

How Taisabaki Works

Taisabaki translates to "body management" and refers to moving an opponent in a circular direction or pattern, leading to a specific attack or technique. There are two primary directions when moving an opponent with taisabaki: 1. Steer the opponent to your tsurite (lifting hand) side, or 2. steer the opponent to your hikite (pulling hand) side.

How Tsugi Ashi Works

Tsugi ashi translates to "follow foot" and is done in two primary directions, lateral or at an angle. The reason this pattern is called "follow foot" is because the attacker (the person initiating the movement) moves so that his rear foot slides up immediately behind his front foot and then the front foot slides forward. The attacker uses his back foot to initiate the movement either laterally or to the front right angle, front left angle, rear right angle, or rear left angle. When doing okuri ashi barai (send after foot sweep), what we call a lateral or side-moving "tsugi ashi" is more specifically a movement pattern called okuri ashi ("send after foot"). This is a direct lateral movement pattern where the foot in the direction of the movement is moved first. This is why okuri ashi barai has its name. For instance, when moving his opponent to his right direction, the attacker initiates his direct lateral movement with his right foot and his left foot follows. The reason okuri ashi isn't used at front or rear angles is because a judoka who leads with his foot and then brings his behind foot following it puts the judoka in jeopardy of having his lead foot swept out from under him. This is how de ashi barai (advancing foot sweep) works.

Knowing how the human body moves as well as knowing how to move it give us the foundation to work on. Now let's put all of this into practical use and analyze some selected throwing techniques that are common and effective in competitive judo.

Analysis of Selected Throwing Techniques

There are defining features in all judo throwing techniques. While each technique has a form or structure all its own, every technique uses the same formula of kuzushi (breaking balance and posture), tsukuri (building the throw), kake (execution), and kime (follow through or finish). And in fact, many throwing techniques have characteristics and similarities that can be easily seen and are common elements that make every throwing technique work. Kodokan judo has an established classification of throwing techniques based on how and why a technique functions. These classifications are: 1. te waza (hand techniques), 2. ashi waza (leg/foot techniques), 3. koshi waza (hip techniques), and 4. sutemi waza (sacrifice techniques). Additionally, sutemi waza is further defined as 1. masutemi waza (back sacrifice techniques) and 2. yoko sutemi waza (side sacrifice techniques). This system of classification does a good job of providing structure to the basic theory and practice of throwing techniques, and I am not attempting to replace it with my way of analyzing throws. But the many throwing techniques used in competitive judo have some definite patterns and similarities, and it's these patterns and similarities on which I am grounding my analysis, and I hope it's helpful in understanding how, why, and when different throwing techniques work in judo.

While there are sixty-eight primary throwing techniques listed in the Kodokan judo syllabus, there are really an unlimited number of ways one human can throw another human through the air and onto the ground. The central idea for a successful throwing technique in judo is to throw an opponent with control and force. With these parameters, the only limiting factors are the imagination of the person doing the throw and the physical constraints of how the human body works. What follows in this section will be an analysis of different throwing techniques based on how they are applied in competitive judo. Since not every throwing technique can be analyzed, some key techniques have been selected to explore. As mentioned previously, there are defining features in every judo technique, and it is these defining features that will be examined.

Attacker's Legs Close Together: Forward Throwing Techniques

Throwing techniques where the attacker starts and remains standing when applying the throw are called tachi waza (standing techniques) and in many cases, the attacker's feet and legs will be positioned so that they are directly under his hips.

Defining Features

The defining features of standing throwing techniques with the attacker's feet close together are: 1. The attacker starts his throw by standing on both feet that are placed in close proximity to each other, and he rotates or turns his head and body into the direction of the throw, producing the necessary torque for the throw to work. 2. The attacker uses both his feet to drive off the mat to generate force into the throw, with the knees flexed initially and contracted at the power peak of the throw. 3. The attacker's body usually tilts into the direction that he is throwing his opponent. 4. The attacker's feet and knees are often pointed in the same direction in which the throw is directed. 5. The attacker often uses a koshi waza (hip technique) where the axis or hinge point of the throw located at the attacker's hip or a te waza (hand technique) where the hinge point of the throw is across the attacker's back. 6. The attacker usually has a fairly straight back so that his hips can be used effectively to close the space between the attacker's body and the defender's body during the action of the throw. 7. The attacker uses the hikite (pulling hand) to direct where he wants the throw to go and uses the tsurite (lifting hand) to lift and steer the defender's body.

Two types of throwing techniques that are considered basic skills, yet continue to be used at all levels of competitive judo will be analyzed here. The first is a series of koshi waza (hip techniques) that are similar in appearance: ogoshi (major hip), tsuri goshi (lifting hip), and uki goshi (floating hip). After that, another workhorse of judo, ippon seoi nage (one-arm back carry throw), will be analyzed.

Tachi Waza: The attacker's hip is the hinge point of the throw in this example of uki goshi (floating/straddling hip throw). Also, look at how the attacker's knees and feet are pointed in the direction of the throwing action, and she is looking into the direction of the throw.

Ogoshi/Tsuri Goshi/Uki Goshi

Ogoshi: Ogoshi is called "major hip" because the attacker uses a tightwaist grip (grabbing around the defender's hips and waist) and pulls the front of the defender's body onto the side and back of the defender's hips. This major pulling and controlling action locks the defender's body onto the attacker's body. The attacker's feet and knees are placed close to each other and are pointing in the direction of the throw.

The attacker has successfully locked the defender's body onto his hips and rotates his body and head so he can add more torque and power into the throw. Also, look at how the attacker's body is driving forward and into the direction of the throw as he drives off the mat with his feet.

Here's the kake or power peak of the throw with the attacker steering and controlling the defender over his hip and down onto the mat.

Ogoshi 4: The attacker used a makikomi (wrapping or winding action) to finish the throw, which resulted in a resounding ippon score.

Tsuri Goshi: The name of this throw (tsuri goshi or lifting hip) describes how the attacker uses his hand and arms to lift his opponent up and onto his hip before turning his hip in order to throw him. The attacker uses his tsurite (lifting hand) to lift up on the defender's belt or jacket at the hip area. The attacker lifts the defender up and onto his hip before throwing him over his hip. There are two types of tsuri goshi and both are used effectively at all levels of competitive judo: o tsuri goshi (major lifting hip) and ko tsuri goshi (minor lifting hip). In o tsuri goshi, the attacker uses his hand and arm to reach around the back or shoulder of the defender, often trapping

the defender's arm. In ko tsuri goshi, the attacker reaches under the defender's arm and around his waist. The o tsuri goshi type grip around the defender's arm or over his shoulder is an effective grip for many applications of other throws such as harai goshi (sweeping hip) or uchi mata (inner thigh). Tsuri goshi is a popular and effective throw, used in all weight classes. Look at how the attacker uses both hands to lift the defender up and onto his hip.

This photo shows how the attacker uses his tsurite to grip and lift the defender. This is the o tsuri goshi (major lifting hip) grip.

The attacker has slid his hip in front of the defender as he lifted the defender up and onto his hip. From this point, the attacker will throw the defender over his hip. Tsuri goshi is a basic throwing skill that has many applications. As a result, this rather simple hip throw has a good rate of success at all levels of competition.

Uki Goshi: The name of this throws translates to "floating or straddling hip," which describes how the defender's body straddles over the hip of the attacker. Like ogoshi and tsuri goshi, this is a rather simple throw requiring just a few small body movements for it to work. In many situations, the attacker will break her opponent's balance by stepping across the defender's body. While uki goshi is considered a basic technique, it continues to be used with effective results at all levels of judo competition.

The attacker uses her left foot and leg to step across in front of the defender. As she does this, she uses her left hand to pull the defender to her front left corner then uses her right arm grab around the defender's waist.

The attacker lifts and pulls the defender up and onto her right hip as the defender straddles or "floats" over the attacker's right hip.

This is the power peak of the throw where the attacker throws the defender over her hip.

Seoi Nage

The name of this throw describes what takes place: the attacker carries the defender's body across and over the attacker's back (seoi), throwing him to the mat (nage). There are three primary applications of seoi nage: ippon seoi nage (one-arm back carry throw), morote seoi nage (both arms back carry throw), and eri seoi nage (lapel back carry throw). This analysis will focus on ippon seoi nage because of its versatility and popularity. In ippon seoi nage, the attacker uses one point of his body to connect to the defender (ippon) and carry the defender over and across the attacker's back (seoi), throwing him to the mat (nage).

Defining Features

These are the defining features of ippon seoi nage. 1. The attacker makes initial contact in the tsukuri (building) phase of the throw with his arm trapping and hooking the defender's arm. 2. The apex or hinge point in this throw is the connection of the attacker's upper arm and the front of the defender's shoulder. 3. As the attacker turns his body into the direction of the throw, he loads the defender up and onto his back and then throws the defender across and over the back of his torso.

Ippon Seoi Nage: The attacker breaks the defender's balance as he starts his body rotation into the throwing action. Look at how the attacker uses his right arm to hook under the defender's right upper arm. Also look at how the attacker's left foot is about to touch the mat as part of his initial back step into the throw.

The attacker has rotated his body fully into the throwing action. Look at how the attacker's entire body (including his head) is leaning into the direction of the throw. The attacker initially used both of his feet to drive off of the mat and, because of his body rotation, he is now driving off his left foot to generate force into the throw.

This shows the throw at the peak of power. Look at how the attacker is driving off of his left foot to continue to generate for force into the throw. This photo also shows why this throw is called "seoi nage": the defender has been carried across and over the attacker's back.

The attacker finishes the throw with a makikomi (winding finish) action.

This shows the connection at the hinge point of the throw by the attacker to the defender. The attacker uses her right arm to hook and trap the defender's right upper arm, pulling it to the attacker's shoulder area as she rotates her body into the direction of the throwing action. Look at how the attacker has rotated her body, and her knees and toes are pointed to the direction of the throw.

Attacker's Legs Wide: Tai Otoshi/Kubi Nage

Throwing techniques where the attacker's feet and legs are split wide apart provide a solid and stable base and have a good rate of success as a result. Tai otoshi (body drop) is probably the most obvious technique that comes to mind, but there are others as well. One is kubi nage (neck throw).

Tai otoshi (body drop) is classified as a te waza or "hand technique" in judo. In this throw, the attacker uses his hands and arms to lift and direct his opponent's body. This action of lifting and directing is used in many judo throwing techniques, but the defining feature of tai otoshi is the use of the hands and arms by the attacker to lift and steer the defender in a forward direction over the attacker's extended leg. When throwing with tai otoshi, the attacker could conceivably use only his hand/arm control and not have to use his lower in any way. This is why tai otoshi is classified as a te waza (hand technique) in judo. However, the addition of the extended leg provides for a strong and reliable throwing technique.

Defining Features

There are two defining features of tai otoshi: 1. The attacker's use of his hands and arms to lift and steer his opponent as the major feature. 2. In the standard application of tai otoshi, the axis or hinge point of the throw is where the attacker's extended leg meets the defender's leg or legs. The attacker uses his hands and arms to lift and steer the defender up and forward, and the attacker's extended leg provides the block that trips the defender and throws him forward. In the kubi nage application of the throw, the axis or hinge point of the throw is where the attacker's hips meet the defender's torso. 3. The attacker's legs are split wide. Some athletes will have a wide distance between his feet/legs, and some athlete will have a narrower distance. In most cases, the attacker places an equal amount of weight on each of his feet that are in contact with the mat.

Practically speaking, there are two types of tai otoshi used in competitive judo (with many variations depending on the athlete doing the throw). The grip that the attacker uses determines how close he pulls the defender forward into contact with the attacker's body as he applies the throw. In the standard application of tai otoshi, the attacker's hands and arms do the majority of the work in pulling and lifting the defender over the attacker's extended leg. In this standard application, there is not a great deal of contact between the attacker's torso and the defender's torso. The attacker's hands and arms pulling and lifting do a lot of the work in throwing the opponent. In another application of tai otoshi that is often used, the torso of the attacker and the torso of the defender are closely connected. This form of tai otoshi resembles kubi nage (neck throw). Using his hands, the attacker pulls his opponent's body close to his own body so that the two bodies are connected. As the attacker pulls with his hands, he rotates the torso of his body, creating torque and throwing his opponent. In kubi nage, the attacker uses his hands in the same way he would in tai otoshi and uses a wide leg split; however, the axis of kubi nage is the attacker's hip (and not his leg as in tai otoshi) making it more of a koshi waza (hip technique). Here's an analysis of these two types of tai otoshi. Both forms of tai otoshi are effective; it's a matter of choice as to which works better for you.

Standard Tai Otoshi: The first is the more standard application where the attacker places emphasis on using his hands and arms to lift and steer his opponent forward and over the attacker's leg as shown. There is space between the attacker's body and the defender's body.

Another View of the Standard Tai Otoshi: The attacker's hikite (pulling hand) pulls the defender up and forward and then steers the defender over the attacker's extended leg. The attacker's tsurite (lifting hand) is gripping on the defender's lapel and is used to lift the defender up and off the mat and assist the hikite in steering the defender over the attacker's extended leg.

Close-Contact Tai Otoshi/Kubi Nage: This variation of tai otoshi is called kubi nage (neck throw) and requires close body contact where the attacker pulls the defender in close to her body and uses a strong rotation of the torso in the action of throwing. The attacker pulls the defender onto her torso with her hands and arms, with no space between the two bodies. This throw is sometimes called kubi nage (neck throw) when the attacker grips around the defender's head and shoulders as shown here. This type of throw blurs the lines between a hand technique and a hip technique as the axis of the throw is at the attacker's hips. But the attacker uses her hands and arms to pull her opponent in tight to her torso, coupling the bodies together.

The attacker uses her left hand (the hikite or pulling hand) to pull inward and in a rotational type of movement rather than pulling up and forward as in the more classical application of tai otoshi. The attacker uses her right hand (her tsurite or lifting hand) to lift and pull her opponent's upper body (head and shoulders) in close to her torso. The attacker uses a strong rotation of her body to initiate and complete the throw. This form of tai otoshi relies less on using the hands than the more traditional form does.

In this form of tai otoshi, the attacker will usually do a makikomi (wrapping or winding) finish and land heavily on her opponent. Although she lands heavily on her opponent, the attacker maintains control of the action. This heavy landing takes the fight out of an opponent, making it easier for the attacker to immediately transition into a pinning technique.

Usually, this type of tai otoshi is an ideal combination of a throw and transition where the attacker will immediately land on her opponent and pin her, getting points for the throw and finishing with the pin for the win.

Close-Contact Tai Otoshi Loop Grip: The attacker is using a back grip with his right hand to trap the defender's upper arm by grabbing around it and gripping onto the defender's back as shown. The attacker uses his left hand to pull the defender's right elbow in close to the attacker's body. This is sometimes called a "loop grip." The attacker pulls his opponent close to his body and steers the opponent using both hands and arms as well as the rotation of his body.

This back view shows how the attacker has pulled the defender in close to his body so that there is no space between the two bodies. This is a tai otoshi (and not kubi nage) because as the attacker uses his hands to pull, lift, and steer the defender; the attacker is not throwing the defender over his hip. But, if someone wants to call it kubi nage, that's okay too. Just call it ippon.

Tai Otoshi with a Tightwaist Grip: Here is a tai otoshi where the attacker is using the same grip he would for ogoshi (major hip throw) by gripping around his opponent's waist. The argument could also be made that this is a variation of ogoshi using a wide leg stance. However, the attacker isn't throwing his opponent over his hip; he's throwing him over his extended leg. Whatever name is given to it, it resulted in an ippon score for the thrower in this photo and is an example of how different techniques blend together in actual use in competitive judo.

Using the Legs in Tai Otoshi: The distance between the feet and legs of the attacker varies with every judo athlete when applying tai otoshi. Some athletes have a wide-leg split and others have a narrower split. This is entirely a personal choice of each person who uses tai otoshi. Generally, the distribution of weight on each foot is equal with 50 percent on each foot. Sometimes, the attacker will place more weight on his base leg (70 percent) and less weight on his extended leg (30 percent). Often, the attacker's extended leg and foot will be placed with the knee pointed downward toward the mat and the foot pointed inward and positioned on the ball of the foot with the heel up. Doing this allows the attacker to flex his leg as he applies the throw giving him more power into the throw.

Knee-Drop Throwing Techniques: Seoi Nage, Seoi Otoshi, Hiki Otoshi

A popular series of throwing techniques at all levels of competitive judo are the knee-drop throws, often called knee-drop seoi nage (back carry throw). First, an explanation of the name "seoi nage" may be helpful. The phrase seoi translates to "carry over or across the back." The usual word in English that is used for this phrase is "shoulder." But this can be confusing to a new student who thinks he has to throw using his shoulder to do it. What really takes place is that the attacker throws his opponent over his back using his hands and arms to lift, pull, and steer the defender over the attacker's body. This emphasis on using the hands to lift, pull, and steer is why seoi nage is considered a te waza (hand technique) in judo.

Defining Features

The defining features of a knee-drop throw are: 1. The attacker's body is low and under the defender's center of gravity. 2. The attacker generates torque by spinning and rotating his body under the defender. 3. The attacker uses his arms to lift and steer the defender up, over, and across his back. 4. The attacker generates more force into the throwing action by driving off the mat with one or both of his feet.

When analyzing the knee-drop application of seoi nage, the most common use of a knee-drop throw is for the attacker to go to the mat on both knees. However, there are three primary methods of knee-drop throws: 1. The attacker goes to both knees, often called suwari seoi nage (kneeling seoi nage). 2. The attacker goes to one knee called seoi otoshi (seoi drop). 3. The attacker goes to one knee and extends her leg (called hiki otoshi or pulling drop as well as knee-drop tai otoshi or body drop). Here are the three primary knee-drop throws.

Suwari Seoi Nage: In this double knee-drop throw, the attacker spins under the defender's center of gravity. This type of spinning knee-drop generates a great deal of torque, which supplies the force for the throw. Additional force for the throw is provided by the attacker driving off of her feet/toes into the direction of the throw. Look at how the attacker's knees are together and pointed in the direction that she intends to throw the defender. The attacker's body is round, much like a cannonball hitting a target. The attacker doesn't lift her opponent straight up and over her body as much as she lifts and then pulls the defender onto her body, propelling or throwing the defender forward and onto her back.

Seoi Otoshi: In this single knee-drop throw, the attacker has a base on one knee and an extended leg, with her foot stabilized on the mat and providing the force necessary to throw the defender. The attacker's body is more upright in this one-knee throw than in the double-knee throw.

Hiki Otoshi: The name hiki otoshi translates to "pulling drop." This throw is also called a knee-drop tai otoshi. The attacker is positioned on one knee with her other leg extended in front of her opponent as shown. The basic concept of this throw is for the attacker to pull her opponent down and drop her over her extended leg. The attacker's body is upright with a fairly straight spine. The attacker will lift the defender up and over her extended hip and leg area.

Knee-Drop Seoi Nage Back View: This photo shows the back view of a knee-drop seoi nage. The attacker is using an ippon seoi nage (one-arm back carry throw) grip. Look at how the attacker is low and under his opponent's center of gravity and deep between the defender's legs. The attacker's knees are together and pointed in the direction of the throw. Both of the attacker's toes are driving off of the mat to generate more force and power into the throwing action.

Knee-Drop Seoi Nage: This photo shows how the attacker has spun under his opponent's center of gravity and is in the process of throwing him. Look at how the attacker's knees are driving in the direction he will throw his opponent. Also notice how deep the attacker is positioned between the legs of the defender. Often, an effective knee-drop throw will force the defender's legs to split wider apart. The attacker's body is round and compact in order to better rotate under the defender's body. Rather than trying to lift his opponent, the attacker is throwing his opponent forward and over his body.

Look at how the attacker is driving off his foot into the direction of the attack. Ideally, he would have driven off both of his feet, but this was still sufficient to complete the throw.

The attacker threw his opponent but the opponent managed to post his hand on the mat to stop the momentum of the throw, resulting in a waza-ari score. The attacker is now preparing to follow up with a pin to secure the victory.

Knee-Drop Upper Body Control: There are a variety of ways that the attacker can control his opponent's upper body in a knee-drop throw. This photo shows the attacker hooking under his opponent's arm to control his upper body.

Knee-Drop Tsuri Goshi Grip Throw: The attacker can use any method in order to control the defender's upper body when applying a knee-drop throw. In this photo, the attacker uses the same grip she would for tsuri goshi (lifting hip throw).

Do Not Flop and Drop: Never drop straight down onto your knees in front of your opponent. This is called "flop and drop" and is not an effective way to apply a double knee-drop throw. By dropping straight down, all the kinetic energy goes straight down to the mat and provides no torque for the attacker to throw her opponent forward and over her body. Flopping straight down and landing with all of your weight on your knees can cause knee injuries. Also, don't drop down with your knees apart. The attacker's knees should be together and pointed into the direction she intends to throw her opponent.

O Soto Gari/O Soto Gake/Harai Goshi

One of the real workhorses of judo is o soto gari (major outer reap) and for good reason: it works and can be easily adapted to fit any body type and works for both males and females. O soto gari is one of the most versatile and effective throwing techniques in judo. In o soto gari (and related throws), the attacker uses his right leg (in a right-sided attack) to reap or hook the defender's right leg (right leg attacks the opponent's right leg). The attacker goes outside the midline of the defender's body to reap his leg. Unlike o uchi gari (major inner reap) where the attacker goes between (or "inside") the defender's legs with his attacking leg to throw him, the attacker goes "outside" the midline of the defender.

Defining Features

The defining features of o soto gari are: 1. The attacker forces the defender to place most of his weight on one foot, and that is the foot the thrower focuses his attack on. 2. The attacker uses a strong reaping or sweeping (and sometimes hooking) action with his attacking leg. 3. The attacker points his toes on the foot of his attacking leg for more control and power in the reaping movement. 4. The attacker uses his hands and arms to pull, push, and steer the defender into the direction of the throw. 5. The attacker reaps with his leg "outside" of the midline of his opponent's body. 6. The defender is thrown in one of three directions: directly backward, to his back corner, or laterally to his side.

The name o soto gari (major outer reap) accurately describes the basic concept of this technique. The attacker reaps his opponent's leg much like a scythe reaps wheat. For our purposes in judo, when describing o soto gari, a reap is a curved or bent leg that is used in a hooking and cutting motion aimed at an opponent's leg or legs. Some variations of o soto gari (major outer reap) could be correctly called o soto gake (major outer hook). A reap and a hook are similar; both are a curved or bent device (such as the attacker's leg in o soto gari) used for catching, ensnaring, or holding something, with the exception that a reap is done in more of a broad, cutting movement. In some applications of o soto gari, the attacker hooks with his attacking leg to catch and hold his opponent's leg in place as he drives in to complete the throw without using a cutting or sweeping-type movement.

O Soto Gari Basic Application: The attacker slides his left foot forward as he uses his left hand (his hikite) to pull the defender's right elbow to down to the mat. The attacker uses his right hand (his tsurite) to push on the defender's lapel. As he does this, the attacker uses his right leg to reap the defender's right leg and throw him.

O Soto Gari: This sequence of photos shows how the attacker's body is driving directly forward. He uses his hands and arms to control and break the defender's balance to the defender's rear direction.

The attacker uses a strong reaping action with his right leg against the defender's right leg. Look at how the attacker is driving off of his left foot to gain more power in the throwing action.

The attacker completes the throw by using a makikomi finish (follow through by turning and winding). This type of finish isn't always used, but it often is in competitive judo situations. Look at how the attacker's right foot is pointed, indicating how it was used to control and reap the defender's leg in order to throw him.

O Soto Gake: Sometimes the attacker's reaping leg may actually be used as a hook. A hook is when the attacker makes contact with his attacking leg on one of the defender's legs, trapping the defender's leg. In this photo, the attacker reaches out with his attacking leg in order to use the heel of his foot to hook and snare the defender's leg at the knee. Look at how the attacker's left foot is driving off of the mat to generate force. The attacker seemingly overextended himself with this risky attack but it paid off for him.

This back view shows how the attacker used his right leg to hook his opponent's ankle and lower leg. This is an example of hooking an opponent's leg rather than reaping it.

The attacker successfully hooked his right heel on the back and side of the defender's right leg and dropped onto his knees to continue with the hooking and snaring control that he started.

This view shows how the attacker hooked and trapped the defender's right leg. Notice that the attacker's foot slid down the defender's right leg from its initial contact with the knee and is now at the defender's ankle. This hooking action controlled the defender's lower body as the attacker used his hands to steer his opponent down to the mat.

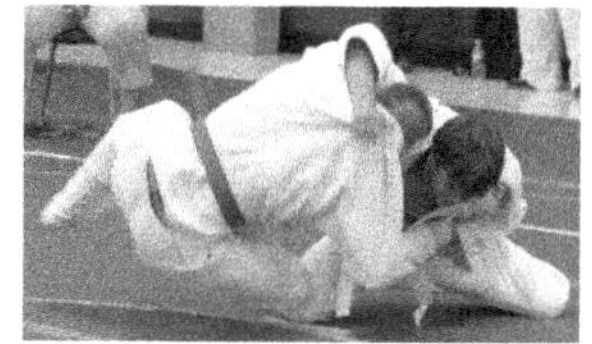

This photo shows how the attacker throws the defender using his right leg to hook the defender's leg for control as the attacker uses his hands and arms (as well as the rotation on his body) to steer the defender to the mat.

Hooking with the Foot in O Soto Gari: This photo shows how the thrower attacks laterally and uses the heel of his right foot to hook behind the defender's right knee. This hooking action traps and controls the attacker's right leg, making him vulnerable to being thrown. The attacker can throw the defender laterally or use a "ken-ken" attack as shown below.

In this situation, the attacker may use a "ken-ken" or hop-hop type of attack where he makes short hopping movements on his base foot/leg to move around the defender's body and throw him. The attacker's initial direction was to the side, but if the opponent defends or resists the initial attack, the thrower will round the corner, using a ken-ken hopping action to throw his opponent to the defender's back (and not laterally).

Lateral O Soto Gari/Harai Goshi: This photo shows the lateral or "crossbody" movement pattern that throws the defender sideways. Mechanically, the human body is not as stable when moved laterally as it is when moved forward, backward, or to the front or back corners. The attacker will throw the defender in the same direction that his toes are pointing.

In the reaping action, the attacker's leg should be bent with the toes of the foot pointed down and should be done in a short compact movement. The attacker should not make an exaggerated sweeping action with his leg. But there are some reaping throws such as a lateral or side direction o soto gari that resemble a sweeping action with the legs that is similar to how the leg is used in throws like harai goshi (sweeping hip) or uchi mata (inner thigh throw). As shown in this photo, the lateral or side direction o soto gari resembles a harai goshi or sweeping hip throw.

Lateral O Soto Gari/Harai Goshi Cross-Body Attack: This attacker moved to his left sideways and used his right leg to sweep the defender's right leg resulting in this harai goshi and scoring ippon. Often, an opponent's balance can be more easily controlled and broken by moving across his body and attacking him at his side.

Lateral O Soto Gari/Harai Goshi: This spectacular harai goshi that resulted in ippon started with the attacker moving in across his opponent's body laterally to his left. The opponent made the mistake of following the attacker, stepping sideways to his right, allowing the attacker to use his right leg to sweep the defender and throw him.

Throws Between the Legs: O Uchi Gari and Similar Throws

Some of most unexpected throwing techniques are the ones where the attacker drives between the legs of his opponent and throws him by reaping or hooking one (or both) of the defender's legs. These throws include o uchi gari (major inner reap), ko uchi gari (minor inner reap), ko uchi makikomi (minor inner wrapping), and others. One of the most often-used throwing techniques in judo is o uchi gari, and this throw has been selected for this analysis. This throw often produces a big ippon score and is an effective transition into groundwork if necessary. O uchi gari (major inner reap) is the mirror technique of o soto gari (major outer reap), but in o soto gari, the attacker goes "outside" the midline of his opponent's body and in o uchi gari, the attacker goes "inside" the defender's midline.

Defining Features

The defining features of o uchi gari are: 1. In o uchi gari, the attacker uses his right leg (in a right-sided attack) to hook and then reap the defender's left leg. 2. The attacker uses his attacking leg to reach between the defender's legs (going "inside" the defender's midline of his body) and reaps the defender's leg, throwing the defender to his back. This reaping action takes the defender's leg out from under him and throws him. 3. The attacker breaks the defender's balance to the defender's rear or back side (throwing him onto his back). 4. The attacker usually initially hooks with his attacking leg to snare or trap the defender's leg and then uses a reaping action to finish the throw. 5. The attacker closes the space between his body and the defender's body, which often results in chest-to-chest contact. 6. The attacker makes sure that his hips are close to the defender's hips, enabling him to make this close body contact possible. 7. The attacker uses his tsurite (right hand in a right-sided throw) as the primary hand to steer or direct where he wants the defender to land. But the attacker also uses his hikite (sleeve hand) to push and direct the defender to his back.

O Uchi Gari: Initially, there is a great deal of space between the attacker and defender. Look at how far apart their hips are. The attacker must close this space with a strong and direct explosive drive.

The attacker close the space between his body and his opponent's body. As he does this, the attacker uses his right leg to hook and trap the defender's left leg. Look at how the attacker's right (attacking) leg is located directly under his right hip for maximum control of the hooking action. Also, take note of how the attacker is using his right hand and arm to direct and steer the defender to the defender's back.

The attacker is at the power peak of this throw and has total control of his opponent's body. Look at how the attacker's torso is coupled to his opponent's torso for maximum control of the opponent's body. The attacker drives off of his left foot to deliver maximum force and power into the throwing action. The attacker's right leg hooked and trapped the opponent's left leg and is in the process of reaping it out from under the opponent in order to throw him.

The attacker scored ippon with this throw but could have quickly transitioned to a pinning technique if necessary.

O Uchi Gari Body Control: Look at how the attacker uses his left leg to hook the defender's right leg just below the knee joint. The attacker has turned his body so he has chest-to-chest contact with the defender for maximum control. The attacker used a strong back grip and steered the defender to the mat with it.

O Uchi Gari Reaping Action: This shows how the attacker reaps with his attacking leg after initially hooking or snaring it. This powerful reaping action literally takes the defender's leg out from under him, throwing him to the mat.

Attacker Is Supported on One Leg: Uchi Mata and Similar Throws

In some throws like uchi mata (inner thigh), harai goshi (sweeping hip), hane goshi (springing hip), o guruma (major wheel), and others, the attacker is supported by standing on one leg. And before we go on with this analysis, you might have noticed that o soto gari (major outer reap) and o uchi gari (major inner reap) have something in common with the throws that are now being analyzed: they are throws where the attacker is supported on one leg. So, you can see how just about every throwing technique in judo has some similarity to others. With that being said, let's get to uchi mata. An entire book can be written on these techniques, so we will focus on one of the most popular: uchi mata. Uchi mata (inner thigh throw) is classified as an ashi waza (leg technique) in judo for good reason. The axis or hinge point of the throw is where the attacker's leg meets the defender's leg. Many in judo consider uchi mata (inner thigh throw) to be the "king" (or for that matter the "queen") of all throwing techniques. Whether you share that opinion or not, there is no doubt that throwing an opponent with uchi mata often finishes the match and is quite a sight to see. Uchi mata in judo can be compared to the straight right-hand punch in boxing. Both are used to finish an opponent with one shot. Much like in boxing where there are many ways to set an opponent up for a straight right punch to land the knockout, there are many ways to set up an opponent for an uchi mata to land the ippon.

Uchi Mata: The name uchi mata provides a good description of this throw because the attacker uses his leg to sweep between the defender's legs. The name uchi mata implies an inner thigh throw because the attacker's sweeping leg makes contact with the defender's inner thigh, but the word "mata" actually translates to being the crotch between the legs or the split in branches of a tree. The implication of this name means for the attacker to make contact with his leg between the middle of the defender's legs and that's exactly what this throw does.

Defining Features

The defining features of uchi mata are: 1. The attacker makes use of his attacking leg to sweep between the defender's legs in order to throw him. 2. The axis or hinge point where the attacker and defender make contact is the back or backside of the attacker's leg and the inner thigh of the defender's leg. 3. In the standard or lifting style uchi mata application, the attacker's base (supporting) leg is positioned between the defender's feet and legs. 4. In the spinning style uchi mata application, the attacker's base (supporting) leg is positioned out and to the side of the defender's feet and legs.

While there are many variations of uchi mata, there are two primary applications of the throw. The first is the standard entry (which will be called the lifting entry in this book) where the attacker uses a strong tsurikomi (lifting-pulling) action enabling him to lift and steer the defender up and forward into the direction of the throw. The thrower's attacking leg is used in a strong sweeping action, making contact with the defender's leg at the inner thigh in the process. In the second application, the attacker uses a spinning entry, enabling him to use his attacking leg to sweep the inner thigh of the defender as the fulcrum of the throw.

Uchi Mata Lifting Entry: This photo sequence shows the same athlete using uchi mata from two different angles. This shows how the attacker has completely broken the balance and posture of the defender. Look at how the defender's feet have been lifted off the mat. The attacker extends his right foot and places it between the defender's feet to pivot on in order to make his rotation into the throwing action.

The attacker pivots off of his right foot and uses his left foot to swing around as he uses his hands and arms to start his lifting and pulling action.

Look at how the defender's left foot/leg is positioned between the defender's feet. This is the attacker's base or supporting leg and is one of the defining features of the lifting-style uchi mata. Look at how the attacker uses his right hand to steer and control the defender.

This photo shows why this throw is called uchi mata. The attacker's leg sweeps deeply, throwing the defender.

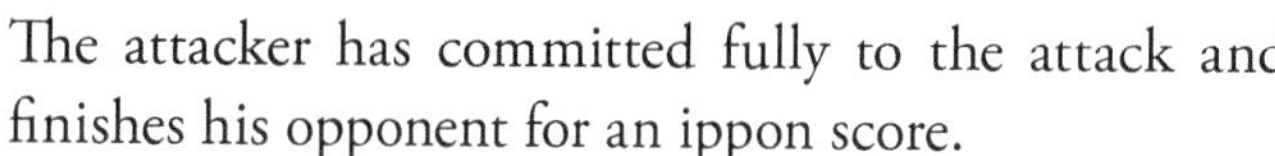

The attacker has committed fully to the attack and finishes his opponent for an ippon score.

Uchi Mata Spinning Entry: The attacker starts his throw by placing his right foot slightly on the inside of the defender's left foot as shown. This permits the attacker to quickly pivot on this right foot and spin into the throw.

The attacker pivots off of his right foot and uses his right foot to step back to the outside of the defender's left leg.

The attacker's left foot is firmly placed on the mat as he uses his right leg to sweep the inside of the defender's left leg at the thigh area. Look at how the attacker uses his left hand to grip the defender's right sleeve and pull it close into his body. The attacker's right hand is using a back grip and pulling the defender's body in close to the attacker's body. The attacker does not lift the defender up and off the mat as much as he pulls the defender's body in close to him.

The attacker uses his right leg to sweep the inside of the defender's left leg as shown. Rather than sweeping his leg up and through the middle and between his legs (as used in the lifting-style uchi mata), the attacker's goal is to sweep the defender's left leg.

The strong spinning action of the attacker creates momentum and builds the torque necessary to throw the defender forward and over the attacker's body. This spinning action of the attacker culminates in his total commitment to the action of the throw.

Foot Sweeps and Foot Props

Some of the most spectacular throws in judo are foot sweeps. Foot sweeps are the embodiment of how judo works. In most cases, the defender literally doesn't know what hit him until he ends up on his back. Foot props are similar to foot sweeps, but in foot props, the attacker uses his foot to prop or block the attacker's foot or leg, and in foot sweeps, the attacker uses his foot and leg to sweep the defender's feet out from under him.

Defining Features

The defining features of a foot sweep or foot prop are: 1. The attacker makes contact with his foot (or leg in some cases) with the foot or leg of the defender. 2. Foot sweeps and foot props are based on how the attacker coordinates the movement of the throwing action with when he sweeps or blocks the defender's foot or leg. This coordination is what is called timing. 3. In foot sweeps, the attacker uses his foot or leg to sweep the defender's foot or legs. 4. In foot props, the attacker uses his foot (or leg in some cases) to prop or block the defender's foot or leg as the attacker pulls the defender's body over the blocked foot. 5. Foot sweeps almost always result from a fast tempo that has been established by the attacker. The velocity (speed and direction of the attack) is the primary controlling action used by the attacker. 6. In foot props, the attacker relies less on a fast tempo and more on using his hands and arms to lift and pull the defender over the attacker's foot that has propped or blocked the defender's foot. 7. In foot sweeps, the attacker uses his hands and arms to control and steer the defender in the action of the throw, allowing the movement of the throw to do most of the work.

Foot Sweep Contact: In this photo, the attacker used his right foot to make contact with the defender's lower leg and ankle area. The attacker generated power from his base foot against the mat and is extended onto his toes. The attacker used a fast tempo to increase the velocity of the movement and used his hands to control and steer the defender's body to the mat.

Okuri Ashi Barai Thigh Contact: This photo shows how the attacker used his bent knee and inner thigh to sweep the defender's legs instead of using his foot. In this case, the name okuri momo barai (send-after thigh sweep) is an accurate description of this throw, but it's usually referred to as a variation of okuri ashi barai.

Foot Prop: This is a good example of how a foot prop is performed. The attacker in this photo used his right foot to prop or block the defender's lower leg. The axis or hinge point of the throw is where the attacker's foot makes contact with the defender's leg. Look at how the attacker uses his hands and arms to lift, pull, and steer the defender's body. In foot props, the attacker doesn't often sweep with his foot or leg but rather uses it to prop or block the defender's leg as shown here.

One of the most common, versatile, and effective foot sweeps is okuri ashi barai (send-after foot sweep) and is a good example when analyzing how foot sweeps work in general.

Okuri Ashi Barai: The attacker's initial stance, measured from his feet to the defender's feet, is fairly close at about twelve inches. The attacker will move to his right in a lateral movement pattern. Look at how the attacker's left foot and leg are positioned slightly to the left of the defender's right foot. The attacker does this so that when he sweeps with his left foot and leg, he has room for the sweeping action.

As the attacker moves to his right, the defender moves to his left. At the point where the defender's feet come together, the attacker will begin his foot sweep. The attacker makes sure to move laterally at a rapid pace. The faster he goes, the more momentum he builds in the throwing action.

Here is the power peak of the throw. The attacker uses his left foot to sweep the defender's feet together as shown. The fast-paced movement is what breaks the defender's balance, and the attacker uses his hands and arms to control and steer the defender to the mat.

This shows the defender in mid-flight with the attacker using his hands and arms to control and direct the defender down so that he hits the mat flat on his back.

The attacker finishes the throw with control and force.

Lifting and Pick-Up Throws

These are the throwing techniques where the attacker lifts the defender high up in the air before depositing him onto the mat on his back. In lifting throws, the defender lands on a big boom on the mat and there is no doubt who won the match. To some, these throws may appear to be the result of brute strength, but that's not the case; but yes, it does take physical strength to perform lifting throws. Throws like ura nage (rear throw), obi tori gaeshi (belt grab reverse direction throw), morote gari (both hands reap), and te guruma/sukui nage (hand wheel/scooping throw) are examples of lifting throws.

Defining Features

The defining features of lifting throws are: 1. The attacker uses his hands and arms to control and start the lifting movement, as well as to finish the throw. 2. The attacker often lowers his body in order to get under the defender's center of gravity in order to lift him. 3. The attacker usually starts the throwing action with both of his feet firmly placed on the mat for stability and to generate force into the throw. 4. Sometimes, the attacker will use one foot or leg to sweep, prop, block, or lift the defender's legs or hips in order to generate more control and power into the throwing action. 5. The defender's body is often taken straight up into the air before being thrown over the defender's body. As a result of this, the defender has more "airtime" when being thrown with a lifting throw and could have a better opportunity to turn out of the throw to avoid landing on his back. 6. In some lifting throws such as morote gari (both hands reap), kata guruma (shoulder wheel), and others, the attacker uses his hands and arms to grab and control the defender's legs or hips. As of the writing of this book, the International Judo Federation (IJF) does not permit grabbing below the defender's hip area or legs, but these throws are very much part of judo and should be learned. In order to satisfy the current contest rules, you can modify these leg grab type of throws or not use them when competing in tournaments using the IJF contest rules.

Lifting Throw Ura Nage: Here is the result of an ura nage (rear throw). In this match, the thrower's head slipped under his opponent's left arm and this resulted in a waza-ari score rather than ippon. Had the thrower managed to use his head to steer this opponent's body, the throw would have been harder and with more control.

Lifting Throw Obi Tori Gaeshi: Obi tori gaeshi is the belt grab reverse direction throw and has its early roots in Georgian Chida-Oba wrestling and later in Russian sambo.

Lifting Throw Te Guruma: Also called sukui nage (scooping throw), te guruma (hand wheel) was a popular counterattack before the IJG rules changes around 2016.

Lifting Throw Leg Lift: This type of knee or thigh lifting throw is something of a cross between ura nage and obi tori gaeshi. Sometimes called momo barai (thigh sweep), this throw is popular among the Mongolian judo athletes with a background in the Mongolian wrestling style of Bak.

Lifting Throw Morote Gari: Morote gari translates to both hands reap and resembles wrestling's double leg takedown, although this isn't simply a takedown as it usually results in a big ippon. With the IJF restriction on grabbing the legs, morote gari is not seen at elite-level competition but is still very much part of judo. Eventually, the rules will change again, and morote gari will continue to be used with great effect.

Lifting Throw Kata Guruma: Another victim of the IJF rules changes, kata guruma (shoulder wheel), in its original form where the attacker uses his hands and arms to grab the defender's legs, is not permitted. However, there are numerous variations of kata guruma where the attacker does not grab the defender's legs. The defining feature of kata guruma is for the attacker to wheel the defender over his shoulder, so grabbing the legs isn't necessary.

Ura nage (rear throw) is a primary lifting throw that readily leads to the development of other lifting and pick-up throws.

Ura Nage: In this basic application of ura nage, the attacker (right) uses a lapel and sleeve grip.

The attacker has moved to her left so that her left hip is directly behind the defender's right hip and buttocks. The attacker uses his right hand to grip and control the defender's left lapel in order to control the defender's upper body. The attacker wedges the left side of her head against the defender's right chest area. Look at how the attacker has lowered her level and is squatting with her knees and toes pointing forward.

This rear view shows how the attacker has used her left hand and arm to use a tightwaist grip to control the defender's hip area. Look at how the attacker is squatting so that her hips are lower than the defender's hips (and center of gravity). The attacker has a stable base with both feet on the mat.

The attacker lifts the defender by driving upward using her feet to drive off the mat as she uses her knees to spring upward. As she does this, the attacker arches her back to elevate the defender's body higher into the air. The attacker uses her head to steer the defender's chest area into the direction of the throw.

This is the power peak of the throw with the attacker driving off of her feet with her body arched. The attacker uses his head to steer the defender. This action of the defender arching her body adds more elevation to the throw.

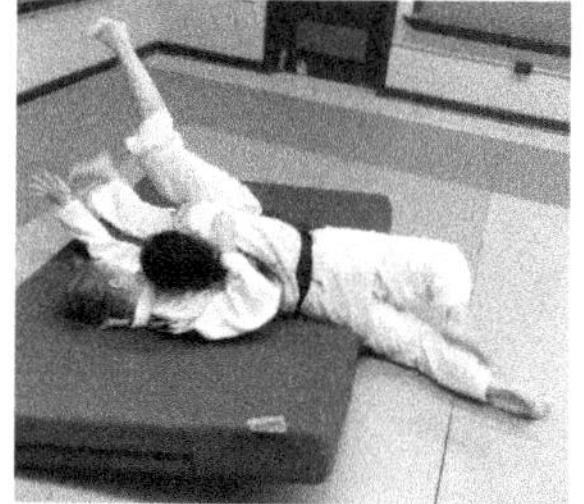

The attacker finishes the throw by turning so that she is chest-to-chest with the defender as the throw is completed. Doing this ensures that the attacker can transition to a pinning technique if necessary.

Sacrifice or Bodyweight Throws: Hikikomi Gaeshi and Similar Throws

Sutemi waza translates to "sacrifice techniques," and the concept of how they work is that the attacker "sacrifices" his standing position and drops to the mat in order to throw his opponent. In every case, the attacker uses the weight of his body to pull his opponent down and over some part of the attacker's body. So, the attacker is sacrificing his body by going to the mat and using his bodyweight to do it in order to throw his opponent. Throws such as hikikomi gaeshi (pull-down reverse direction throw), sumi gaeshi (corner reverse direction throw), tomoe nage (circle throw), uki waza (floating technique), and others all are part of this type of throwing technique. Sacrifice throws are subdivided into two groups: masutemi waza (back sacrifice techniques where the attacker goes onto his back to throw the opponent) and yokosutemi waza (side sacrifice techniques where the attacker goes onto his side or backside to throw the opponent). One of the most often-used sacrifice throws used in competitive judo is hikikomi gaeshi. It has a good rate of success as a throw for scoring points but is also used as an effective transition to groundwork, so this analysis will focus on this throw.

Defining Features

The defining features for sacrifice throws are: 1. The attacker uses the weight of his body to fall to the mat, taking the defender with him. 2. The attacker's body goes under the defender's center of gravity. 3. In some throws (such as tomoe nage or circle throw), the attacker's body is round. In others, the attacker's body is more linear (such as in uki waza or floating technique). 4. Sacrifice throws are often used as transitions to groundfighting in addition to scoring points for the throw itself. This analysis of hikikomi gaeshi (pulling down reverse direction throw) is a good example of how a sacrifice throw can score points as well as serve as an effective transition to groundfighting.

Hikikomi Gaeshi: The attacker uses a strong back grip with his right hand to control his bent-over and defensive opponent.

The attacker swings his body under the defender as shown, using his back grip to pull the defender down and into the direction of the throw. Look at how the attacker uses his bent right leg (using his shin) to jam under the defender's right upper leg.

Here's the power peak of the throw. The attacker has rolled under his opponent and lifted him off the mat.

The attacker uses his right leg to control and steer the defender over and into the direction of the throw. The attacker uses his hands and arms to also steer the defender over.

In this photo, the defender tried to turn out of the throw but was unable due to the defender's effective use of his hands and arms to control and steer him.

The attacker immediately turned and started to apply a kami shiho gatame (upper four corner hold).

The attacker finished with a secure pin.

This well-executed hikikomi gaeshi was double trouble for the defender; the attacker scored a waza-ari and transitioned directly into a pin to pick up the second waza-ari and finish the match. This leads us to the next part of the book: transitions.

CHAPTER 7

Transitions

I would get them to the mat and have my way with them.

—AnnMaria DeMars

Transitions are an essential part of competitive judo and deserve the same attention that throwing and grappling techniques get. A transition is a continuous and planned link from one technique or situation to another. In this sense, a transition is a renzoku waza or continuation technique because there is continuity in the movement from start to finish. Often, a judoka will use a transition from a standing position to set something up in groundfighting, and to most judo athletes and coaches, this planned continuation from standing to the ground is what they envision a transition to be. But techniques can be linked to another in groundfighting as well, and for that matter, from one standing situation to another standing technique. Another transition situation is for the attacker to start a transition from groundfighting against a standing opponent. A great thing about judo is that you can make an attack from any position, even if you are on the mat and your opponent is standing over you. In this section, we obviously can't analyze all transitions, but we will examine some selected situations that happen frequently.

Three Types of Transitions from Throwing to Groundfighting

There are three types of transitions from standing to the mat. The defining feature in all three is that each is a sequence of events that finish with the attacker controlling the defender to secure the winning score.

Finish with a Specific Technique: In the first type, the attacker has a specific attack he wants to finish his opponent with. An example is to use a yoko tomoe nage (side or spinning circle throw) as the attack used to get the opponent down onto the mat in order to apply juji gatame (crossbody armlock). In this type of transition, the attacker visualizes his opponent in the finished position; it's just a matter of executing the move after that. The attacker elicits a response from the defender with a pre-determined outcome. This type of transition is not so much an actual throwing technique that leads to groundwork; rather, the initial attack is made to look like a throw in order to convince the referee that it is a legitimate throwing attempt, ending in groundwork. The contest rules of judo stipulate that a legitimate throwing attack is the only way to get an opponent to the mat; dragging, pulling, or snapping an opponent down to the mat isn't permitted. In this type of transition, the attacker really has no intention of throwing his opponent; he simply wants to get his opponent on the mat and apply a submission technique. What may look like a yoko tomoe nage is really a good disguise for getting the opponent to the mat in order to finish him off with a juji gatame.

The Insurance Policy: The second type of transition is to think of a transition as an "insurance policy" in case the referee doesn't award a score for your throw. An immediate transition from the throwing attack to the mat using a pre-planned pin, choke, or armlock to finish the opponent is the "insurance" needed to secure the win. This type of transition is used when the attacker knocks his opponent to the mat but either doesn't get a score for the throw or receives a score less than ippon. In this case, the attacker will immediately transition to a pin, choke, or armlock to finish his opponent.

Makikomi: A third way to transition is a makikomi. The word makikomi translates to "winding or wrapping around a fixed object." A makikomi is the finishing action where the attacker lands on or near his opponent with considerable force. Getting thrown by an opponent who finishes with a makikomi is not a pleasant experience, to say the least. Throwing an opponent and using a makikomi to finish the throw often results in a definite ippon score. However, that may not always be the case, so in many situations, the attacker who finishes with a makikomi can quickly transition to a pin in order to finish the opponent in case the referee didn't call ippon.

Everything in judo is connected somehow and in some way. Transitions provide a natural link between throwing techniques and groundfighting techniques, and the only limitations on how to use transitions from standing to matwork are an athlete's imagination and the physical limitations of the human body. Here are some selected transitions that have good rates of success in all levels of competition.

A Throw to Pin Transition Type 1: Here's a sequence that every judo athlete has seen and done: completing a throw and immediately finishing an opponent with a pin. In this case, the attacker scored ippon for his efforts but had his "insurance policy" handy by immediately pinning his opponent upon landing on the mat. In this type of a throw/pin transition, the attacker's intention is to throw his opponent for an ippon, and the transition to the pin ensures victory for the attacker.

Throw to Pin: The attacker has his opponent at the power peak of the throw and is controlling the entire action.

Upon landing, the attacker uses a makikomi (winding finish) to add more force to the landing for his opponent, all the while maintaining control.

The attacker finishes the throw with a hard landing for his opponent. This hard landing momentarily stuns the opponent and takes the fight out of him, making a quick transition to a pin easier for the attacker.

The attacker transitions to kesa gatame (scar hold) to finish his opponent in the event an ippon wasn't called by the referee.

Throw-to-Pin Transition Type 2: This is another common throw-to-pin transition sequence, but in this case, the attacker's main purpose is to get the opponent to the mat in order to apply a pin. Getting a score for the throw is secondary to getting the opponent to the mat. One of the most common and effective of this type of transition is the knee-drop seoi nage (back carry throw) to a pin (most often the pin used is kesa gatame or scarf hold).

Knee-Drop to Pin: The attacker goes under the defender's center of gravity with a suwari (both knees) ippon seoi nage (one-arm back carry throw). A good score can be gained with this throw, but the attacker's primary intent is to get low under her opponent and to the mat in order to pin her. If the referee calls ippon to secure the win, all the better for the attacker.

The attacker finishes the throw, making sure that her body is solidly connected to her opponent's body and there is no space between them. This is a low, short, and compact throw designed to get the defender onto her back and permit the attacker to immediately apply the pin to secure the victory.

The attacker has completed the throw and immediately works to secure the pin.

Ko Uchi Makikomi to Pin: Another effective transition that is difficult for an opponent to counter and has a high rate of success is using ko uchi makikomi (minor inner wrapping throw) to get an opponent to the mat and quickly apply a pin. This technique is low to the ground and hard for an opponent to counter. The primary purpose of this throw is to get the opponent to the mat in order to secure the pin, but in many cases, this throw produces a hard landing for the defender and may result in an ippon.

Ko Uchi Makikomi to Pin: The attacker comes in low with a hard-driving action with the intention of getting the defender onto his back as quickly as possible. Ko uchi makikomi is considered a "safe" throw for the attacker because it is hard for the defender to block or counter.

Look at how the attacker drives forward using her left leg and foot to hook the defender low on his leg, near his ankle. Also, look at how the attacker uses his left hand to drive and steer the defender onto his back.

The attacker completes the throw but makes sure to not remain between her opponent's legs. If she remains between the legs, the defender may be able to wrap his legs around her and stop her from continuing on to the pin.

The attacker immediately swings her right leg over the defender's left leg to start the transition to the pin. If you don't immediately pass over your opponent's leg, you will get stuck between your opponent's legs and be at a stalemate.

The attacker passes over the defender's left leg and hip to start the pin.

The attacker finishes with mune gatame (chest hold) to secure the ippon.

A Throw to an Armlock Transition: This is a transition where the attacker has no intention of throwing the opponent; he merely wants his initial attack to look like a throw and get the opponent to the ground in order to apply a submission technique. If the attack looks enough like a throw to fool the referee, good for you and bad for your opponent. You will notice that the armlock used in these transitions is juji gatame (crossbody armlock). This is because juji gatame is such a versatile armlock that can be applied from just about any position. Several transitions where the attacker starts from a standing position and finishes with an armlock will be analyzed.

Yoko Tomoe Nage to Juji Gatame: In this first sequence, the attacker uses a yoko tomoe nage (side or spinning circle throw) to get his opponent to the mat in order to apply juji gatame (crossbody armlock). This is a popular and effective transition that has been used for years and continues to be effective at all levels of competition.

Yoko Tomoe Nage to Juji Gatame: The attacker faces his opponent and leads with his left foot as shown. The attacker uses his right hand to grip his opponent's left lapel and his left hand to grip his opponent's right sleeve.

The attacker places his right foot on his opponent's left hip as shown. As he does this, the attacker spins to his right and under his opponent, using his right hand to pull down on the opponent's left lapel.

The attacker spins under his opponent as shown. As he does this, he pulls his opponent down so that the opponent is bent over forward.

The attacker swings his left leg over his opponent's neck as he continues to spin under him.

The attacker rolls his opponent over and finishes in the leg press position ready to apply juji gatame.

Foot Push to Juji Gatame: In this transition, the attacker must make his initial foot push look like a failed throw and then immediately transition to the juji gatame. Often, the defender is taken to the mat and lands face down. This disorients him for long enough to allow the attacker to apply the juji gatame. This transition has a good rate of success, especially against skilled opponents who may more easily stop a yoko tomoe nage to juji gatame transition.

Foot Push to Juji Gatame: The attacker uses his right foot to jam in the left hip and upper leg area of his opponent as he rolls to his right side.

The attacker is on his right side and uses his right foot to push his opponent's hip and upper leg area. Doing this extends his opponent's right arm.

The attacker uses his left foot and leg to swing over his opponent's extended right arm and head.

The attacker swings his left leg over his opponent's head as he uses both of his hands and arms to pull his opponent's extended right arm tightly to his chest. The attacker is rolling to his right as he does this.

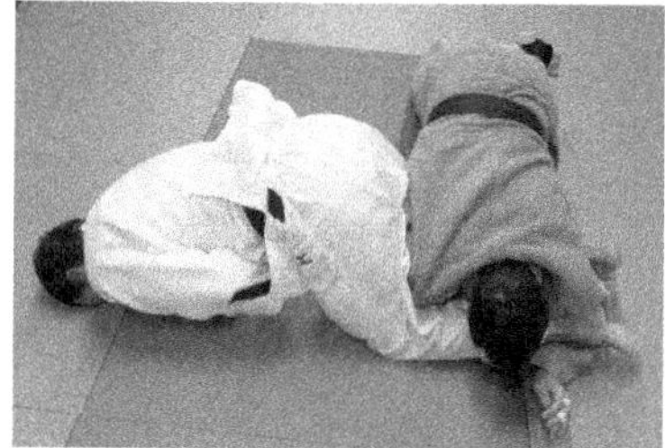

The attacker has rolled over onto his front as shown and thrusts his hips forward. Doing this creates pressure on his opponent's extended arm.

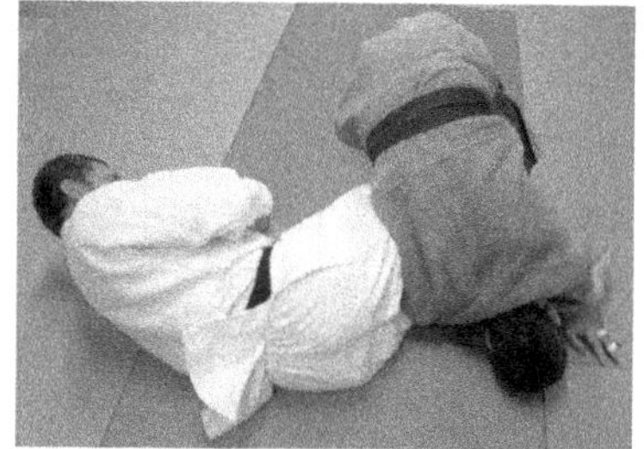

If the attacker chooses, he can add more pressure to the armlock by continuing to roll onto his left side as shown.

Knock Down to Juji Gatame: Keeping in mind that in order to enter into groundfighting from a standing position, the attacker must attempt what appears to be an actual (and legitimate) throwing technique. Often, the attacker will use his hands and arms to snap his opponent down to the mat or fake a foot sweep or prop to knock his opponent to the mat in order to make it look like a valid throwing attempt to fool the referee. This sequence shows how the attacker has snapped or knocked his opponent to the mat and follows through with a rolling juji gatame.

Knock Down to Juji Gatame: The attacker uses his hands and arms to pull his opponent down to the mat.

As his opponent goes to the mat, the attacker places his left leg near the opponent's right shoulder and starts to swing his leg over the opponent's right shoulder.

The attacker steps over his opponent with his right leg and starts to roll over his right shoulder. Doing this extends the opponent's right arm.

As the attacker rolls over his right shoulder, he uses his feet and leg to hook and control his opponent's head. As he does this, the attacker continues to use both of his hands and arms to pull and control the attacker's extended right arm.

The attacker rolls his opponent over and onto his back.

The attacker immediately applies juji gatame.

Knee-Drop Throw to Juji Gatame: In the same way a judo athlete can use a knee-drop seoi nage (back carry throw) in order to transition to a pin, the same can be done with a knee-drop seoi nage to juji gatame. The attacker's intent is to get the defender to the mat and apply juji gatame, but if the referee awards as score for the throw, that's even better.

Knee-Drop to Juji Gatame: The attacker uses a knee-drop ippon seoi nage (one-arm back carry throw) to throw his opponent.

The attacker immediately springs up and onto his feet and jams both of his knees into the side of his opponent's torso and neck as shown. As he does this, the attacker uses both of his hands and arms to pull his opponent's right arm to his chest.

The attacker swings his left leg over his opponent's head as he uses both hands and arms to trap his opponent's extended right arm to his chest as shown.

The attacker rolls back and applies juji gatame.

Transitions from a throw to an armlock are effective, and every judo athlete should have at least one transition from a throw to an armlock in his or her arsenal of skills.

Transitions When Opponent Attempts to Stand: A good time to catch an opponent in a transition is when he is on the mat and attempts to stand up. It's a smart tactical move to make it look like you are attempting to throw him as he stands, but the referee may or may not award a score. One way to possibly get a score is to "sell" your attack by using a loud kiai (spirit shout) as you apply the transition.

Transition to Pin: Sometimes your opponent will hop up quickly onto his hands and feet if he has been down on the mat.

The attacker quickly uses his left arm to hook under the opponent's right shoulder and upper arm. The attacker uses his right hand to grab his opponent's jacket for control.

The attacker uses his right hand and arm to reach down his opponent's back and firmly grab the belt as shown.

The attacker uses his left hand to firmly grab his right arm. As he does this, the attacker starts to move to his left and under his opponent's right shoulder.

The attacker spins his opponent over and onto the mat.

The attacker immediately follows through and lands on his opponent to pin him.

Drill Training for Transitions

As with any other set of skills, the best way to become proficient in transitions is to learn the correct way to perform linking standing throws to groundwork and then do a lot of drill training so that it becomes ingrained as a good habit.

Here are three drills that are effective in training for effective transitions and should be done on a regular basis. They are: 1. Spin and Pin Drill. 2. Spin and Stretch Drill. 3. Spin to Win Drill. The defender starts on her knees to better simulate taking a fall. Rather than taking a lot of hard falls from throws, you can perform many repetitions to develop skill in transitions by having the defender start on her knees.

Spin-and-Pin Drill: This drill is highly effective to teach and reinforce the skill of immediately following through with a pin after a throw. Doing this drill on a regular basis will significantly increase a judo athlete's skill in transitioning from a throw to a pin.

Spin and Pin: The attacker places his right foot in front of the defender's right knee as shown. As she does this, the attacker uses her right hand to reach around the defender's neck and grabs the defender's jacket at the right shoulder area. The attacker uses his left hand to grab the defender's right sleeve.

The attacker uses her left hand to pull on the defender's right sleeve and spin the defender over her extended right foot and leg as shown.

The attacker spins the defender over and onto her back.

The attacker immediately transitions to kesa gatame (scarf hold).

Spin-and-Stretch Drill: This drill simulates doing a throw and transitioning immediately into juji gatame (crossbody armlock). This drill is highly recommended for every judo athlete, but especially for those who compete at advanced or elite levels. Here's a personal story to illustrate how effective this drill is. Several years ago, in the first round of the World Sambo Championships, one of my athletes was paired against the previous year's silver medal winner. One of the primary drills we used in preparation for the tournament was this spin-and-stretch drill. My athlete had an effective tai otoshi (body-drop throw) but had also spent many hours doing this transition drill. With just nineteen seconds into the match, my athlete threw his opponent with tai otoshi and immediately transitioned to a juji gatame to get the tap out. After the match, my athlete said to me, "Coach, I owe you an apology." I asked him why. He said, "I've cussed you under my breath for the last four months in training because you made me do the spin-and-stretch drill over and over and that's exactly how I beat that guy. Thanks for making me do that drill."

Spin and Stretch: The attacker is standing in front of the kneeling defender. The attacker uses his left hand to grab the defender's right sleeve and uses his right hand to grab the defender's jacket at the upper back.

The attacker extends his right foot and leg, placing it in front of the defender's right knee as shown.

The attacker pulls the defender and spins him over his extended right foot and leg as shown.

The attacker spins the defender over and onto his back.

The attacker immediately squats low on the defender's right shoulder and head area as shown. The attacker swings his left foot and leg over the defender's head. Doing this traps the defender's head and upper body.

The attacker rolls back and applies juji gatame.

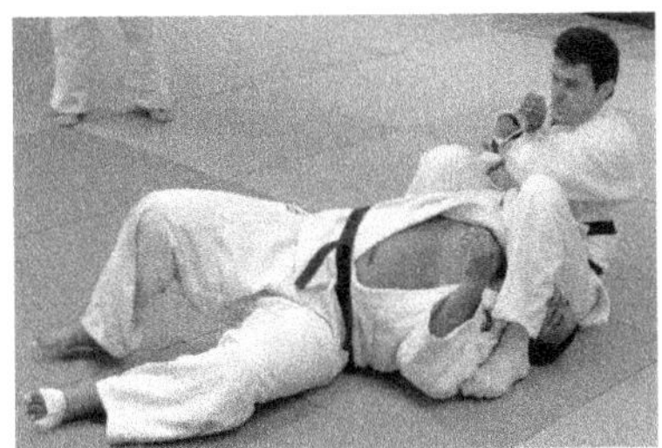

Spin-to-Win Drill: This drill teaches an athlete to pursue an opponent after a throw if the opponent attempts to get a stable base after being thrown by rolling over onto his or her front and getting onto all fours. This is an effective drill based on what really happens in a judo match, and doing this drill on a regular basis will increase a judo athlete's skill in transitions against opponents who roll out and get onto hands and knees.

The attacker uses her left hand to grab the defender's right sleeve and uses her right hand to grab the defender's upper back and shoulder area on the jacket. As she does this, the attacker places his right foot in front of the defender's right knee as shown.

The attacker uses his hands and arms to pull the defender over her extended right leg.

The defender is spun over onto her back but immediately rolls over onto her elbows and knees as shown. This is an important part of this drill as it simulates an opponent rolling out of a throw.

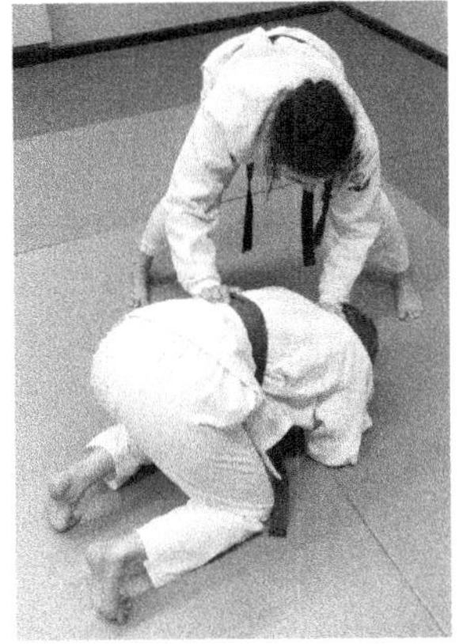

The attacker quickly moves to her right side and to the defender's left side and uses her left hand to hook and pull on the defender's right elbow. As she does this, the attacker uses her right hand and arm to grab around the defender's left upper leg.

The attacker rolls the defender over and onto his back as shown.

The attacker immediately applies mune gatame (chest hold) to pin the defender.

Only a few transition skills were analyzed in this section, but if you make it a point to develop your skills in transitioning from one technique to another, you will add another layer of skill to your judo. A good way to think about transitions is that they are the mortar that holds the bricks of a house together. Just like mortar, transitions firmly bind techniques together into a cohesive and efficient sequence of movements, resulting in control for the judo athlete who applies them.

CHAPTER 8

An Aggressive Defense

Make him sorry for attacking you.

—Rene Pommerelle

Defense is more than simply avoiding defeat; it's an integral part of imposing your will on your opponent. This section of the book focuses on an aggressive defense. An aggressive defense is based on the tactical combat concept of kobo ichi where offense and defense are one and the same thing and are used interchangeably as the situation dictates. This means that you not only defend yourself; you force your opponent into making mistakes that can be used to defeat him.

An Aggressive Defense Wins Matches

Don't simply seek to avoid or evade an opponent's attack; prevent it from taking place. But if it does, stop it dead in its tracks. There is both a physical difference and a psychological difference between avoiding or evading an opponent's throwing attack as opposed to shutting it down and stopping it dead in its tracks. Avoiding an attack is passive in nature. A judoka reacts to what his opponent does. Stopping an attack is aggressive in nature because it's proactive. This proactive approach is what defines an aggressive defense.

More About Kobo Ichi: Counterattacks

Kobo ichi is discussed elsewhere in this book; it is the central concept in the tactics of a judo contest. A practical example of kobo ichi as a tactical aspect of an aggressive defense is that it will lure an opponent into a trap. Much like the concept of counterpunching in boxing, an intelligent judoka can set his opponent up into making a mistake and then capitalize on that mistake with his counterattack. A good example of how you can use this is to use a "sugar foot" to lure an opponent into extending his foot and leg in his attempt to sweep or reap you. A sugar foot is where you place your foot and leg out just far enough to tempt your opponent into going for it. When he does, you can quickly launch your counterattack that you had planned all along. This is an old tactic, but it continues to work at all levels of judo. Kobo ichi is a state of mind as well as an actual occurrence. If an athlete constantly seeks to control or attack his opponent and views the time when he has to defend himself as an opportunity to turn it around and beat his opponent, he has the advantage over his opponent. Knowing that a good defense limits and nullifies what an opponent can do is part of imposing your will on your opponent and gives you a psychological edge.

Training for Defense

As with any skill, if you don't practice defense, you won't be very good at it. An athlete is as only good as what his training produces. Probably one of the most neglected aspects of training in judo is in the area of defense against throwing techniques. This is true from both a technical aspect (the physical act of defending against a throw), but also from a tactical aspect (using defense to control the action in the match).

There are two effective methods for practicing an aggressive defense.

The first is drill training on the hip block and cut-away defense on a regular basis. The hip block and cut-away defense (more on this a bit later) is the most effective defensive skill used in standing judo. Perform this drill with the training partners doing a specified number of attacks on the left side and the same number of attacks on the right side. This can also be done as a timed drill where each judoka has thirty or sixty seconds to attack and defend. This is a skill drill where there is cooperation between the athletes. This drill can progress to a more realistic drill where one judoka attacks his partner (with varying degrees of intensity) for a specified time period and the partner must defend against all of them using a hip block and cut-away defense. This is what I call "defense randori" or "hip block randori."

The second drill for working on an aggressive defense is grip-fighting randori (or grip randori). Actually, grip randori is a drill that develops technical and tactical skill in more areas than defense, but grip randori permits judo athletes to work on the grip-fighting skills that stop an opponent from launching an attack. A useful drill for this is to assign one judoka to be the one doing the grip fighting to shut down his partner's throwing attacks. Assign the other partner the task of attempting throwing attacks. The coach can specify what type of throw is to be used or allow the athletes to use their own initiative. This can be done as a timed drill. Another drill that is simpler is for the athletes to engage in grip randori. Grip randori is the same as regular randori with the exception that only grips can be used (no throwing attacks).

Lines of Defense

There are several lines of defense. Depending on individual needs and preferences, each athlete will use one of more of these. During practice, work on defense as part of your overall fight plan and use it to not only defend against an attack but to shut down or stop an attack before it develops. As with anything, there may be some other lines of defense not mentioned here that work for you, but the important thing is that you make it a habit to spend some time working on these on a regular basis.

Grip Fighting as Defense: Grip fighting is the first line of defense. Both offensive and defensive gripping skills are used to put an opponent into position so he can't attack effectively. In very real terms, using gripping as a means of defense is actually "preventative" defense. In other words, shutting your opponent down as much as possible with good grip fighting so that he can't launch an attack against you. Just as in medicine, an ounce of prevention is worth a pound of cure.

Body Movement and Body Posture as Defense: The second line of defense is body movement and control of the opponent's posture. This includes an effective use of your body space—how close or far you are from your opponent. Making sure that you are in a position that doesn't allow your opponent to attack effectively is an effective defensive skill, and you achieve this by your use of posture, grip, or how fast you move about the mat. A bent-over body with poor weight distribution is much easier to throw than a body that's well balanced.

Hip Block and Cut-Away Defense: Using the hips to block an attack is probably the most effective method of stopping a throw, especially a forward throw. For instance, in the hip block, the defender will use his left hip to block or jam his opponent's right sided throwing attack. The defender won't allow the attacker to get past his left hip. From this, the defender stops the momentum of the forward throwing attack and regains his balance to reestablish himself as a threat to his opponent. Basically, you cut with your opposite hip, hit him hard with that hip, and don't let your opponent get past your hip. If he slips his hip in, he can still catch you in a throw, so block his attack hard. The defender should also "cut away" from the attack if possible. As you block with your left hip, tear your right hand away from his grasp and maybe even step back a bit with your right leg and foot. The defender, on the right, has used a hip block with his left his as he cuts away to negate the momentum of his opponent's attack.

Jamming with the Hand: The defender (left) is using the hip block and cut-away defense and adds another line of defense by jamming his left hand and arm against the attacker's body as shown. This type of defense is aggressive because it doesn't simply evade an attack but rather stops the attacker dead in its tracks.

Hop-Around Defense: Another line of defense is to hop around your opponent's attack in order to avoid it. This is one of the most common defenses used in judo. When the attacker comes in for a right-sided forward throw, the defender will react by hopping around the throw to his right, avoiding the throw.

Hip Block and Hop-Around Defense: Sometimes, a combination of a hip block and hop-around takes place. The defender initially stops the attacker's throw with a hip block, but the attacker's momentum in the throw is so strong that the defender has no time to cut away but has to hop around to avoid being thrown. This photo shows how the defender, on the right, has used a hip block but has to hop around the attacker as well to keep from being thrown.

Sag Defense or Lower-the-Body Defense: This line of defense is to lower your body below his center of gravity and sag. You will often do this in combination with a hip block, but not always. When using this line of defense along with a hip block, you set your opponent up for a great counterthrow with an ura nage (rear throw) or other types of rear lifting throw. The defender (on the right) has lowered his hips below the attacker's hips and has stopped the forward momentum of the throw. Now he's ready to use a counterthrow such as ura nage.

Jigotai Defense: Probably the oldest and most obvious form of defense against a throwing attack is the jigotai position of bending over at the waist. Jigotai translates to "defensive posture," and this is the most used defense in judo. By bending over and crouching, the defender is attempting to make as much space as possible between his hips and his opponent's hips.

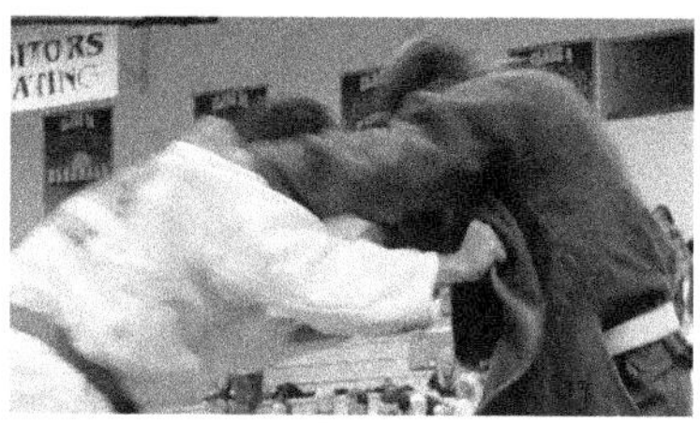

Stiff-Arm Defense: Another line of defense that is quite common is for the defender to extend his arms out straight and "stiff arm" his opponent. Although the referees (rightly) quickly penalize a judo athlete for excessively using the stiff-arm defense, it's still an effective way to make space between the defender and his opponent. Knowing how to stiff-arm an opponent is what will prevent the referee from penalizing a judoka. Use your arms like springs with the elbow slightly bent to start. By doing this, the defender doesn't extend his arms out straight and make the stiff-arm action so obvious.

Jam Defense or Ride-Down Defense: The next line of defense is to drive through your opponent's attack and jam him to the mat. This often starts out as lowering the body and sagging, but then the defender drives his hips forward and completely negates the throwing action of the attacker. This defense is a good one when the attacker uses a throw with only one leg or foot on the mat such aa harai goshi (sweeping hip throw).

In this series of photos, the attacker is using harai goshi). The defender, with his back to the camera, has successfully done a hip block but chooses not to cut away from the throw. He will make sure to stay low and below the attacker's hips and drive the attacker to the mat.

The defender drives the attacker to the mat and "rides" him down, controlling the action.

The defender has successfully stopped the attacker's throw and continues on to control him on the mat.

Cut-Against-the-Grain Defense: A common and effective line of defense is to cut against the grain of the throw. When your opponent attacks you with a forward throw, you cut against the direction, flow, or "grain" of the throw. This movement stops his momentum and throws him off balance, giving you an opportunity to counter him with a throw or takedown of your own. This photo shows the attacker attempting a harai goshi. The defender has cut against the grain of the throw to his left, stopping the forward momentum of the throw. This also has thrown the attacker off balance and caused him to lean to his left rear corner.

Sprawl Defense: Another common line of defense is a sprawl against a front double leg takedown or other move where your opponent shoots a takedown at you. Work hard on not only your sprawl technique, but also hitting him hard with your hips as you sprawl back aggressively, forcing him down to the mat. While the current IJF contest rules prohibit grabbing the legs, it's still a good idea to have the ability to sprawl, especially is you compete in sambo, BJJ, or submission grappling.

Hop-Around and Sprawl Defense: Sometimes, you may have to combine a sprawl with a hop-around defense to avoid being thrown. This is the case when an opponent attacks with a low knee-drop shoulder throw and you may have to sprawl out and away as you hop around him to keep from being thrown. This photo shows a good knee-drop attack that almost catches the defender. The defender initially tries a hop-around defense.

As the defender hops around, he sprawls out wide.

The defender continues to hop around as he sprawls to negate the forward momentum of the throwing attack.

The defender has also managed to post his left hand on the mat for stability as he continues to sprawl around the attacker's body.

The defender has successfully sprawled out and hopped around the throwing attack and continues in to groundfighting.

Evade-the-Attack Defense: This line of defense is to evade the throw. The idea is to open the space between the defender's hips and the attacker's hips. This is called "sukashi," which translates to evade. As your opponent attacks with a forward throw, you sidestep out and away from his attack and can counter by using your hands to turn him over forward. The attacker's forward momentum can be used against him and the defender can counterattack with a throw of his own. The defender, on the left, has managed to move his hips away from the attacker, giving him room to mount a counterattack.

Hand-Post-on-Mat Defense: If the defender's been caught and is being thrown, this line of defense is often used. The defender uses his hand to stop the action of the throw. It's not a particularly safe defense as the defender has the real chance of injuring his arm or shoulder as he posts on the mat. However, it's one of the last lines of defense if someone's been caught in a throw.

Roll-Out Defense: If the defender's been thrown, he can turn or roll his body away from the action of the throw in order to land on his front or side to lessen the score. This is a common defense and is used as a last option to avoid landing on the back.

Turn-Out-of-Throw Defense: The last line of defense is to turn out of the throw, which is a last-ditch attempt at avoiding being thrown onto your back. This is the least recommended line of defense and should only be done by skilled, elite athletes who have excellent kinesthetic awareness. Turning out is when the attacker has thrown you and you must twist your body enough to land on your front or front side so that a minimal score is awarded.

IMPORTANT: Under no circumstances should you ever land in a bridge position when thrown on your back. Landing in a bridge position to avoid landing on your back is extremely dangerous, and you could break your neck or suffer other serious injuries. This is also true when the defender uses his head to post onto the mat as shown in this photo. Serious neck or head injuries can take place by posting on the head to turn out of a throw.

Plant him there until he quits.

—Shawn Watson

CHAPTER 9

The Groundfighting of Judo

Groundfighting in modern competitive judo takes place in many positions and situations. Often, the tempo in groundfighting in judo is fast, especially in contrast to the tempo in other forms of submission grappling. And, as in the standing aspect of competitive judo, groundfighting has changed over the course of judo's history, both from external sources such as Western-style wrestling and sambo, and just from the natural development of this aspect of judo. This section of the book will examine selected pins, chokes, and armlocks of competitive judo, as well as practical ways of applying them using the different breakdowns, turnovers, and other entry methods used in judo.

Newaza, the Guard, Groundfighting, and Groundwork

The earliest position for grappling on the mat in judo was "newaza" or "newaza no semekata." Newaza translates to "supine techniques" and newaza no semekata translates to "attack forms of supine techniques." (This phrase "newaza no semekata" was popularized in the book *Newaza of Judo* by Sumiyuki Kotani, Yoshimi Osawa, and Yuichi Hirose and published in 1968 by Koyo Bussan Kaisha, Ltd.) From a technical standpoint, newaza places emphasis on osaekomi waza (pinning), shime waza (strangling), and kansetsu waza (joint locks). Early in judo's history, striking, leglocks, neck cranks, wristlocks, and other submission techniques were permitted, but as injuries increased and the safety of the contestants was constantly at risk, the rules gradually changed. Kodokan judo's emphasis was (and continues to be) placed on nage waza (throwing techniques) over katame waza (grappling techniques). All contests start standing up, but in reality this simply reflects the nature of real fighting. A good way to look at the rules of judo, especially in groundfighting, is that they mirror what actually takes place in a self-defense situation. If you throw an assailant hard onto the ground, you will injure him and it often ends the fight. In the rules of judo, if you throw an opponent hard onto the mat, it ends the match with ippon. If for some reason, in a street fight, you throw your opponent but not with enough control or force to injure him, you may have to engage him in fighting on the ground. Your goal then is to control him and pin him until you can get help or inflict further damage on him (osaekomi waza), lock his arm, and end the fight (kansetsu waza) or strangle him to end the fight (shime waza). Looking at it logically, the rules of judo simply reflect what can take place in real personal combat.

Newaza Position: Unlike Western wrestling, where being on the back is considered to be a disadvantage, judo views fighting off the back, backside, buttocks, or flanks as just another opportunity to beat an opponent. Kyuzo Mifune, in his classic book *Canon of Judo,* featured most of the groundfighting techniques from this position. The exponents of Kosen judo in pre-World War II Japan were highly skilled in all phases of groundfighting but especially in fighting from this position. The Kosen judo movement was organized at a number of Japanese universities and emphasized the groundfighting of Kodokan judo over the throwing techniques. After the war, only a few universities continued Kosen judo, but its influence on Japanese judo remained. One of those influences is probably why, in judo, the term "newaza" has become the general term used to describe all ground grappling. This newaza position is called the "guard" in Brazilian jiu-jitsu and mixed martial arts. No matter the name, it's an effective position for groundfighting.

Speaking of groundfighting, what is called "groundfighting" is a descriptive name for all grappling and fighting on the mat or ground. In mixed martial arts, this includes both grappling and striking, so it's accurate to call it groundfighting because that's what it literally is: fighting on the ground. While many people call grappling on the mat "groundfighting," some call it "groundwork," "ground grappling," or "ground play" but whatever you call it, do it skillfully.

Strategies for Groundfighting

Here are some strategies that have proven over time to be effective for successful groundfighting at all levels of competition. Many (if not all) of these strategies are interdependent and form an overall plan of attack based on efficient movement. Always remember that efficient movement translates to effective control.

Fitness Is a Weapon

Groundfighting is tough, physically demanding, and not for the faint of heart. The better conditioned you are in all aspects of fitness, the better you will control your opponent and apply your technical skills. An athlete with superior fitness will better be able to reflexively apply his technical skills over an opponent who may be technically more skilled but isn't fit enough.

Make It Tough for Your Opponent

Make life tough for your opponent and do everything you can (within the rules as well as while being safe) to wear your opponent down so that he not only gives up physically, but mentally as well. Impose your will on your opponent and make him fight under your terms. In the same way a snake squeezes its victim, keep the pressure on your opponent. From a psychological point of view, he's thinking of how bad it is for him rather than how he can beat you.

Work to Control the Position

Always work to control the position that your opponent is in. If you are in a superior position in relation to your opponent and to where you are located on the mat, you will have a better chance of securing a winning move. The old saying "control the position and get the submission" is true. Mobility is essential in effective groundfighting, both for you and your opponent. Always work to gain as much freedom of movement as possible for yourself and always work to limit your opponent's freedom of movement.

Shiho: Control the Four Corners

Always work to control your opponent's head, shoulders, and hips. These are the key control points of the human body. Almost always, by controlling these points you will control the rest of your opponent's body and thereby his movement. In Kodokan judo, the concept of "shiho" or "four corners" is applicable here. This is a situation where the attacker controls the defender's hips and shoulders and is useful in controlling an opponent (keeping in mind that the hips and shoulders are the four corners of the human body that need to be controlled).

Use Time Holds

Think of a pin as a "time hold" where you hold your opponent to the mat for a specific period of time (in the current judo rules, it's twenty seconds) to secure the victory or control him long enough to apply a submission technique. Additionally, think of a "ride" as a controlling position. In amateur wrestling, a wrestler can gain points from a ride, but in all other grappling sports, a ride is used to control an opponent in an effort to apply a submission technique or pin. All effective rides operate on the basis of controlling an opponent's head, hips, or shoulders.

Improve Your Position: Keep Working to Get Better Control

After controlling the position, immediately attempt to control your opponent better. Constantly probe, pry, grab, or manipulate with your hands, arms, elbows, feet, legs, knees, or even your head to better control your opponent. Continually work to break your opponent down from a stable to an unstable position or situation.

Even if you are in a defensive position, look to see how you can improve your position and gain further control.

Break Your Opponent Down

A breakdown is when you take your opponent from a stable position or situation to an unstable position or situation. A breakdown is taking your opponent from his stable base and gain control over him. You may break him down to a flat, face-down, and prone position in order to apply a submission technique or gain further control of him. You may break your opponent down from an all-four or turtle position and turn him over onto his back for a pin. By continually working to break down your opponent, you will improve your own position and control your opponent.

Constantly Try for a Submission

The ultimate goal is to force your opponent to submit or tap out. If pinning an opponent for twenty seconds ensures you the victory in a judo match, take it, but in other forms of submission grappling, a submission technique guarantees your victory. If you make an opponent give up to you, he'll never forget you and never forgive you.

Everything Is a Handle

Use every part of your opponent's body or uniform as well as every part of your body or uniform to grab, grip, hold, and manipulate to get control, maintain control, and get more control of your opponent.

Always Work to Gain a Stable and Fluid Base

Use all the parts of your body to provide a stable base from which you can work. A stable base permits you to generate force and attain control, and a fluid base permits you to flow from one move to another, all the while maintaining control of the situation.

Kobo Ichi: Adapt to the Situation and Work to Control It

Use the concept of kobo ichi where you turn a defensive situation into an offensive one. Kobo ichi means that defense and offense are interchangeable and work together fluidly as the situation dictates. Move seamlessly and fluidly from defense to offense and back to defense and then to offense as necessary and as the situation arises. This is the ability to have an "aggressive defense." Develop the ability to turn a defensive movement into a counterattack.

One Thing Leads to Another

This is the ability to move from one situation to the next as fluidly as possible. One thing always leads to another, so make sure you have control of what is going on. Much like putting pieces of a puzzle together, work so that one move fits into the next in a sequential manner.

Have a Back-up Plan

In other words, have a "plan B" or "backdoor" skill or tactic available. Not everything works as planned, so plan for when it doesn't work.

Avoid a Scramble

A scramble takes place when neither athlete has the advantage and both are working to gain control on pretty much equal terms. Scrambles are inevitable and when one takes place, work to gain control of the position and situation.

Work to Get to the Top Position

Continually work to get to the top position where you have more freedom of movement and mobility. Think of the mat as a wall. No one wants to fight with his back to the wall.

Work to Get to a Stable Base

When on the bottom (especially when you are on all fours in a turtle position or lying flat on your front in a prone positions), work to get to a stable base and then work to get to a better position. One of the worst places to be in a match is flat on your face and prone with an opponent on top of you working to apply a scoring move.

Don't Get Your Head Trapped

When you are on all fours or face down in a prone position, make sure you don't get your head trapped between your opponent's knees or legs. Get your head out of the middle so you can see what you are doing and use your head as a weapon.

If Your Opponent Is Flat and Face Down on the Mat, Take Control

The flat, face-down, and prone position is known as utsubuse in judo. Your opponent gets into utsubuse either because he has been put there temporarily and is working to get to a stable (and better) position, or (and often more likely) because he is waiting for the referee to call a halt to the action and get him out of trouble. In either case, you are in control of the situation, so start working to get your hooks in and take advantage of it.

Your Hooks and Your Third Arm

Use your feet and legs in the same way that you use your hands and arms. Your head is your "third arm" in the sense that you can use your head to control and steer your opponent (as well as use as a base for stability). Your appendages (including your head) are your "hooks."

Get Your Hooks In

This is a common saying and it's true. Use your feet and legs to control and manipulate an opponent but also be sure to get your hooks in using your hands as well. If an opponent is balled up defensively in a turtle position and you are unable to get a foot or leg in to get control with your legs, use your hands and arms to "swim" in (slide your hands and arms into a gap in your opponent's body) and use a wrist ride or shoulder grip to control him.

Control Your Opponent's Lower Body

Often, controlling an opponent with your feet and legs will put you in a better position to apply a submission technique or break an opponent down. There are two old sayings related to chokes that pretty much mean the same thing: "all chokes start with the legs" and "before you can control an opponent's neck, you have to control his legs and hips." The best way to do this is to get your hooks in with your feet and legs to control his lower extremities (hips and legs). If you control your opponent's lower extremities, you've taken control of his ability to get to a stable base or escape.

Get Your Opponent's Back

Work to get behind your opponent in a ride or controlling position. He doesn't have eyes in the back of his head and can't see what you are doing. Keep glued to his back and control him as long as necessary to break him down or turn him over to apply a submission technique or pin.

Stay Round

In many situations, you will roll your opponent into a choke, armlock, or pin. Sometimes you will need to be more linear in your movement, but if you are too linear, you will not be flexible or adaptable in your movement. By staying round, you have more flexibility of movement and freedom of movement.

Be Compact

Do not extend your hands, arms, feet, and legs too far (and this includes your head, so keep your chin tucked). Never reach out too far or extend an appendage because doing this allows an opponent to use it as a handle. Keep your elbows in close to your body, and when reaching to gain control of your opponent, make your movements sharp and deliberate.

Where You Look Is Where You Go

Keep your chin tucked and point your head in the direction where you want your body to move. Keep your eyes on your opponent and where you want to take your movement. Where your head goes, your body follows; more importantly, where you look is where you go.

Always Know Where Your Head, Arms, Feet, and Legs Are

Don't lose sight of where your hands and arms are unless you are using them to manipulate and control an opponent and you know where they are and what they are doing.

Work Off Your Flanks

When working off the bottom newaza (bottom guard) position, work off of your flanks (buttocks and hips). Position yourself so that you have as much freedom of movement as possible. Mobility is essential. As mentioned earlier, think of the mat as a wall. You limit your moment when your back is flat on the mat. There are times when it's necessary to lie flat on the mat, but for the most part, doing so limits your mobility. You can launch an attack from this bottom position only if you have mobility and as much freedom of movement as possible.

Stay South of the Border

When between an opponent's legs (when he is in the bottom newaza or guard position), do not reach out and extend your arms. If you reach out too far, he can better control your arm and put you in an armlock or triangle choke. Stay positioned below his hips or belt line (south of the border) and control his hips by pinning them to the mat with your hands and arms (or knee and leg) and then work to get past his legs.

Take Your Time, But Do It in a Hurry

Work efficiently and don't rush things, but just as important, don't waste movement. Everything you do should have a purpose. Move as efficiently and effectively as possible from one situation to another and always work to control the position and control your opponent's body.

Groundfighting Positions

In groundfighting, there are a variety of different situations you'll find yourself in. These different situations are simply the different positions a human body is at any given time and in any given place. Listed below are some of these positions.

1. When you are on your knees with your opponent on his hands and knees and you are at his side.
2. When you are on your knees with your opponent on his hands and knees and you are at his head.
3. When your opponent is on all fours and you are behind him or in the rodeo ride position where you control him with your legs.
4. When your opponent is lying flat on his front.
5. When you are on all fours and your opponent is on his knees to your side in a wrestler's ride position.
6. When you are on all fours and your opponent is on his knees at your head.
7. When both you and your opponent are on your knees.
8. When you are standing and your opponent is on both or one of his knees.
9. When you are on your knees and your opponent is standing.
10. When you are fighting off your buttocks, hips, or backside with your opponent between your legs in the guard position or when you are on your back and your opponent is on top of you in the mount position.
11. When you are on your knees between your opponent's legs in his newaza or guard position.

Breakdowns and Turnovers

No opponent will ever lie down and let you pin, choke, or armlock him willingly. You have to put him there. The way to do this is to break your opponent down from his stable base or position and put him into an unstable position where you can apply a pin, choke, or armlock. What are called hairi kata (entry forms) are the breakdowns and turnovers that put an opponent in a vulnerable position.

"Breakdown" is a generic term to describe taking an opponent from a stable position to an unstable position in order to put him in a vulnerable position in order to apply a pin, choke, or armlock. Many people in judo call these moves "turnovers," but a turnover is more specific than a breakdown. In a turnover, the attacker turns his opponent over on the opponent's back or back side in order to apply a pin, choke, or armlock. When using a breakdown, you may not turn him over onto his back; you may simply put him flat on his face and apply a submission technique or work for a turnover where you can put him on his back and pin him.

A breakdown or turnover is very much like a throw. One instant your opponent is stable and secure, and then he's on his back. You put him there. Good breakdowns require plyometric power and explosiveness. Sure, there are times when you roll your opponent onto his back in an almost gradual or incremental way, but usually you break him down or roll him onto his back with sudden and controlled force, much like you do when you throw him from a standing position onto his back. You actually break an opponent's balance when you break him down for a pin in much the same way you would if you throw him. There are several phases that take place in groundfighting, regardless of your starting position or your opponent's starting position. He can be on his knees, between your legs in your guard, or any groundfighting position, and these principles of groundfighting come into play.

1. **Kuzushi:** Control your opponent by how you grab him and how you use the handles on his (and your) body or judogi. Control your opponent's position and balance. By controlling how he moves, you dictate the terms of the fight. You break your opponent's balance by taking his supporting arm, leg or knee (or any body part) from him. Breaking down a human body is like breaking down a table. If you pull in one of the supporting legs of a table, it will collapse. So will a human body. You have fit your body into place to best break him down and are about to execute the breakdown.

2. **Tsukuri:** Start to form or build your technique after breaking your opponent down. This is when you start moving your body into position and actually start applying the pin, choke, or armlock. This phase of the action flows direction from the kuzushi phase and flows directly into the next phase, the kake phase.

3. **Kake:** Execute your specific breakdown: This is when you manipulate and use your arms, hands, legs, and feet as well as body position to perform the actual breakdown. At this point, you are breaking your opponent down and putting him to the position you want him to be in.

4. **Kime:** Finish: You've followed through from the breakdown and have him in the pin. At this point, you tighten the control of the pin and immobilize him. It's now a matter of controlling him for the time required to score ippon or apply a submission technique if necessary.

The Concept of Shiho

Shiho translates to "four corners." You've no doubt heard and read about pins such as yoko shiho gatame, tate shiho gatame, or kami shiho gatame. The defining feature of these pinning techniques is the "shiho" in the name. This concept of "shiho" describes the major controlling points of the human body. The use of these points was initially developed in Kodokan judo as a practical method of controlling an opponent when pinning him as well as when engaged with him in groundfighting (or even in standing situations). The four corners are the two shoulders and the two hips. While there are other parts of the body used in controlling an opponent, controlling one or both of the opponent's shoulders and hips work with a high rate of success.

Shiho: This athlete is using the concept of shiho (four corners) with good effect. He is controlling his opponent's shoulders and hips with this yoko shiho gatame (side four corner hold).

Transitions from Pin to Submission Technique

Transitions can take place in any situation in judo, including groundfighting. In many cases, a judo athlete will transition from a pin and apply an armlock or a choke in order to finish an opponent. This usually takes place if the judoka pinning his opponent senses that his pin isn't going to hold his opponent for the required time to score ippon. In other cases, such as in sambo, a pin or hold for time doesn't win the match and a submission technique must be applied to secure the victory. The most common submission techniques used when making a transition from a pin are armlocks, but strangles are used as well. So, it's a smart tactical idea to have at least one or two transitions that you can use when necessary.

Pin to Armlock Transition: A common (and effective) armlock that is used as a transition from a pin is ude garami (arm entanglement) as shown in this photo.

Osaekomi Waza

The phrase osaekomi is comprised of two words; "osae" translates to immobilize, pin, or hold in place, and "komi" translates to "put into" and is mostly used to affix to a verb. So, this phrase describes the action of putting someone into a pin or the act of immobilizing someone. Waza translates to "technique." There are ten standard osaekomi waza in the Kodokan judo syllabus, but there are others that are often used in competitive judo that are considered variations of these ten standard pins. This section of the book will examine some of the pins that have a high rate of success in competitive judo as well as the entry forms used to put an opponent into position for the pin. Specifically, the focus in this section will be on showing different entry forms and pins based on the position of both the attacker and defender. Several different positions (along with the entry forms and pins) that often take place in groundfighting will be analyzed.

Osaekomi waza (hold-downs and pins) are the workhorse techniques of judo or any type of grappling. To some people, they are the least glamorous of all grappling skills. Basically, you hold your opponent down on the mat or ground and don't let him up. Nothing spectacular, unless you're the guy on top and who just won the match. Maybe you didn't force your opponent to tap out or submit from an armlock or strangle but you still beat him and proved dominance over him. Holding someone down and not letting him up isn't a fluke. It takes effort and it takes skill. Osaekomi waza is like having a good friend. Let me explain what I mean. Like anything else, techniques in judo are subject to what's stylish or the latest trend. When a great champion or fighter uses a particular move, everyone seems to want to copy it or at least learn it. Trends in techniques, like trends in fashion or in any phase of life, come and go. Pins and hold-downs seem to be the moves that are always there, even when other moves are more fashionable; they're the skills that an athlete can rely on when he needs to beat an opponent. They're like that old friend: they're there when you need them.

Position in Osaekomi Waza

Before you can pin your opponent, you have to control his body. Position is discussed in other parts of this book and is included here because it's important in applying pinning techniques. The more effectively you limit an opponent's movement by controlling his legs, hips, arms, and pretty much everything about your opponent, the better you will be able to pin him. Position is being in the right place at the right time and putting your opponent in the wrong place (for him) every time possible. You want to limit his movement, limit his options, and nullify what he can do. Not only do you want to limit his mobility, you should try to "shut him down" so that he can't put you in a bad position. Good groundfighting is moving from one position to another position to even another position and trying to control your opponent and ultimately make him give up to you. Use your position to set up your breakdown and use the breakdown to get him onto his back or side and pin him. Think of it as a chain of events: position to breakdown to pin.

The Anatomy of Osaekomi Waza

There are two goals when using an osaekomi waza (pinning technique) in judo: 1. Hold your opponent largely on his back or back side with control for the required time to score ippon. 2. Hold your opponent to the mat and control his body so that you can apply a submission technique in order. This is a different concept of pinning than used in Western wrestling where the person being pinned must have his shoulders touch the mat. A judo athlete isn't concerned about pinning his opponent's shoulders to the mat; he's concerned about controlling his opponent for an extended period of time.

So then, from a tactical perspective, the goal of an osaekomi is pretty simple; it's to pin your opponent to the mat for as long as needed to beat him. An osaekomi is what Gene LeBell has referred to as a "time hold." In other words, the goal is to hold him to the mat for a specified period of time. During that time, the attacker continually shifts his body position as necessary in order to maintain control of his opponent. In an osaekomi waza, time is on the side of the athlete applying the pin. In the early rules of judo, there was no established time for holding an opponent with a pin to score an ippon. This changed over the course of judo's history to using sixty seconds for a pin, then to thirty seconds for a pin, and then twenty-five seconds for a pin. In the current IJF contest rules, a pin for twenty seconds scores ippon.

Osaekomi Waza Is Face Up

In feudal jujutsu where the emphasis in pinning was on fighting and not on winning in a sport, the desired position for an osaekomi (immobilization) was to have an opponent face-down on the ground. This face-down position is called utsubuse (face down). When Jigoro Kano first wrote the contest rules for Kodokan judo in 1900, he adapted a more Western-style approach to grappling and required the person being pinned to be lying face-up (aomuke). This change in pinning position was monumental and an important step in changing judo from the feudal systems of jujutsu and making it a modern, competitive activity.

Defining Features of Effective Pins

Presented here are some common, fundamental features used in successful osaekomi waza to control an opponent. All these features work together and may seem redundant, but an isolated, detailed study of all the factors used will help explain why osaekomi waza works.

Legs and Base: Your legs provide your base. A base is another way of calling it a foundation. Make it a mobile foundation (more on that a bit later). Keep your hips low, knees wide, and use your feet to adjust your position as needed. Use the weight of your lower body to provide a solid foundation for the pin. Shift position as necessary to keep him on his back and control his movement. Use your toes to constantly dig into the mat to add power into the hold and allow you to shift position as needed.

Use Your Hips: Use your hips to control your own movement and the movement of your opponent. This is what is called "heavy hips" or "control hips" where you keep your hips as low to the mat as possible and shift your weight as needed to control both your movement and the movement of your opponent. When pinning or riding an opponent, your "heavy hips" are the contact point with the mat or opponent as you maintain control of the position, so make sure your hips are as low to the mat as possible in almost every situation. Your hips control the position, so make it a point to initiate everything from your hips. By good use of your hips, your entire movement in newaza is economical and compact, leaving little room for an opponent to get a handle on you and gain control. This photo shows the attacker with his hips low on the mat, a stable base with his legs, and his toes digging into the mat to provide power, stability, and mobility.

A Mobile Base: Move and adjust your position as needed to keep your opponent held down and control him. You may have to shift from one position to another to keep him under control. Shift your leg position, hip position, or how you control him with your arms or upper body to keep him from escaping. Holding a resisting opponent onto the mat for twenty seconds is not always easy. You may have to shift from one position to another, or even from one pin to another to control him. In the same way we use our elbows to "steer" or control an opponent in grip fighting or throwing, the legs and knees have the same role in newaza, especially in pinning an opponent.

Head Control: Control your opponent's head. Where the head goes, the body follows. Don't allow an opponent to turn his head or use it to bridge off the mat. The head is used as a "third arm" to stabilize the body on the mat or drive off the mat. Don't allow your opponent to use his head as a third arm. Head control is often does along with shoulder control. In most cases, controlling the upper body, especially the head, will enable to attacker to control his opponent's entire body, including the hips.

Control Opponent's Shoulders: Unlike Western wrestling where the goal in a pin is to pin the opponent's shoulders on the mat simultaneously for a victory, the osaekomi of judo is a "time hold" where the goal is to restrain or hold the opponent (mostly, but not entirely) on his back. If you control your opponent's hips, you often control the movement of his shoulders and upper body; and if not controlling his shoulders directly, good hip control always leads, ultimately, to good upper-body control. Likewise, knowing how to control and manipulate an opponent's shoulders, arms, and hands is all part of controlling his hips and total body movement. "Hand wrestling" or "hand fighting" is a skill that should be mastered for effective newaza. Hand wrestling is the effective use of your hands and arms in controlling your opponent's movement and position. When holding an opponent to the mat, controlling his upper body, which includes his head, neck, shoulders, arms, and upper back are all used together to immobilize him for maximum points or the win.

Control Opponent's Hips: We all start our movement from our hips, whether it's in groundfighting or fighting standing up. If you control your opponent's hips, you control his movement. Often, when holding an opponent, you will control either his hips primarily or his upper body (shoulders, neck, and head) primarily. This isn't always the case, but immobilizing an opponent's hips severely limits his movement and ability to escape. When you effectively control your opponent's hips, you control his legs as well. Often, the defender (or athlete being pinned) will attempt to wrap or scissor his legs around the pinner's leg or body to initiate an escape. The pinner, by good control of his opponent's hips, will be able to steer clear of his opponent's legs and not allow the bottom man to use his legs to set up his escape. This photo shows how the top man is using a modified version of kami shiho gatame to control his opponent's hips and restrain him on the mat.

Post to Stabilize: Use your appendages to "post" or place on the mat for stability when holding your opponent. An osaekomi is more than simply pinning an opponent to the mat for a few seconds. Your job is to immobilize and restrain your opponent for at least twenty seconds in order to score an ippon to win the match. This is much like "riding" an opponent so that he has little freedom of movement. Sometimes, you will need to post your head, hand, arm, elbow, knee, leg, or foot onto the mat to stabilize your hold on your opponent.

Position in Judo

Before you can pin your opponent, you have to control his body. The better you limit his movement by controlling his legs, hips, arms, and pretty much everything about your opponent, the better you will be able to pin him. This control of an opponent is called "position." Position is being in the right place at the right time and putting your opponent in the wrong place (for him) every time. You want to limit his movement, limit his options, and nullify what he can do. Not only do you want to limit his movement (or mobility), you should try to "shut him down" so that he can't put you in a bad position. Good groundfighting is moving from one position to another position to yet another position and trying to control your opponent and ultimately make him give up to you. Use your position to set up your breakdown and use the breakdown to get him onto his back or side and pin him. Think of it as a chain of events: position to breakdown to pin.

Analyzing Selected Osaekomi Waza and Entries

There are many applications and variations of the osaekomi waza (pinning techniques) used in competitive judo. One book can't possibly do justice to this technically diverse area of judo, so what will follow is an analysis of only a few osaekomi waza and some of the entry forms (hairi kata or breakdowns and turnovers) that make them happen based on the starting positions of both the attacker and defender. The breakdowns and turnovers shown here are ones that have a high rate of success. What is being shown here is that the pin that is being applied is the end result of the entire movement, with the attacker taking advantage of the situation or position and using the entry form to break the defender down and apply the pin to finish him for the ippon.

Entry to Pin When Opponent Is in Bottom Newaza Position

This is a common situation in judo and there are many entry forms where the top judoka can work past her opponent's legs and apply a pin, choke, or armlock when her opponent is in the bottom newaza (supine) position. This leg pass is simple, quick, and effective with a high rate of success.

Newaza Knee Slide Pass: The attacker (on her knees) uses her hands to grab the pant legs on the inside of her opponent's knees.

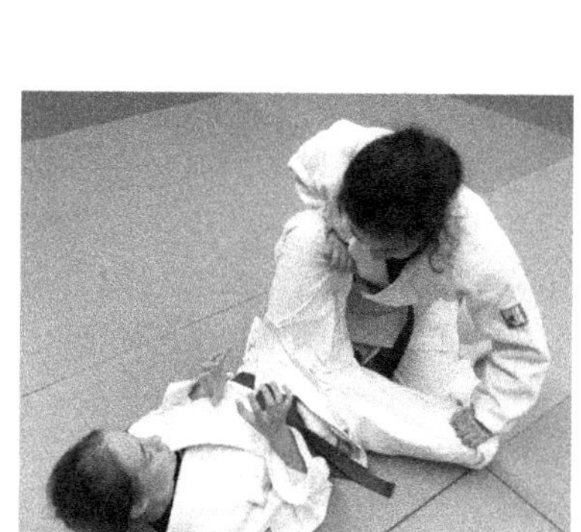

The attacker uses her hands to push her opponent's right knee to the mat as shown.

The attacker uses her right knee to slide across her opponent's right upper thigh.

The attacker moves her body over and across her opponent's right upper thigh.

As the attacker slides her right knee across her opponent's upper leg, she quickly moves her left foot and leg over and across the leg as well.

The attacker applies kesa gatame (scarf hold) to pin her opponent.

Entry to Pin When You Are on the Bottom in Newaza Position

There are many ways to work from bottom newaza (supine position), and this is one that has a good rate of success at all levels of judo competition.

Leg Drag to Tate Shiho Gatame: The attacker (on bottom) is positioned in the bottom newaza position. The opponent (on top) positions his foot and leg up in a kneeling position in order to get a more stable base, or to possibly try to get past the bottom judoka's legs.

The attacker moves his body to his right as he uses his right hand and arm to hook his opponent's left lower leg as shown.

The attacker uses his right arm to hook and pull his opponent's left lower leg out straight. Doing this knocks his opponent down onto his left buttocks as shown.

The attacker has quickly moved on top of his opponent and can apply tate shiho gatame (vertical four-corner hold) from here.

The attacker climbs onto his opponent to further secure his pin. As he does this, the attacker uses his hands and arms to further control his opponent's hands and arms as well as his upper body.

The attacker applies tate shiho gatame (vertical four corner hold) to pin his opponent.

Entry to Pin When Opponent Is in Utsubuse Position (Lying Flat on Front)

This position of lying face down is called utsubuse (face down) and is used often in competitive judo. It's a defensive position with the bottom judoka waiting for the referee to call a halt to the action and allow him to stand. This is often used by athletes who either don't like groundfighting or are not skilled in it. However, sometimes the bottom judoka is temporarily in this position and wants to get onto his hands and knees for a more stable base. In either situation, the attacker should quickly take control of the opportunity. Here is one (of many) breakdowns or turnovers that can be used from this position.

Judo Stack to Yoko Shiho Gatame: The attacker (standing) is positioned at the upper body of his opponent who is lying on his front.

The attacker moves to his left and to the right side of his opponent and quickly uses his right hand to grab the sleeve of his opponent's left upper arm and uses his left hand to grab the opponent's left pant leg just above the knee. The attacker is squatting to provide a strong and fluid base.

The attacker springs up from his squatting position and moves back quickly as he pulls his opponent's sleeve and pant leg up. Doing this pulls his opponent's body up and off the mat as shown.

The attacker uses his hands to control and steer his opponent's body to the mat as shown. The attacker makes sure to immediately lower his body so that there is no space between him and his opponent.

The attacker uses yoko shiho gatame (side four-corner hold) to pin his opponent.

Entry to Pin When You Control Opponent in the Leg-Press Position

The leg-press position is a strong position of control and commonly used in controlling an opponent in order to apply juji gatame (crossbody armlock), but this leg-press position is used for more than simply applying an armlock as shown here.

Leg Press to Tate Shiho Gatame: The attacker (on top) is using the leg press to control his opponent and attempting to apply juji gatame (crossbody armlock). If the attacker is unable to apply the armlock, he can quickly transition to a pin from this position.

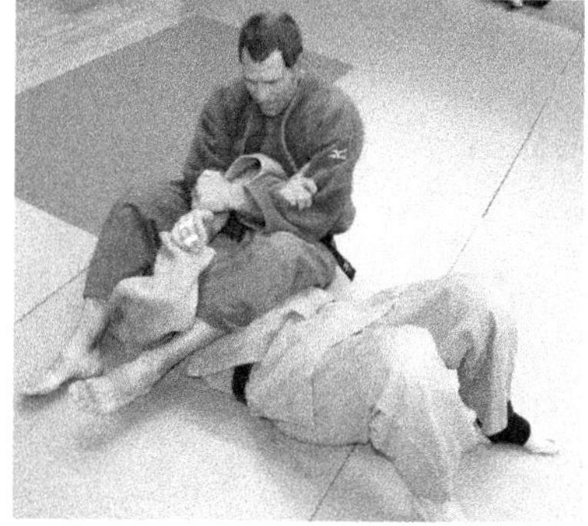

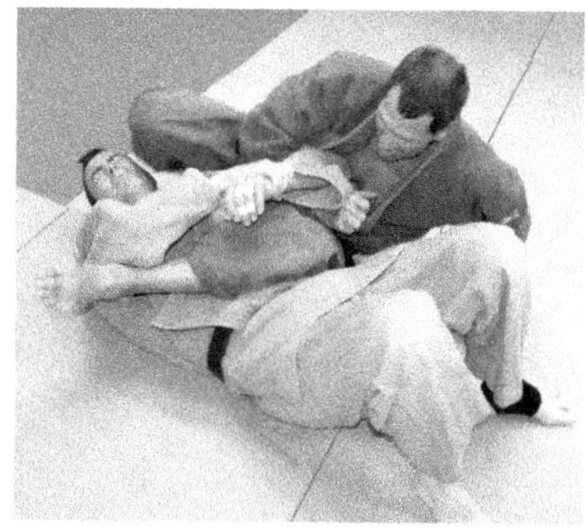

The attacker places his left hand (not shown) on the mat for stability as he shifts his weight to his left hip. As he does this, the attacker bends his right knee as shown and keeps his left leg across his opponent's torso.

The attacker climbs up and onto his opponent's torso as shown. As he does this, the attacker starts to move his body over his opponent's body to start his pin.

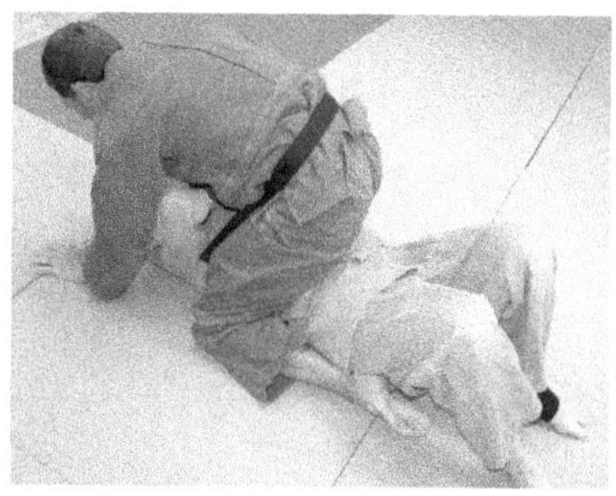

The attacker has moved his body up and over his opponent's body as shown.

The attacker establishes control with tate shiho gatame (vertical four-corner hold) to pin his opponent. If necessary, the attacker can use one hand to post onto the mat for more stability.

The attacker can also apply ude garami (arm entanglement) from here if necessary.

Entry to Pin When Opponent Is on All Fours in Turtle Position

This position, where the bottom athlete is on all fours (often called the turtle position), is a common one. In some cases, the bottom judoka is simply waiting for the referee to call a halt in the action so she can get back to a standing position. In other cases, the bottom judoka may be in this position temporarily and actively trying to get to a better position. In either case, the attacker should immediately and aggressively work for a turnover from here. While this turnover is one of the basic skills often taught in judo, it's effective and has been used at all levels of judo competition with success.

Far Arm Near Leg to Mune Gatame: The attacker (standing) is positioned at the shoulder area of her opponent. Her opponent is positioned on her hands and knees as shown.

The attacker moves to her right and to the left side of her opponent. The attacker uses his left hand to hook her opponent's right elbow as shown. As she does this, the attacker uses his right hand (not shown) to grab her opponent's left upper leg.

This photo from the back side shows how the attacker uses his right hand to grab her opponent's left upper leg.

The attacker uses her left hand and arm to pull on her opponent's elbow as she uses her right hand and arm to lift her opponent's left leg as shown. Doing this rolls the opponent over his right shoulder and onto her back.

The attacker immediately applies mune gatame (chest hold) to pin her opponent.

Entry to Pin When You and Opponent Are Facing Each Other Kneeling

In some situations, both judo athletes are kneeling on one or both knees and facing each other in a neutral position. In this case, the judoka who takes the initiative and attacks first is often the one that will dominate the action. This breakdown is simple and effective and has a good rate of success.

Koshi Guruma Breakdown: This breakdown is basically a koshi guruma (hip wheel) from a kneeling position. The athletes are in a kneeling neutral position facing each other. The first athlete to take advantage of the situation dominates the action.

The attacker (right) uses his left hand to grip the defender's right sleeve. As he does this, the attacker uses his right hand to reach around the defender's left shoulder and grip the defender's upper back as shown.

The attacker slides his right hip in front of the defender's body as shown. As he does this, the attacker uses his left hand to pull the defender's sleeve and uses his right hand to steer the defender's body into the direction of the breakdown.

The attacker rolls the defender over his right hip as shown.

The action of the breakdown rolls the defender over and onto his back, with the attacker immediately applying kesa gatame (scarf hold).

Entry to Pin When You Are Standing and Your Opponent Is Kneeling

If the defender is kneeling on both knees and the attacker is standing, this is considered a groundfighting situation in the contest rules, so no score will be awarded for this technique as a throw, but it's an effective breakdown to kesa gatame (scarf hold).

Spin to Pin: This attacker is standing in front of her opponent and using her hands and arms to grip her. Her opponent is kneeling. The attacker must work quickly in order to take advantage of the situation.

The attacker places her right foot in front of her opponent's right knee with her heel placed directly in front of her opponent's knee. The attacker uses his hands to pull, lift, and control and steer her opponent.

The attacker uses his hands and arms to "spin" or pull her opponent over her extended foot and leg as shown.

The attacker spins her opponent over her foot and leg and onto the mat. The attacker uses her hands to maintain control over her opponent.

The attacker immediately follows through and applies kesa gatame (scarf hold) to pin her opponent.

Entry to Pin When You Are on Bottom on All Fours

Sometimes, you are on the bottom and positioned on all fours. When in this position, make sure you are on a strong base on your elbows and knees with "active feet." This is the term for making sure that your feet are not positioned on the dorsal (top) side of the feet while on the mat and your toes are digging into the mat so you can drive off your feet.

Soto Makikomi on Knees: The attacker (on bottom) is positioned on his elbows and knees with his opponent using a spiral ride from the top as shown.

This photo shows how the attacker uses his right and to grab his opponent's right wrist and how the attacker uses his right elbow to trap his opponent's right arm tightly to the attacker's body.

The attacker starts to roll his opponent over his body as shown.

As the attacker rolls his opponent over, he stays as round as possible and may use his left leg to help lift and prop his opponent's body as necessary to make the rolling action easier.

The attacker completes his roll and immediately uses his left hand to grab his opponent's pants at the left side to start establishing his pin. An important point is that the attacker maintains a firm grasp on his opponent's right wrist and never lets go of it.

The attacker immediately rolls his opponent over onto his back and applies ushiro kesa gatame (rear scarf hold) to pin his opponent.

Entry to Pin When You Are on Bottom with Opponent Above You Vertically

Every judo athlete has been in this situation: you are on the bottom and working to get to a stable base and your opponent is positioned above you vertically. The first thing to do is to make sure you are on all fours and on a stable base. After this, make sure that your head is not stuck in the middle and under your opponent's body. If your opponent controls your head, he will have a better chance of controlling your entire body. This breakdown serves two purposes: 1. it gets you out of trouble when on the bottom position, and 2. it's an effective breakdown or rollover to a pin.

Double Arm Roll to Kuzure Kesa Gatame: The attacker (the bottom judoka) is positioned on his elbows and knees with his head under his opponent.

The attacker moves his head to his right and positions it on his opponent's left hip. As he does this, the attacker uses his hands and arms to grab both of his opponent's arms, pulling them tightly to his body.

The attacker extends his right foot and leg for stability and starts to move out from under his opponent.

The attacker shoots his left leg out and sits out as shown. As he does this, the attacker starts to turn his body to his right and leans back onto his opponent. As he does this, the attacker continues to use both his hands and arms to trap his opponent's arms tightly to his torso.

The attacker completes his sit-through action with his feet and legs and rolls his opponent over onto his back as shown. The attacker continues to tightly hold both of his opponent's arms with his hands and arms.

The attacker completes the rolling action and positions his body so that his right hip is situated next to his opponent's head as shown. The attacker applies kuzure kesa gatame (irregular scarf hold) to pin his opponent.

CHAPTER 10

Armlocks

An armlock is like a throw. Your opponent usually doesn't see it coming.

—Becky Scott

There is an old saying about submission techniques: "If you make your opponent give up to you, he will never forgive you, but more importantly, he will never forget you." In other words, if you force an opponent to tap out, there is a definite psychological advantage for you every time you face him again on the mat. He won't forget you, and it doesn't matter what he may say; he knows that you are the person who made him quit. This is why, from a competitive point of view, it is important to be skilled in armlocks and strangles. If you have the reputation of being the person who makes opponents tap out, then you will have an edge every time you step on the mat. No one likes to have his throat squeezed or arm stretched and if you're known as someone who will do this to others, it certainly gives you an edge.

This section of the book is focused on kansetsu waza. Kansetsu translates to "joint" and waza translates to "techniques." In the sport of judo, the arm is the primary target of joint locks, with the focus on the elbow joint. A secondary target is the shoulder joint, and this is because there is often pain resulting in the shoulder joint when the elbow joint is taken out of its normal range of motion. Based on personal observation and statistics that have been kept through the years, the two most popular armlocks used in judo are juji gatame (crossbody armlock) and ude garami (arm entanglement). Another popular armlock is waki gatame (armpit lock). All three of these armlocks have a high rate of success at all levels of competition. For this reason, this section will focus on practical and functional ways to apply these armlocks. Judo has a wide variety of armlocks and every serious judoka should make a thorough study of them and find what works best for him or her. So, by all means, don't limit your arsenal of armlocks to what is popular or commonly used.

Control the Position and Get the Submission

Position is purposely (and with forethought) placing your body is such a way that you can successfully control how and where your opponent moves. Break him down from a stable to an unstable position and control his movement. Limit his movement, and while doing that, do everything possible to continually put yourself in a better position to armlock, choke, or pin him. A major goal in groundfighting is to establish a position of control and dominate your opponent. This is especially true when attempting to secure an armlock. The armlocks shown in this section all are the result of controlling an opponent's position and taking advantage of the situation. Armlocks often come out of a fast tempo when fighting on the mat. Often, the actual roll or setup to the actual armlock comes out of a fast flurry of activity much in the same way a throw develops in standing judo. Then again, some of the most effective armlocks come out of a grinding, methodical series of movements ending in stretching or bending an opponent's arm.

An Explanation of "Position"

"Position" was discussed earlier in this book, but let's take a closer look at it now. Position is where, how, and when the bodies of the two judo athletes engaged in a contest are in relation to each other and in relation to where they are located on the mat at any given point in time. One athlete will be in the controlling or dominant position in relation to his opponent, or the two athletes will be situated in a neutral position where neither have the advantage. A judo contest is a series of positions and situations that are linked together based on the movement and actions taken by the two judo athletes that are engaged in the match. The goal of each athlete is to control (as much as possible) how his body is positioned, and how his opponent's body is positioned during the course of the match. This control of position leads to applying a technique or movement that results in defeating the opponent. The more effectively a judo athlete controls where, how, and when his opponent moves, the better he will be able to apply an armlock, choke, or pin. Position is also important in standing judo, but for our purposes now, the judoka who controls the position in groundfighting most often is able to apply the submission to win the match.

There are many useful positions. Working from a bottom newaza (supine position) off the buttocks (what has come to be known as the "guard" position) is a useful and often effective position. This position is as old as judo itself and it's an instinctive movement for many of us. Remember, for any position you take, have a goal in mind. Your short-term goal may be to simply get to a more stable or controlling position. It may simply be to get out of a bad position and get out of trouble. Not every position ends in a spectacular, sophisticated submission hold with the opponent tapping out. Being in the wrong position often leads to bad results. When you are in a bad position, do what you can to work out of it (what I like to call "get-out-of-trouble moves."). An example of a bad position is what I've called the "chicken" position for many years when teaching groundfighting to my athletes. The chicken position is when an athlete lies flat on the mat in the utsubuse (prone position), face down, with his hands up around his neck and elbows tucked in. We've seen this for years in judo. It's like an ostrich sticking his head in the sand hoping a threat will go away. But that threat never does go away. It simply takes advantage of the situation. When an opponent is in the chicken position, say a silent "thank you" and then work him over. Here is a great opportunity to do just about any breakdown or setup you want if you are the top person. He's flat on his belly with his face flat on the mat and not fighting back and not in a position to be able to fight back. One of the weakest positions to be in when engaged in groundfighting is flat on the front with your face on the mat. If you happen to be in that position, quickly get to a base on your hands and knees and start to work to improve your position.

Another factor to consider about position is that the body has a lot of handles. Every part of the opponent's judo uniform or clothing is a handle. An opponent's arm is a handle, or a shoulder or hip; just about any part of his body can be used as a handle to pry or lever him into a position where you can gain further control.

Also remember that patience is a virtue in groundfighting. Be methodical and persistent. Go from point A to point B to point C to point D. Remember to take your time, but do it in a hurry!

With all of this in mind, there are specific positions that will often lead to a successful setup of an armlock. Basically, good groundfighting is establishing a series of positions that lead to a successful submission or hold.

Often, an ideal position to get into if you want to secure your armlock is to get behind your opponent, dig your feet in, and aggressively initiate your move. Getting into the ideal position to do an armlock leads us to the next phase of the core skills, and that is the setup.

The "Setup" in Groundfighting

The setup is the actual breakdown, roll, turnover, entry, or application of a particular armlock. No opponent will lie there and let you stretch his arm, so it's your job to put him in a position so that you can do that. The sequence of events that culminate in making an opponent tap out is establishing a strong initial position, followed by gaining further control of the opponent's body by digging the feet in, controlling a wrist or arm, and basically using the body's handles to establish more control, followed by the actual setup, breakdown, or roll into an armlock.

In addition to the concepts of position and setup, the idea of making a technique work for you is vital to being successful in judo. This concept of adapting a technique to make it work best for you has been a constant theme in this book. A skillful application of any move or technique is the ability of a judo athlete to take a technique or skill and make it fit him like a glove, resulting in a high rate of success. A technique doesn't have to be complicated. Years ago, the great football coach Vince Lombardi said, "Do simple things with consistent excellence rather than complicated things done poorly." It really doesn't matter how many armlocks you know, what really matters is that you can do what you know when you need to do it.

The Defining Features of Armlocks

Like every other type of technique in judo, armlocks are based on mechanics and how they apply to the human body. The attacker places the defender's elbow joint (the lever) across some part of either the attacker's body or the defender's body (the fulcrum) and applies force. This application of force takes the joint being attacked out of its normal range of motion and this causes pain for the defender. Fundamentally, there are two positions that the attacker puts the defender's arm in. The attacker either straightens his opponent's arm or he bends the arm at the elbow. The first takes place when the attacker stretches the defender's arm out straight, applying pressure to the elbow joint (but in reality, pressure is also applied to the shoulder joint as well as to the muscles, ligaments, and tendons of the entire arm). The second takes place when the attacker bends the defender's elbow and cranks or wrenches the elbow joint out of its normal range of motion.

Straight Arm Using the Pubic Bone as Fulcrum: This is juji gatame (crossbody armlock). This armlock is the most commonly used joint technique in competitive judo. The attacker stretches the defender's arm straight, placing the defender's elbow joint over the attacker's pubic bone in a classic example of how a lever and fulcrum work. The attacker stretches the defender's arm as he pulls it across his pubic bone to take the elbow joint out of its normal range of motion. As can be seen in this photo, the entire arm of the defender is under a great deal of stress with all the muscles, tendons, and ligaments being strained (as well as the shoulder joint).

Straight Arm Using the Body as Fulcrum: This photo shows an application of waki gatame (armpit lock) where the attacker levers the straight arm of the defender against the side of the attacker's torso at the area of his armpit.

Bent Armlock: When using ude garami (arm entanglement), the attacker bends the defender's arm at the elbow joint and levers the defender's elbow joint against the attacker's arm that serves as the fulcrum. Bent armlocks are quite painful, as they not only place a lot of strain on the elbow, they place a lot of strain on the shoulder joint.

Leg-Press Position

A common position in groundfighting is the "leg press." This position has been called the "juji gatame position" by others, and rightly so, because this position is ideal for applying juji gatame. My preference for calling this the leg press comes from the fact that the attacker literally uses his legs to press the defender to the mat and control him. This is a strong position of control and other skills apart from juji gatame can be applied starting from the leg press.

Leg Press Basic Application: The attacker has turned or rolled his opponent over and onto his back as shown and is seated on his buttocks with his legs extended over the opponent's torso and head for control. This is a common and effective controlling position, where the attacker can launch a variety of attacks including armlocks, chokes, and pins. This position is what has been called the "juji gatame position" previously, but there are many more techniques than juji gatame that can be applied from this position.

Leg Press Control: In order to maintain control over his opponent for as long as necessary, the attacker will use any means necessary that are permitted by the contest rules. This photo shows the attacker using his left hand and arm to grab his opponent's leg in order to better control the opponent's lower body.

Armlocks Are Applied from Any Position or Situation That Takes Place in Groundfighting

Defender is lying belly up. In many situations, the attacker has rolled or turned his opponent over onto his back in the utsubuse (belly-up) position and applies the armlock.

Defender is lying belly down. In some situations, the defender may attempt to roll over onto his front in an effort to escape an armlock. When this happens, the attacker makes sure to never let go of the defender's arm and continues to apply pressure to get the submission.

Attacker applies an armlock from a pin. In many situations, the attacker will apply an armlock as he is pinning his opponent. This is the case when the defender is making a good effort to escape the pin and the attacker can immediately transition to an armlock as he is pinning his opponent.

Defender attempt to stand up. A common defense against being armlocked is for the defender to attempt to stand and pull the attacker up and off the mat. When this takes place, the referee will call a halt to the action, thus permitting the defender to avoid being armlocked. However, a judo athlete who aggressively works for the submission will not let go of the armlock and will continue to apply pressure even as he is being picked up off the mat. In many cases, the effect of the armlock takes place and the defender taps out as he is in the process of attempting to pull the attacker off the mat.

Analyzing Selected Kansetsu Waza and Entries

There are so many applications and variations of armlocks that are used in competitive judo, one section of this book can't do them justice, so what will follow is an analysis of only a few kansetsu waza and some of the entry forms (hairi kata or breakdowns) that make them happen based on the starting positions of both the attacker and defender. The armlocks shown here are ones that have a high rate of success. What is being shown here is that the armlock is the end result of the entire movement; with the attacker taking advantage of the situation or position and using the entry form to break the defender down and apply the armlock to finish him for the ippon.

Entry to Juji Gatame (Crossbody Armlock) When the Attacker Is on the Bottom in Newaza (Supine Position) with the Opponent Kneeling and Between His Legs

In many cases, the opponent who is in the top position will make the mistake of extending his arm too far forward in an attempt to apply a lapel strangle.

Spinning Juji Gatame: The opponent is between the legs and reaches to apply a lapel strangle but is making a crucial mistake by reaching out too far with his arm. The attacker will trap the extended arm and spin under his opponent, applying juji gatame.

The attacker (bottom) uses his left hand and arm to grab and trap to his chest his opponent's right extended arm. As he does this, the attacker spins onto his left hip area, placing his left leg against the opponent's left side as shown.

The attacker spins to his left side as shown and places his left foot and leg over his opponent's head, making sure to bend his knee so that it traps the head of his opponent and pushes it down toward the mat. As he does this, the attacker uses both of his hands and arms to trap his opponent's right arm to the attacker's chest.

The attacker rolls his opponent over onto his back, all the while using both of his hands and arms to pull and trap his opponent's right arm tighter to his chest.

The attacker rolls his opponent over and onto his back as shown. As he does this, the attacker uses both of his hands and arms to trap his opponent's right arm, stretching it out straight and applying the juji gatame.

Entry to Ude Garami When the Attacker Is on the Bottom Position in Newaza and the Opponent Is Kneeling Between Her Legs

This is an aggressive application of ude garami from this bottom position and useful when an opponent attempts to control your leg to pass over it.

Ude Garami from Bottom Newaza: The top judoka uses her right hand to push the bottom judoka's left knee to the mat.

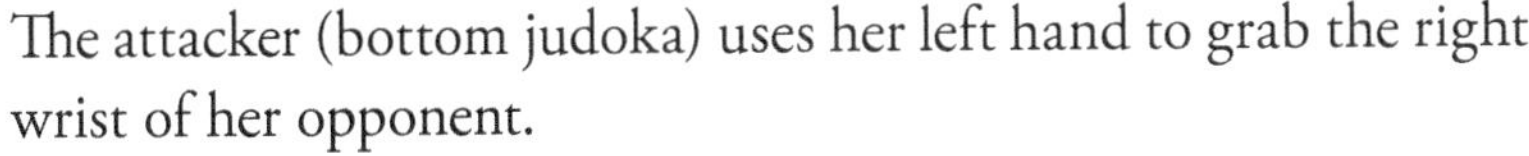

The attacker (bottom judoka) uses her left hand to grab the right wrist of her opponent.

The attacker rolls to her left side as shown and uses her left hand maintain control of her opponent's right arm. As she does this, the attacker uses her right hand and arm to reach over her opponent's right upper arm.

The attacker uses her right hand to grab her left wrist and form a figure-four with her hands and arms.

The attacker pulls her opponent's entangled right arm close to her body as she rolls to her left side.

The attacker rolls onto her back as shown and applies pressure by cranking the opponent's entangled right arm.

Entry from Leg-Press Position to Uki Gatame (Straddle Pin) and Finishing with Juji Gatame (Crossbody Armlock)

Here is a series of techniques that have a high rate of success. If your opponent escapes the pin, you can quickly transition to the armlock. This was made famous in the 1970s by many British judo athletes, most notably Olympic bronze medalist Neil Eckersley.

Leg Press to Uki Gatame to Juji Gatame: The attacker controls his opponent with the leg press.

The attacker uses his left arm to hook under his opponent's right arm as shown. As he does this, the attacker uses his right hand to grab and control his opponent's left leg. The opponent is protecting his arm from being extended for a juji gatame (crossbody armlock) by gripping his hands together as shown.

The attacker moves his left knee under his opponent's head as he pulls himself up and onto his opponent's torso as shown. Doing this puts his opponent into uki gatame (straddle pin). The attacker can hold his opponent with the pin to secure the ippon.

If the opponent loosens his grip in order to escape the pin, the attacker rolls forward to move his left foot and leg over the defender as shown.

The attacker uses his left hand to trap his opponent's right arm to his chest as he moves his left foot over the opponent's head.

The attacker uses both of his hands and arms to trap his opponent's right arm to his chest and rolls back to stretch the arm and secure juji gatame.

Entry from Leg Press Position to Ude Garami (Arm Entanglement)

This variation of ude garami is often called a "biceps slicer" because the attacker traps and entangles his opponent's arm at the elbow joint and wedges his forearm in between the forearm and biceps, causing pain.

Leg Press to Slicer Ude Garami: The attacker controls his opponent with a leg press. As he does this, the attacker places his right forearm under his opponent's right arm as shown.

The attacker uses his left hand to grab his opponent's right wrist.

The attacker moves his right lower leg over his opponent's bent arm at the wrist area.

The attacker uses his left foot and leg to hook over his right ankle, forming a triangle with his legs and causing pressure on his opponent's bent arm.

Entry to Waki Gatame (Armpit Lock) When Opponent Is on Elbows and Knees with His Head Close to You

This is especially useful when an opponent grabs your leg in an attempt to control you from his bottom position.

Waki Gatame Against Flat Opponent: The attacker is kneeling and his opponent has grabbed his right leg as shown in an attempt to gain control of the situation.

The attacker extends his left foot and leg for stability as he leans forward and drives his right elbow into his opponent's right armpit area. As he does this, the attacker uses his left hand to grab his opponent's right elbow.

The attacker slides his right foot and leg forward. Doing this loosens his opponent's grip of his leg and starts to extend his opponent's right arm.

The attacker sits through with his right leg, extending his opponent's right arm as shown.

The attacker uses both hands to grab his opponent's right wrist as he leans forward, placing pressure on his opponent's straight right elbow.

Entry to Head-Roll Juji Gatame When Opponent Is on Elbows and Knees in the Turtle Position

This situation is one of the most common in all levels of judo competition, but this head roll application of juji gatame (crossbody armlock) has a high rate of success. There are numerous steps in it, and it takes some time to master, but this entry into juji gatame is effective and well worth the time and effort you put into in making it part of your arsenal.

Head-Roll Juji Gatame: The attacker stands above his opponent who is on all fours in a defensive turtle position.

The attacker uses his hands to pull on his opponent's collar and belt, pulling him in the direction of the opponent's head.

The attacker climbs onto his opponent using his left foot and leg to hook over his opponent's lower back area as shown.

The attacker leans forward as shown, first placing his left hand on the mat for stability and then placing the top of his head on the mat.

The attacker places his bent right leg over the back of his opponent's head as shown.

This back view shows how the attacker places his feet and legs to control his opponent.

The attacker rolls onto his right side as shown (in the direction of his opponent's head). As he does this, the attacker uses his left hand and arm to grab his opponent's left leg just above the knee in order to drag it over, forcing his opponent to roll.

The attacker rolls over, and as he does, he forces his opponent to roll over his head as shown.

The attacker rolls his opponent over onto his back and as he does, the attacker rolls over and comes to a sitting position as shown.

This front view shows how the attacker is sitting in a leg-press position and controlling his opponent.

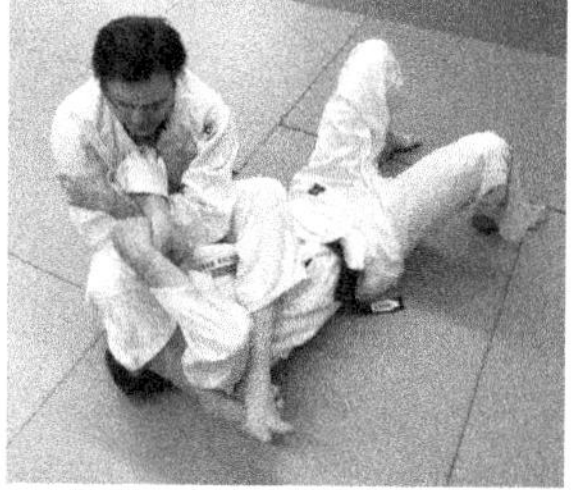

The attacker uses both hands and arms to grab and trap his opponent's left arm to his torso as shown.

The attacker rolls onto his back, extending and stretching his opponent's left arm and applies the juji gatame.

Entry into Hip-Roll Juji Gatame When Opponent Is on Hands and Knees

Sometimes an opponent will assume a "parterre" position from wrestling when he is on the bottom position. This is especially true among wrestlers who compete in judo. When an opponent does this, he is giving you many body gaps and spaces that you can use to control him more efficiently. This head-roll application of juji gatame is ideal for situations like this.

Hip-Roll Juji Gatame: The attacker is positioned at the side and behind his opponent as shown.

The attacker climbs onto his opponent placing his right foot and leg over his opponent's lower back as shown.

The attacker leans forward and places his right hand onto the mat for stability. As he does this, the attacker uses his left hand and arm to trap his opponent's right arm as shown.

The attacker places the top of his head onto the mat for stability. As he does this, he starts to slide his left foot and leg over the back of his opponent's head.

The attacker uses his left leg to hook his opponent's head as shown.

The attacker rolls over his right shoulder in the direction of his opponent's hip as shown. The attacker makes sure to stay as round as possible when rolling.

The attacker rolls over his right shoulder. As he does this, the attacker uses both of his hands and arms to trap his opponent's right arm tightly to his torso.

The attacker rolls over onto his buttocks in the leg press position.

The attacker uses both of his hands and arms to trap his opponent's right arm to his chest as he rolls back, stretching and extending his opponent's arm to apply juji gatame.

Entry into Rolling Ude Garami When an Opponent Is on Hands and Knees

Here is another armlock when an opponent is positioned in "parterre" and on his hands and knees.

Rolling Ude Garami: The attacker stands over his opponent as shown.

The attacker uses his right foot and leg to wrap and entangle his opponent's left arm.

The attacker leans forward as he continues to entangle his opponent's left arm as shown.

The attacker leans forward and uses his right hand and arm to slide under his opponent's head.

The attacker starts to roll over his right shoulder as shown.

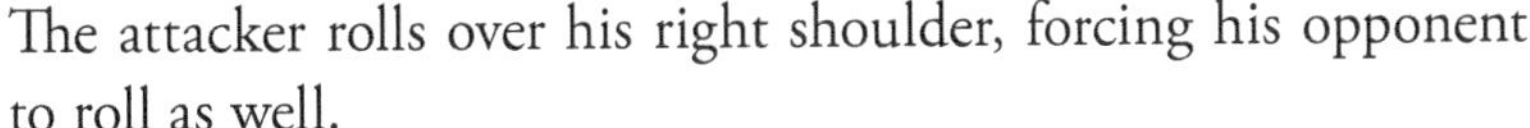

The attacker rolls over his right shoulder, forcing his opponent to roll as well.

The attacker completes his roll and is on his buttocks with his opponent's left arm trapped and entangled with the attacker's right leg as shown.

The attacker moves his left foot back and places it on the mat for stability.

The attacker leans forward as shown and places pressure on his opponent's entangled left arm with his legs.

Entry to Juji Gatame When the Opponent Uses Niju Garami (Leg Wrapping) to Scissor Your Leg

This situation happens fairly often in competitive judo with the bottom judoka using his legs to wrap around and scissor his opponent's leg. Doing this usually causes the referee to call a halt to the action and allow the bottom judoka to escape this situation.

Leg-Scissors Juji Gatame: The attacker is positioned on top of his opponent, but his opponent has wrapped his legs around the attacker's right leg in a defensive maneuver.

This front view shows how the attacker starts to slide his right leg forward to lessen his opponent's control of it.

The attacker leans his body to his left in the direction of his opponent's head in order to give himself room to have more freedom of movement and to move his left foot and leg over his opponent's head.

The attacker sits onto his buttocks for stability. Look at how he has positioned his left bent leg near his opponent's head.

The attacker uses his left hand and arm to trap his opponent's right arm to his torso as he moves his left foot and leg over his opponent's head.

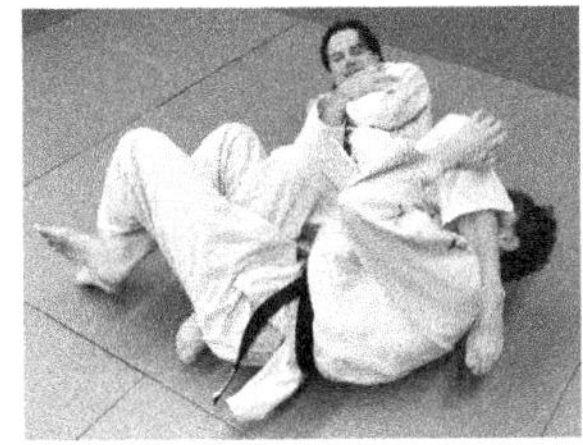

The attacker uses both of his hands and arms to trap his opponent's right arm to his chest as he rolls back applying juji gatame. Look at how the attacker's right leg is still entangled by his opponent's legs.

Entry to Ude Gatame (Arm Lock) from the Bottom When Positioned an Elbows and Knees

This is a sneaky and effective armlock if you are on the bottom and your opponent is working to control you with a wrestler's or spiral ride. This armlock is also called kannuki gatame (latch bolt lock).

Bottom Position to Ude Gatame: The opponent is on top using a wrestler's or spiral ride for control.

The attacker uses his right hand and arm to hook over his opponent's right upper arm (just above the elbow) and uses his left hand to grab his opponent's right wrist.

The attacker rolls onto his left side.

The attacker continues to roll onto his left side and onto his back as he uses both of his hands and arms to entangle his opponent's right arm using a figure-four grip. As he does this, the attacker starts to apply pressure on his opponent's straight right arm at the elbow joint.

To increase the pressure on the opponent's right elbow (as well as the shoulder), the attacker uses his legs to form a triangle on his opponent's arm, increasing the pain.

Entry to Ude Garami (Arm Entanglement) Starting from Kesa Gatame (Scarf Hold)

This is a popular transition from a pin to an armlock. It's popular because it works and has worked for a lot of athletes for a long time. There are other variations of this technique, so make sure to experiment with this armlock in practice to find out which works best for you.

Kesa Gatame to Ude Garami: The attacker is using kesa gatame (scarf hold) to pin her opponent.

If the opponent is attempting to escape, the attacker uses his left hand to grab her opponent's right wrist and arm and move them forward as shown.

The attacker uses his left hand and arm to pull and extend her opponent's right arm as the attacker lifts her right foot and leg in preparation to trap the extended right arm.

The attacker places her right foot and leg over her opponent's extended right arm and traps it. This causes pain in the elbow joint as well as the shoulder joint of her opponent.

If more pressure is required to get the tap out, the attacker will use her left hand to push forward onto her opponent's elbow.

Entry to Ude Garami (Arm Entanglement) from Kami Shiho Gatame (Upper Four Corner Hold)

This transition to ude garami from kami shiho gatame is quite effective and unexpected. What makes this armlock particularly effective is the position of the attacker at the head of his opponent where the attacker can apply more torque to the joint lock.

Kami Shiho Gatame to Ude Garami: The attacker is pinning his opponent with kami shiho gatame (upper four corner hold).

The attacker shifts his body to the right as shown and as he does this, he uses both of his hands and arms to trap his opponent's left upper arm.

The attacker uses left hand to grip his opponent's left wrist and uses his head to push onto his opponent's left elbow and arm in a downward direction.

The attacker uses his hands and arms to form a figure-four. Doing this entangles his opponent's left arm.

The attacker applies pressure to secure the armlock.

Entry to Ude Garami (Arm Entanglement) from Mune Gatame (Chest Hold)

This transition to ude garami from mune gatame has a high rate of success at all levels of judo competition. The strong and stable base that mune gatame provides allows for the attacker to manipulate the defender's arms more easily.

Mune Gatame to Ude Garami: The attacker holds her opponent with mune gatame (chest hold).

The attacker uses his right hand and arm to grab her opponent's left lower arm and pushes it downward toward the mat.

The attacker uses both of her hands to grab and pin her opponent's left arm to the mat.

The attacker uses his left hand and arm to move under her opponent's bent left arm. The attacker continues to use her left hand (that is under her opponent's head as shown) to grab and control her opponent's left wrist.

The attacker slides her left bent elbow over her opponent's head and face. As she does this, the attacker jams her left elbow into the left side of her opponent's neck. The attacker then uses his right arm to lift upward on her opponent's bent elbow and upper arm, applying pressure to secure the tap-out.

Entry to Juji Gatame (Crossbody Armlock) as a Transition from Tai Otoshi (Body Drop)

Applying a juji gatame immediately after throwing an opponent is a good way to make sure of an ippon score for the win. Juji gatame is such a versatile armlock that it is an ideal armlock to transition to from a throwing technique. A particularly effective and popular combination of a throw-to-armlock transition is tai otoshi to juji gatame.

Throw to Juji Gatame: The attacker applies tai otoshi (body drop). We are using tai otoshi, but any throwing technique will work.

The attacker throws his opponent with tai otoshi.

The attacker finishes in control, but the referee may not have awarded ippon for the victory. In this situation, the attacker will transition to juji gatame (crossbody armlock).

The attacker immediately sits on his opponent's right shoulder as he uses both arms to trap his opponent's right arm to his chest. The attacker uses his left foot and leg to hook over his opponent's head and uses his right foot and leg to jam in the right side of his opponent's torso as shown. Doing this controls the opponent's entire upper body, including his shoulder and arm.

The attacker leans back as he applies pressure on his opponent's extended and stretched right arm to secure juji gatame for the ippon.

Entry to Ude Garami (Arm Entanglement) When Standing over a Kneeling Opponent

Transitioning from a standing position to an armlock when your opponent is kneeling is effective in a variety of situations, including this one. In this situation, the attacker uses sumi gaeshi (corner reverse direction throw) to transition to the mat. The attacker has knocked her opponent to the mat, and the opponent attempts to stand. As the opponent gets to her knees, the attacker can quickly use this sumi gaeshi transition to the mat and apply ude garami to get the tap-out. This is also effective because it's a "double trouble" technique where the attacker applies the ude garami as she pins her opponent with mune gatame (chest hold).

Sumi Gaeshi to Ude Garami: The attacker stands over his opponent, who is kneeling.

The attacker slides her right hand and arm over her opponent's head as shown.

The attacker uses her left hand to grab her opponent's right wrist as she continues to slide her right hand and arm over her opponent's shoulder.

The attacker uses her right arm to trap her opponent's right shoulder area as she uses her right hand to grab her left wrist, forming a figure-four grip.

The attacker moves her right foot and leg to the middle and under her opponent as she steps forward with her left foot and leg. As she does this, the attacker uses her hands and arms to pull her opponent's entangled right arm closer to her body.

The attacker rolls backward onto her buttocks as she uses her right shin and foot to wedge under her opponent's right upper leg area. As she does this, the attacker continues to use her hands and arm to pull her opponent's entangled right arm close to her.

The attacker rolls to her left rear corner as she uses her right foot and leg to lift her opponent's right leg as shown.

The attacker continues to roll to her right rear corner, throwing her opponent over and onto her back.

This front view shows how the attacker has rolled her opponent over onto her back and finishes with ude garami as well as pinning her opponent with mune gatame (chest hold) for a "double trouble" situation for her opponent using both the armlock and pin.

CHAPTER 11

Chokes and Strangles

Everybody's got a neck.

—Dewey Mitchell

Strangling is the great equalizer in judo. Everyone has a neck, and it doesn't matter how thick the neck is—it can be strangled or choked. This section of the book focuses on shime waza. The word "shime" translates to "squeeze" or "tighten" and is a good description of what happens to the neck of an opponent. The tightening or squeezing effect on an opponent's carotid arteries or trachea are effective and unforgiving. "Waza" means "technique" and implies a broad approach in its application. Strangles are the subtlest of all grappling skills. They aren't spectacular; choking an opponent isn't nearly as exciting for spectators as seeing an opponent slammed to the mat with a throw. There's no loud thud, just a tap-out, but there is a definite winner and a definite loser. As with armlocks, strangling an opponent is an emphatic way to win. As I said earlier, once you strangle an opponent, he'll never forget you and certainly never forgive you. You have a psychological edge over him, and the next time you fight him, he'll remember you're the person who made him give up.

A good strangler seems to sneak the choke in on his opponent; his hands and wrists seem almost loose, but always gripping, controlling, and manipulating his opponent. A good strangler also knows how to use each hand independently. One hand may grip the lapel in a certain way and the other may wing the opponent's arm or pull the other lapel to gain the best leverage in the strangle. I've always told my athletes that you need to "get to know your chokes." Knowing how to strangle takes a lot of time, experimentation, effort, thinking, and practice. It's not a set of skills are quickly acquired. What happens is that after a lot of hard work and time on the mat, and once you've developed enough skill, you get a "feel" in your hands and arms for applying strangles. I'm not sure how to explain it other than it's a kinesthetic awareness you develop after having done it for so long. After a while, you can actually feel when your opponent is going out and can control the flow of action in applying the strangle.

Defining Features of Shime Waza

It may be simply a matter of terminology, but there is a difference between the terms "strangle" and "choke." A strangle is a generic name in the English language for any form of shime waza but is usually specifically aimed at the carotid arteries, cutting off the blood supply to the brain. These are the "sleeper holds" that the old-time professional wrestlers made famous. Someone will "go to sleep" or go unconscious quickly if strangled. I've heard this type of shime waza called a "blood strangle" by some people because of how it cuts off the blood supply to the brain. A "choke" usually refers to any shime waza aimed at the trachea. Squeezing the trachea shut is, if not painful, certainly a very unpleasant experience for the victim and cuts off the air supply, often producing a gagging reaction. This shime waza has been called an "air choke" by some old-timers for obvious reasons.

Historically, the neck and throat were not the only targets of shime waza; the opponent's body was fair game as well as the neck and throat. The use of dojime (trunk or body squeezing) was included as a method of shime waza in the early years of Kodokan judo. Eventually, changes in the contest rules in the early part of the twentieth century eliminated attacking the body with dojime so that shime waza was directed toward the throat and neck.

Strangles Start with the Legs

It may sound odd, but most (if not all) strangles start with controlling an opponent's lower extremities. Strangles and chokes simply work more efficiently when you are in the right position and have good lower body (leg and hip) control over your opponent. Isolating an opponent's legs and hips effectively controls his entire body. Don't be in such a hurry to get your hands around his neck that you forget to set him up and control his body before applying the choke. So an important aspect of shime waza is controlling an opponent with your legs. In other words, make sure to control your opponent's body and the movement of his body (that is, control the position) with your legs before attacking his neck.

The Anatomy of Shime Waza

The action of strangling often (but not always) hurts. It can be painful and dangerous. You could kill someone if you applied a strangle hard enough and long enough. That's why they used to hang bad guys in the Old West. It hurt and it was effective. Aside from that obvious point, cutting off the blood supply to the brain deprives the brain of oxygen and causes unconsciousness. The fact is, when you strangle or choke someone you are depriving him of his breath, and it doesn't matter how tough a guy is—he still has to breathe. Aside from the physical effects, depriving someone of his ability to breathe has a big psychological impact.

The neck connects the body to the head and as a result is an important part of the body. When you choke someone, attacking the front of the throat and neck, you usually want to get your focus of the choke directed at, or directly below, the Adam's apple (thyroid cartilage). The thyroid cartilage is located directly under the hyoid bone, a small bone that has many functions in swallowing and supports the thyroid cartilage. The trachea (windpipe) is located below the thyroid cartilage and is a flexible tube made up of cartilage. All these things are tough but not really made for having somebody else squeeze them with great intensity! The sides of the neck contain the carotid arteries, which are large arteries and the brain's major source of blood. When they are constricted, most of the blood going to the brain doesn't get there anymore. Deprived of oxygen for even four or five seconds, the brain starts to shut down and unconsciousness occurs. If the brain is deprived of oxygen for four to six minutes, clinical death occurs. Whether you make an opponent pass out from constricting his carotid arteries or constricting his windpipe and connected organs, you still deprive him of oxygen.

Using strangles and chokes is serious business and is not for the immature. I've coached for many years, specializing in submission techniques, and sincerely believe strangles and chokes are more dangerous than armlocks. A broken arm can mend, but the effects of the brain cells lost from being choked could always stay with you. The lack of oxygen to the brain kills brain cells and these brain cells don't grow back. Lose enough of them and neurological damage can take place.

It's better to tap out than pass out, especially in training. Don't risk serious injury and possible problems later in life. By the same token, if you're strangling an opponent or training partner and he taps out, he means it. Release the pressure and stop choking him for his safety. An old saying is, "When in doubt, tap out." You're not any less brave, less tough, or less of anything. You're using your survival instinct to let your opponent know it's time to stop choking you. Don't risk your health. It's better to tap out than pass out.

Using the Appendages in Shime Waza

There are two primary sets of appendages used in shime waza: 1. the hands and arms, and 2. the feet and legs. While the hands and arms are used in the majority of chokes and strangles, leg chokes are used almost as often and are equally effective.

Using the Hands and Arms: Most shime waza are the result of using the hands and arms to apply pressure to an opponent's neck.

Using the Leg and Feet: The legs are powerful tools in shime waza, and there are numerous applications and variations of leg chokes used in judo.

Using the Judogi in Shime Waza

Shime waza can be applied either using the judo uniform or not using the judo uniform. There are some shime waza that require the use of clothing (either the attacker's or the defender's jacket, belt, or pants) and there are some shime waza that don't require the use of clothing.

"Naked" Chokes That Don't Require Clothing: This example of hadaka jime (naked choke) shows how it's possible to apply shime waza without using clothing. This type of strangle has an appropriate name: "hadaka jime." While there is a series of stran-

gles specifically named hadaka jime, the name also refers to this type of shime waza. "Hadaka" means anything without a garment. It can be the opponent's neck and throat (we're not using his lapel or jacket to strangle him) or it can be our bare arms. "Jime" means to squeeze or to tighten. Like a neck in a noose, the action of this strangle is as effective as it is unrelenting. It can be a slow squeeze or a sudden action that causes your opponent to tap out. The skills classified as naked strangles are probably the most basic and simplest of all neck and throat submissions. As is often the case, the simpler the better, and the naked choke or strangle is one of the most commonly used and reliable chokes in judo.

Shime Waza Using Clothing: The opponent's lapel is often the tool used to strangle an opponent, but any part of the opponent's (or attacker's) uniform can be used. Professor Jigoro Kano believed that shime waza was so important, and his fondness of lapel strangles was so apparent, that he redesigned the uwagi (training jacket used in judo and jujutsu) so that it had wider, thicker lapels with which to secure a lapel strangle. The thicker lapels also stood up to the rigors of gripping, so they served a dual purpose, but the lapel strangles were common in the early days of Kodokan judo and continue to be popular today. In those early years, attacking an opponent's neck from the front with a lapel strangle was more common than in judo competition today, but strangling an opponent with the lapels of his jacket is an effective and emphatic way to end a contest and continues to be one of the most popular ways of strangling. While the lapels are most often used, you can use any part of your clothing or any part of your opponent's clothing to strangle him.

Position in Shime Waza

The two primary positions for applying shime waza are strangling an opponent from the front or facing him and strangling an opponent when behind him. Strangles are versatile in that they can be applied from any direction. Generally, the attacker will either face his opponent or strangle his opponent when behind him. The preference of most judo athletes is to get behind an opponent and control the position and apply the strangle, but this isn't always possible, so having a reliable choke when facing an opponent is a valuable tool. In the feudal jujutsu schools before the Meiji Restoration in Japan in 1868 and before Jigoro Kano devised Kodokan judo, shime waza focused on combat effectiveness and was used to finish off an opponent if a weapon was lost on the battlefield and when engaged in hand-to-hand combat. Often, the man who did the strangling was the one sitting on top of his downed opponent. In the modern application of judo as a sport, the athlete doing the strangling is just as often the one on the bottom as much as the one on top. Obviously, knowing how to strangle an opponent from any position is important for success in judo.

Shime Waza Applied from the Front: The lapels are the most-often used part of the judogi, but the sleeves, pant leg, apron of the judo jacket, and belt are also used in strangling an opponent.

Shine Waza Applied from Behind the Opponent: This lapel strangle from the rear is tight and the lapel of the judogi is being used in the same way a rope is used in a noose.

Control the Legs and Body and Control the Neck: Before you can choke your opponent, you have to control his body. The better you limit his movement by controlling his legs, hips, arms, and pretty much everything about your opponent, the better you will be able to strangle him. If you control the position, you control the match. Position is being in the right place at the right time and putting your opponent in the wrong place (for him) every time. This photo shows the top judo athlete controlling the position using a rodeo ride. Also referred to as "getting your hooks in," this position is one of the best ways of controlling an opponent used in judo (or any form of sport combat). "Getting his back" is what is referred to as getting behind an opponent, digging the feet into his opponent's hips and crotch, and controlling him. World Judo Champion Neil Adams once said to me, "The best way to control your opponent is to get behind him. He doesn't have eyes in the back of his head." The rodeo ride proves the wisdom of this advice.

Hand Fighting in Shime Waza: Good newaza is moving from one position to another position to yet another position and trying to control your opponent and ultimately make him give up. Controlling the movement of an opponent's body is the initial step in strangling him. After controlling his opponent with his legs and position, a good strangler continually uses his hands to control, probe, pull, push, or do what is necessary to further isolate and strangle his opponent's neck or throat. Likewise, the defender will use his hands to fight off his opponent and defend himself. This is what is referred to as "hand fighting" and is an essential skill in strangling. The athlete on the bottom has good control with his rodeo ride and has rolled his opponent over to attempt to work in a strangle or armlock. Look at how both contestants are fighting with their hands and using them to gain control of the situation. The attacker is doing his best to secure a strangle, and the defender is doing his best to protect his neck and "peel" the attacker's hands away.

Applying the Strangle: Adding Torque

There are two strategies in strangling an opponent's neck. The first strategy is very direct and to the point. The attacker isolates his opponent's neck and methodically squeezes it until the strangle takes effect. The second strategy is to gain momentum to make the strangle work. In many cases, the action of strangling an opponent relies on more than simply using your hands or legs to get the job done. You can add considerable pressure into the strangle by the use of momentum. There are two principal ways of gaining momentum when applying a strangle: the attacker will roll his opponent, or he will flatten his opponent out. This added momentum works in the same way a noose tightens around a neck in hanging.

Isolate Opponent's Neck and Methodically Squeeze: Here's a good example of the bottom athlete isolating his opponent's body (and ultimately his neck) and methodically tightening the strangle. Look at how the bottom athlete is using his right hand to hold his opponent's left leg, keeping it from moving. The bottom athlete is controlling his opponent's position and movement by use of his sankaku (triangle) leg position and using his left hand to tighten the triangle hold and make this sankaku jime (triangle strangle) work.

Roll Opponent and Finish on Your Buttocks to Increase Torque: When applying a rolling strangle, the attacker should finish the rolling action so that he is positioned on his buttocks. This provides a strong and stable base to apply more torque (and produce a quicker and more effective choke) and also ensures that the attacker has the mobility he needs to transition to another move or position if necessary. By finishing the roll on the buttocks, the attacker does not bear the weight of his opponent on him and has more freedom of movement to apply the strangle or transition to another move if necessary.

Flatten Opponent to Increase Torque: The top athlete used his legs in this match to control his opponent's legs and lower body to flatten him onto his front. As the top athlete flattened his opponent out, he applied the strangle, in this case an okuri eri jime (send-after lapel strangle). The movement of flattening his opponent on his front and using his hands to tighten the strangle produced the momentum necessary to get the tap-out.

Analyzing Selected Shime Waza and Entries

There are many applications and variations of shime waza and many more ways to apply them in competitive judo, and this section of the book can't do them the justice they deserve, so what will follow is an analysis of only a few shime waza and some of the entry forms (hairi kata or breakdowns) that make them happen based on the starting positions of both the attacker and defender. A shime waza can be applied from just about any position or situation in a judo match, but chokes and strangles are particularly effective against an opponent positioned on all fours or lying flat on his face in a prone position.

Pull on Belt to Apply Hadaka Jime Against a Flat Opponent

In many situations, an opponent will lie flat on his face in the prone position, which is usually a mistake, and this is a solution that makes an opponent pay for that mistake. This is a common entry into hadaka jime (naked choke), and while it's probably one of the first entries to hadaka jime learned by judo athletes, it is used at all levels of competition with success.

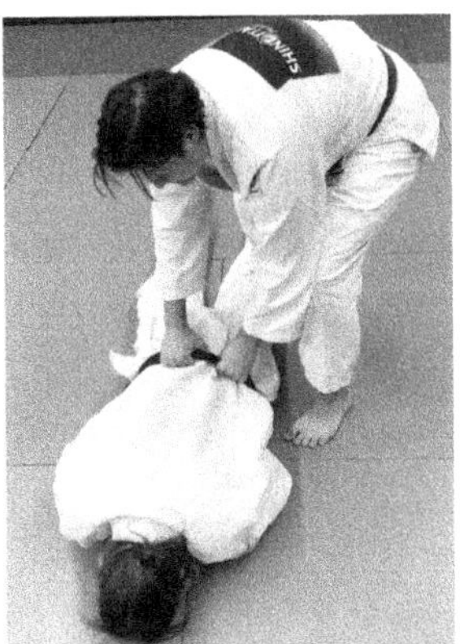

Hadaka Jime Against Flat Opponent: The attacker stands above his opponent who is lying flat on his front in a defensive position waiting for the referee to call a halt to the action.

The attacker stands above his opponent, using both hands to grab his opponent's belt in order to lift him.

The attacker lifts his opponent off the mat by pulling up on his belt. This raises the opponent's hip enough so that the attacker can drive his feet and legs under his opponent's hips.

The attacker drives his feet and legs under his opponent's hips and upper legs and drives his opponent forward and flat onto the mat.

The attacker places the weight on his body onto his opponent's upper back area as the attacker digs in with both of his hands to start applying hadaka jime (naked choke).

This close view shows how the attacker uses his head to help trap his opponent's head to prevent his opponent from moving as the attacker uses a square-grip application of hadaka jime to apply the choke.

Rolling Okuri Eri Jime Against an Opponent on All Fours

Often, an opponent will get onto a compact position on his hands and knees (in what many call the "turtle" position). This is an ideal time to use a rolling strangle, and okuri eri jime (send-after lapel strangle) is an effective technique.

Rolling Okuri Eri Jime: The attacker uses his left hand to grip his opponent's right lapel.

The attacker moves to his right as he uses his left hand to move under his opponent's neck (gripping his opponent's right lapel). Doing this starts the strangling action.

The attacker uses his right foot and leg to step over his opponent's lower back as shown. This starts the rolling action.

The attacker rolls over his opponent's back, all the while tightening the lapel strangle with his left hand.

As the attacker rolls over his opponent, he uses his right hand and arm to grab his opponent's right leg at about the knee area. The attacker uses his left foot and leg to wrap around his opponent's left arm to trap it. As the attacker rolls, he continually tightens the lapel strangle with his left hand. The accumulative effect of rolling and wrapping the lapel around the neck forces the opponent to tap out.

Jigoku Jime Against an Opponent on All Fours

This is a well-named strangle. Jigoku translates to "hell," and this strangle does indeed hurt that much. There are many applications and variations of jigoku jime. Generally, when a strangle is called "jigoku jime" it implies that the attacker uses his leg to trap the opponent's head and apply pressure to the strangle.

Jigoku Jime Against Opponent on All Fours: The attacker uses his left hand to grip his opponent's right lapel and uses his left hand and arm to loop under his opponent's neck and head as shown. As he does this, the attacker moves to his right and to the left side of his opponent.

The attacker uses his right hand to grab his opponent's belt as the attacker starts to move his left foot and leg in order to step over his opponent's head.

The attacker uses his left foot and leg to step over his opponent's head. As he does this, the attacker uses his right hand that is gripping his opponent's lapel to wrap the lapel tighter around his opponent's throat.

The attacker uses his left foot wedge under his opponent's right shoulder and upper arm area as shown. The attacker is now sitting on his opponent's head and upper shoulder area.

The attacker leans backward to his left hip as he applies pressure to his opponent's throat with his left hand gripping his opponent's lapel. The attacker adds more pressure to the strangling action by using his right hand to pull on his opponent's belt as shown. Look at how the attacker is using his left leg to trap his opponent's head, driving his opponent forward. This adds torque to the strangle.

To add pressure to the strangle, the attacker can place his right foot and leg over and onto his opponent's lower back.

Wrist Ride Control to Yoko Sankaku Jime Against Opponent on All Fours

A "wrist ride" is the term used when the attacker controls and traps his opponent's wrist in order to control his opponent long enough to apply another move or technique. In this situation, the attacker is using a wrist ride to control his opponent who is on all fours. This application of yoko sankaku jime (side triangle choke) is popular at all levels of judo competition.

Wrist Ride to Yoko Sankaku Jime: The attacker uses his right hand to grab and control his opponent's right wrist.

The attacker uses his right hand and arm to pull his opponent's right wrist in and trap it to his opponent's torso for control.

The attacker moves to his right and around his opponent's body in order to get to his opponent's head and shoulder area.

The attacker is in a kneeling position as shown and starts to trap his opponent's right wrist and lower arm by using a "judo key lock" where he wraps the apron of his opponent's judo jacket around the opponent's wrist in order to trap it, making it useless to the opponent.

This back view shows how the attacker uses his right root and leg to hook under his opponent's left upper leg and hip. The attacker uses his right hand to grab (palm down) onto his opponent's belt.

The attacker uses both of his hands and arms to pull his opponent over and onto his side as shown.

The attacker is now lying on his right side and extends his right leg under his opponent's head and upper shoulder area. As he does this, the attacker uses his left leg to hook under his opponent's left upper arm as shown. This is the start of forming a triangle with the legs.

The attacker uses his left hand to pull on his opponent's left wrist area to cinch the triangle action tighter. As he does this, the attacker uses his feet and legs to form a triangle as shown. Once the triangle with the legs is formed, the attacker applies pressure by squeezing his legs together to get the tap-out.

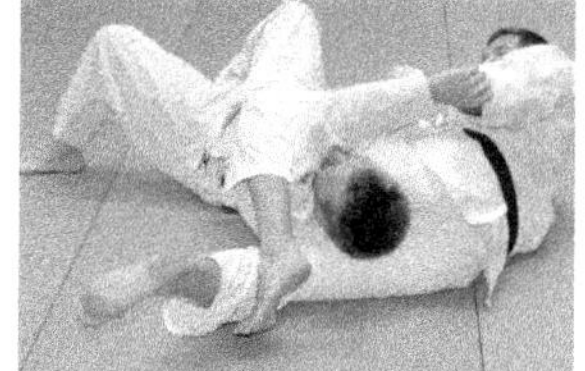

Koshi Jime Against Opponent on All Fours

This application of koshi jime (hip choke) produces a quick tap-out based on how the attacker uses his leg to hook his opponent's arm and the suddenness of the attacker forcing his opponent to flatten out onto his front. There are numerous variations of koshi waza, and in all cases the attacker uses the power of driving his hip forward to create the torque necessary to make the strangle work.

Koshi Jime Against Opponent on All Fours: The attacker stands above his opponent from behind as shown. As the attacker does this, he uses his left hand to reach under his opponent's neck and throat and grips his opponent's right lapel.

The attacker uses his right foot and leg to entangle his opponent's left arm. By doing this, the attacker controls and restricts the movement of opponent.

The attacker uses his right hand to reach over his opponent's back, grabbing the inside of his opponent's upper right leg. As he does this, the attacker drives his body forward, leaning slightly to his right. Doing this flattens his opponent and starts to add pressure to the strangling action.

By driving forward and flattening his opponent, the attacker increases the torque being applied to the lapel strangle he is using with his left hand and gets the tap-out.

Ura Sankaku Jime Against Opponent on All Fours

This application of a triangle choke is ura sankaku jime (rear triangle choke) because when the attacker applies the choke, he is positioned behind his opponent. This variation of ura sankaku jime is exceptionally powerful because the attacker grabs his leg as he rolls his opponent over into the choke, cinching his leg in tightly as he rolls.

Ura Sankaku Jime Against Opponent on All Fours: The attacker is positioned as shown at the front of his opponent who is on all fours in the turtle position.

The attacker wedges his right foot and leg between his opponent's right arm and head.

The attacker uses his left foot and leg to step over his opponent's back. As he does this, the attacker uses his left hand to grab his right ankle.

This photo shows how the attacker uses his left hand to grab his ankle and lower leg.

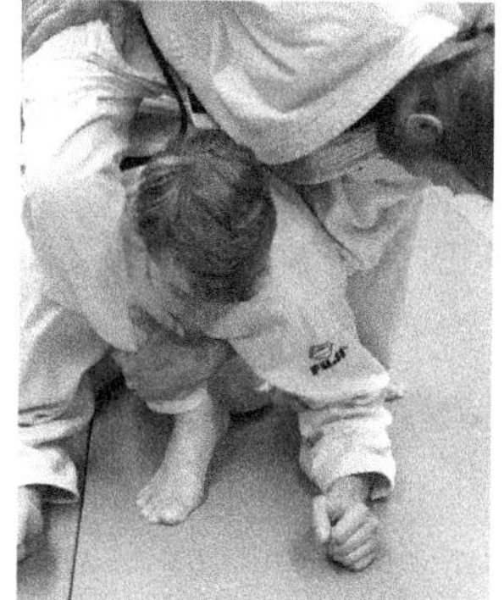

The attacker rolls over his right shoulder as shown. As he does this, the attacker continues to use his left hand to grab onto his right ankle area. As the attacker rolls, he pulls with his left hand on his right ankle tightly. Doing this tightens the triangle the attacker is forming with his feet and legs.

The attacker has rolled onto his side as shown and swings his left foot and leg over as shown to start forming a triangle with his feet and legs.

The attacker has formed a triangle with his feet and legs and uses both of this hands and arms to trap and pull his opponent's left arm straight.

This back view shows how the attacker uses his left foot to wedge under his opponent's left torso to anchor the foot and make the triangle stronger. The attacker squeezes with his legs to create the choke.

Leg Prop Rollover Using Kata Juji Jime

This rollover works well whether the opponent is lying flat on his front or is positioned on his elbows and knees in the turtle position. This is a "double trouble" technique where the attacker can apply a strong kata juji jime (half cross-lapel strangle) or pin his opponent with a variation of tate shiho gatame (vertical four-corner hold).

Leg Prop Rollover Using Kata Juji Jime: The attacker is positioned on his knees at the top of his prone opponent.

The attacker uses his left hand and arm to reach under his opponent's right arm.

The attacker uses his left hand to reach under his opponent's right armpit area to tightly grip the left side of his opponent's lapel as shown in this photo.

The attacker uses his right hand (palm down) to grip the right side of his opponent's jacket at the shoulder.

This photo shows how the attacker's hands and arms are positioned as he applies the kata juji jime (half cross strangle).

The attacker extends his left leg and uses his left foot to prop his opponent's right hip area as shown.

The attacker uses his hands and arms that are applying pressure to the lapel strangle to roll his opponent over.

The attacker applies more pressure with the lapel strangle as he rolls over on top of his opponent and into this tripod position. If the strangle does not work, the attacker can use this position to lie down on his opponent and pin him.

The Trap Choke from the Bottom Newaza Position

This is a variation of kata juji jime (half cross-lapel strangle) and is often called the "trap choke" because the bottom judoka is laying a trap for his opponent. It is also called the "baseball bat choke" because the attacker's hands and arms are held the way you hold a baseball bat.

Trap Choke from Bottom Newaza: The attacker is on the bottom in newaza (supine technique) position and uses his right hand to grip (palm up) his opponent's left lapel and his left hand (palm down) to grip his opponent's right lapel.

The attacker lowers his right leg and knee. This lures his opponent to attempt to pass over the lowered right knee as shown. This is the point where the "trap" starts to take place in this trap choke.

As his opponent passes over this right knee, the attacker quickly rolls onto his left side.

This photo shows how the attacker's hands and arms are positioned as he applies the trap choke.

To tighten the effect of the choke, the attacker swings his right leg over his left leg.

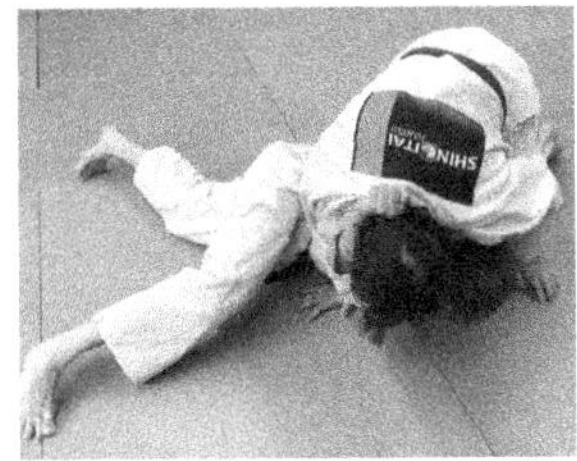

The attacker finishes the choke in this position. This is a tight and sneaky choke.

Sankaku Jime Starting from Kesa Gatame

This application of the triangle choke is called gyaku sankaku jime (reverse triangle choke) because the attacker applies the choke from a reverse or upside-down type of position. The starting position for this choke is with the attacker pinning his opponent with kesa gatame (scarf hold). The attacker can transition from the pin to the triangle choke as his opponent is escaping from the pin or this can be used in other grappling sports where a submission is necessary to secure the victory.

The attacker is pinning his opponent with a variation of kesa gatame (scarf hold). Look at how the attacker's right hand and arm are positioned under his opponent's left shoulder.

The attacker uses his left hand to grab his opponent's right forearm and drives it downward.

The attacker lifts his left leg over his opponent's right arm as shown to start the process of controlling it as he proceeds to form the triangle.

The attacker uses his left hand and arm to grab under his opponent's head as the attacker rolls his body to his left.

The attacker rolls to his left and starts to lift his left leg over his opponent's head.

The attacker forms a triangle with his feet and legs as he continues to roll over on top of his opponent as shown.

The attacker applies pressure with his leg and gets the tap-out.

Sankaku Jime Starting from the Leg-Press Position

The leg-press position is a versatile and strong controlling position and provides a stable and secure base in order to apply numerous techniques. Although often called the "juji gatame position," the term doesn't do justice to this position of control, and this application of sankaku jime (triangle choke) proves it.

Sankaku Jime from Leg Press: The attacker controls his opponent using the leg-press position.

The attacker slides his right leg under his opponent's left arm as shown.

The attacker rolls to his right hip area in order to more easily slide his right leg deeply under his opponent's arms and over his upper body as shown. As he does this, the attacker places his left knee under his opponent's head and uses his knee to lift his opponent's head up.

The attacker continues to use his left knee to lift his opponent's head and upper body up. As he does this, the attacker starts to slide his right foot and leg closer to his left leg.

The attacker forms a triangle with his feet and legs. As he does this, the attacker starts to apply pressure on his opponent's neck with his legs.

To add additional pressure to the choke, the attacker rolls to his left and onto his buttocks as shown. As he does this, the attacker squeezes his opponent's neck with his legs to complete the choke and get the tap out.

EPILOGUE

If you find that a particular technique works best for you in an unorthodox manner, then by all means practice it that way. As you continue to learn and improvise, you will be developing your own style. Remember that if every judoist were to execute a move in an identical fashion, a lot of fascination for the sport would be gone. The sport would cease to improve and degenerate into a series of stylized exercises.

—Gene LeBell and L. C. Coughran (from their book *The Handbook of Judo* published by Cornerstone Library)

Some Closing Thoughts

As I was contemplating writing a book on judo and what it should be about, I was reminiscing with my friend and colleague John Saylor about the books we owned and read when we were starting out in our respective careers in judo and how they influenced us. It was then that John suggested to me that I should write the kind of book we wish we had when we were young men, a book focused on practical information that both newcomers and experienced judo athletes could use. David Ripianzi, my publisher at YMAA Publication Center, had been encouraging me to write another book on judo as a follow-up to my earlier book *The Judo Advantage*. The more I thought about John's suggestion, the more it appealed to me, so David and I met and decided to get to work. But, getting back to what John and I were reminiscing about, I would like to tell you how much the first book on the subject of judo influenced me and why, many years later, I've written a book in the hope of achieving the same positive results for other people as that first book did for me.

When I started learning judo back in the mid-1960s I was fortunate that some outstanding books were produced during that era, and even more fortunate to discover a book that literally shaped my career in judo. That book was *The Handbook of Judo* by Gene LeBell and L. C. Coughran. I bought it sometime late in 1965 when I was thirteen years old, having started judo earlier that year as a twelve-year-old boy. I had the habit of taking the public transit bus on Saturday mornings (it was about a thirty-minute trip each way on the bus) to the dojo where I was learning judo and would arrive early to help clean the tatami and lend a hand doing some light janitorial work to keep our dojo clean. My sensei, Jerry Swett, encouraged us to do this, and there were usually about four or five of us kids who showed up early. After about an hour of cleaning our dojo, we would practice judo for about two hours. Sometimes, I would arrive early, and to kill some time before the dojo opened, I would go to the drugstore across the street and browse through the display of paperbacks. One Saturday morning, I saw *The Handbook of Judo* for sale for $1.00. I rifled through my wallet and pockets and was fortunate enough to have a little more than the required dollar to buy the book as well as a few cents for the tax. I packed the book in the bag that I kept my judogi in and, through those early years of my judo career, read it from cover to cover, studying the photos of the techniques. If you are aware of Gene LeBell's career as a professional wrestler as well as a judoka, it will come as no surprise that there were all sorts of leglocks, shoulder cranks, and headlocks included along with many standard judo techniques in that book. I figured the best way to try these new things out was with my training partners at the dojo. On one occasion when I had attempted something that I saw in the book on one of the other kids during randori (I think it was some kind of leglock), my sensei stopped me and asked me where I learned that technique. I proudly told him about my new book and showed him my copy that I always kept in my judo bag. My sensei, Jerry Swett, told me, "I admire your interest in learning more techniques, and I want you to keep reading books, but the technique you're doing isn't normally done in judo. Why don't you show me the techniques you would like to learn from the book and we can work on them?" Later, he encouraged me to buy what would become the second book in my judo library, *The Sport of Judo* by Kiyoshi Kobayashi and Harold E. Sharp. This was good advice, as the contents of that book certainly increased both my enthusiasm and knowledge of judo.

My sensei was a good and patient teacher. He could have told me to stop reading the book, but instead he saw that I was an inquisitive kid and encouraged me to continue to explore the world of judo through the medium of books. While these books taught me much and motivated me to learn more, they didn't prepare me for the world of competitive judo I was about to enter. In reality, they couldn't have because judo, as a sporting activity, was still in its developing years. It would take some time for books focused on the practical process of achieving success in the sport of judo to be written, and the book you are reading now is one of them.

Fast forwarding to the present, I believe books are still the most effective way of transmitting knowledge, but we also now have video and as well as the different forms of social media to supplement what we learn on the mat. Only time will tell as to what the future holds for us in the way of teaching and transmitting knowledge in the future. But, if it hadn't been for that chance encounter at the drugstore when I found my first judo book and the patience of a wise judo sensei who encouraged me to learn everything possible about judo, my life would have been different. Those two books are still in my library along with hundreds of others in many languages that have been accumulated through the years, and I continue to read them on a regular basis.

Years later, I was fortunate enough to meet Gene LeBell, and later, when I was starting the manuscript for my first book, I asked his advice on writing a judo book. This is what he told me: "Remember that a reader buys your book to find out something he doesn't know, or to find out a different way to do something he already knows. He wants to read what you have to say, so say it." He also said that if the writer doesn't make the book interesting, that book can have a lot of great information, but no one will see it because they haven't read it. He said, "A reader won't know what's in your book if he doesn't buy it." As best that I can remember, he also told me, "Writing is an art, but publishing is a business," emphasizing the fact that a writer should produce something that a publisher will want to put on the market and that the public will find worth buying and reading. I hope this book meets Gene LeBell's criteria.

As mentioned earlier, this book would not have come about if it hadn't been for the patient yet firm insistence of David Ripianzi, the owner of YMAA Publication Center. Thank you, David, for your belief in this project. Doran Hunter, my skilled and patient editor, and Barbara Langley, our fantastic publicist at YMAA, are also deserving of much credit. Additionally, the encouragement of my wife Becky Scott, as well as the encouragement of my friends, John Saylor, AnnMaria DeMars, Ken Brink, Tom Crone, and Bill Montgomery, as well as their ideas and input, made this book possible. The photographs for this book were provided by several talented professionals. Terry Smemo, Mark Lozano, Sharon Vandenberg, Jorge Garcia, Jake Pursley, and Joe Mace all contributed their talent and enthusiasm by supplying the photographs for this book as well as to many of my other books. Also, I wish to thank all the athletes and coaches at Welcome Mat for their efforts at our photo shoots and enthusiasm for this project.

Providing practical information on how to achieve success in competitive judo has been the focus of this book. No single book can give an answer to every question or provide a solution to every situation that will be encountered in a dynamic sport like judo. The information offered on the pages of this book is based on what actually takes place on a judo mat and what it takes to succeed in one of the most difficult sports ever invented. Success in judo is a long-term process, and the better you control that process, the better chance you have of winning in the sport of judo with a high rate of success. But it is important to bear in mind that achieving success in competitive judo is just one aspect of the totality of judo. If you are fortunate, the effort needed to succeed in judo as a sporting activity will open new doors of understanding and appreciation for you as to how judo can enrich your life in many ways. You will never stop learning judo. If you have gained any new knowledge, insight, or appreciation of judo as a result of what is on the pages of this book, then I have succeeded as an author and as a coach.

Books are marvelous things for many reasons, but two come to mind as this is being written. First, reading in a dynamic activity. The act of reading makes a person think, and thinking leads to action. So, the ultimate purpose of this book, as Gene LeBell said, is to provide you something new to think about, or at least a new way of thinking about the subject of competitive judo. The second reason books are marvelous things is that you can come back at a later time to reread it and gain fresh insights. You and the author will have an ongoing conversation for as long as you continue to read and reread what that author has written. I never personally met two of my favorite judo authors, Donn Draeger and Geof Gleeson, but every time I read one of their books, I get to know them better because they help me get to know myself better. It is my hope that as an author and as a coach, you and I have an ongoing conversation for a long time to come.

—Steve Scott

This book is dedicated to the memory of Bob Corwin,
a great friend, a great coach, and a great man.

REFERENCES AND BIBLOGRAPHY

Abrahams, Peter. *The Atlas of the Human Body*. London: Amber Books, 2002.

Barnett, Peter M. *Judo Groundplay to Win*. Merrick, NY: USJA Publishing, 1974.

Barnett, Peter M. *Judo to Win*. Merrick, NY: USJA Publishing, 1973.

Catanese, Anthony J. *The Medical Care of the Judoka*. Tucson: Wheatmark Publishing, 2012.

Clarke, Christopher M. *Saving Japan's Martial Arts*. Huntington Town, MD: Canyon Press, 2011.

Clarke, Michael. *Shin Gi Tai*. Wolfeboro, NH: YMAA Publication Center, 2015.

DeMarco, Michael. *Judo Kata: Practice, Competition, Purpose*. Santa Fe: Via Media Publishing, 2016.

DeMars, AnnMaria, and James Pedro. *Winning on the Ground: Training and Techniques for Judo and MMA Fighters*. Chicago: Black Belt Communications, 2013.

Draeger, Donn. *Modern Bujutsu & Budo*. New York: Weatherhill Publishers, 1997.

Epstein, David. *The Sports Gene*. New York: Portfolio/Penguin Publishing, 2014.

Gladwell, Malcom. *Outliers*. New York: Black Bay Books, 2013.

Gleeson, Geof. *All about Judo*. Cranford, UK: EP Publishing Ltd., 1984.

Gleeson, Geof. *Judo Inside Out*. Rutland, VT: Lepus Books, 1983.

Gleeson, Geoff. *Judo for the West*. Cranford, UK: A.S. Barnes and Company, 1967.

Greene, Robert. *Mastery*. New York: Penguin Books, 2017.

Hacker, Michael J. *The Language of Aikido*. N.p.: TalkingBudo, 2017.

Hepburn, James Curtis. *A Japanese and English Dictionary*. Tokyo: Charles E. Tuttle Publishing Company, 1987.

Hoare, Syd. *A History of Judo*. London: Yamagi Books, 2009.

Inman, Roy. *Judo for Women*. Ramsbury, UK: Crowood Books, 2004.

Inokuma, Isao, and Nobuyuki Sato. *Best Judo*. Tokyo: Kodansha International, 2009.

Ishikawa, Takahiko, and Donn Draeger. *Judo Training Methods*. Tokyo: Charles E. Tuttle Company, 1961.

Kano, Jigoro. *Judo and Education*. Tr. Tom Kain. Judo and Education. Tokyo: Japan Publishing Industry Foundation for Culture, 2020.

Kano, Jigoro. *Mind Over Muscle, Writings from the Founder of Judo*. Naoki Murata, comp. Tokyo: Kodansha International Publishing, 2013.

Kashiwazaki, Katsuhiko and Hidetoshi Nakanishi. *Attacking Judo*. London: Ippon Books, 1995.

Kawaishi, Mikonosuke. *My Method of Judo*. E.J. Harrison, ed. London: W. Foulsham & Company, Ltd., 1955.

Kerr, George and Peter Seisenbacher. *Modern Judo*. Ramsbury, UK: Ippon Crowood Books, 1997.

Kobayashi, Kiyoshi, and Harold E. Sharp. *The Sport of Judo*. Rutland, VT: Charles E. Tuttle Company, 1974.

Kodansha. *Illustrated Kodokan Judo*. Tokyo: Kodansha, 1964.

Koizumi, Gunji. *My Study of Judo*. New York: Sterling Publishing, 1960.

Kotani, Sumiyuki, and Yoshimi Osawa, and Yuichi Hirose. *Kata of Kodokan Judo*. Kobe: Koyano Bussan Kaisha, Ltd., 2022.

Kotani, Sumiyuki, Yoshimi Osawa, and Yuichi Hirose. *Newaza of Judo*. Kobe: Koyano Bussan Kaisha, Ltd, 1973.

LeBell, Gene, and Laurie Coughran. *The Handbook of Judo*. New York: Cornerstone Library, 1975.

Martens, Rainer. *Successful Coaching*, 2nd edition, by Human Kinetics Publishing, 2004.

Mifune, Kyuzo. *Canon of Judo*. Tokyo: Seibundo-Shinkosha Publishing, 1958.

Moshanov, Andrew. *Judo from a Russian Perspective*. Vaihinigen an der Enz, Gemany: Ipa-Verlag, 2004.

Nishioka, Hayward. *Judo Training for Competition*. Chicago: Black Belt Communications, 2010.

Okan, Isao. *Vital Judo Grappling Techniques*. Tokyo: Dai Nippon Printing, 1982.

Pulkkinen, Wayland. *The Sport Science of Elite Judo Athletes*. Guelph, ON: Pulkinetics, 2001.

Saigo, Toshiro. *Kodokan Judo Throwing Techniques*. Tokyo: Kodansha Publishing, 2016.

Sato, Tetsuya, and Isao Okano. *Vital Judo Throwing Techniques*. Tokyo: Dai Nippon Printing, 1982.

Saylor, John, and Steve Scott. *Conditioning for Combat Sports*. Sante Fe, NM: Turtle Press, 2013.

Scott, Steve, and John Saylor. *Vital Jujitsu*. Kansas City, MO: Welcome Mat Books, 2013.

Scott, Steve, *Triangle Holds Encyclopedia*. Wolfeboro, NH: YMAA Publication Center, 2022.

Scott, Steve. *Coaching on the Mat*. Kansas City, MO: Welcome Mat Books, 2005.

Scott, Steve. *Juji Gatame Encyclopedia*. Wolfeboro, NH: YMAA Publication Center, 2019.

Scott, Steve. *Sambo Encyclopedia*. Wolfeboro, NH: YMAA Publication Center, 2020.

Scott, Steve. *The Judo Advantage*. Wolfeboro, NH: YMAA Publication Center, 2019.

Scott, Steve. *Winning on the Mat*. Sante Fe, NM: Turtle Press, 2011.

Scott, Steve. *Winning on the Mat*. Sante Fe, NM: Turtle Press, 2011.

Simmons, Louie. *Explosive Strength Development for Jumping*. Tokyo: Seibundo-Shinkosha Publishing Company, 1956.

Stevens, John. The Way of Judo. Boston: Shambhala Publications, 2013.

Takagaki, Shinzo, and Harold E. Sharp. *The Techniques of Judo*. Tokyo: Charles E. Tuttle Company, 1989.

Thalken, Jason. *Fight Like a Physicist*. Wolfeboro, NH: YMAA Publication Center, 2015.

Verkhoshansky, Yuri, and Mel C. Siff. *Supertraining*. 6th ed. N.p.: Ultimate Athlete Concepts Publishing, 2009.

Watanabe, Jiichi, and Lindy Avakian. *The Secrets of Judo*. Tokyo: Charles E. Tuttle Company, 1960.

Watson, Brian N. *Judo Memoirs of Jigoro Kano*. Victoria, BC: Trafford Publishing, 2008.

Yessis., Michael. *Kinesiology of Exercise*. Indianapolis: Masters' Press, 1998.

ABOUT THE AUTHOR

Steve Scott has authored over twenty published books on judo, sambo, jujitsu, submission grappling, fitness, and coaching. He is an 8th dan in judo and has been a professional judo coach for fifty years, developing numerous national and international medalists in a variety of grappling sports at his home club, the Welcome Mat Judo Club. Steve served as the US team coach at the World Championships in the sports of judo and sambo, as well as at the Pan American Championships and many other international events. He worked as the national coordinator/coach for junior (ages twenty and under) development with US Judo, the national governing body for judo. In this capacity, Steve coached at many national and international training camps at the US Olympic Training Centers. He is a graduate of the University of Missouri–Kansas City. Steve started learning judo in 1965 and hasn't stopped.

BOOKS FROM YMAA

101 REFLECTIONS ON TAI CHI CHUAN
108 INSIGHTS INTO TAI CHI CHUAN
A WOMAN'S QIGONG GUIDE
ADVANCING IN TAE KWON DO
ANALYSIS OF GENUINE KARATE
ANALYSIS OF GENUINE KARATE 2
ANALYSIS OF SHAOLIN CHIN NA 2ND ED
ANCIENT CHINESE WEAPONS
ART AND SCIENCE OF STAFF FIGHTING
THE ART AND SCIENCE OF SELF-DEFENSE
ART AND SCIENCE OF STICK FIGHTING
ART OF HOJO UNDO
ARTHRITIS RELIEF
BACK PAIN RELIEF
BAGUAZHANG
BRAIN FITNESS
CHIN NA IN GROUND FIGHTING
CHINESE FAST WRESTLING
CHINESE FITNESS
CHINESE TUI NA MASSAGE
COMPLETE MARTIAL ARTIST
COMPREHENSIVE APPLICATIONS OF SHAOLIN CHIN NA
CONFLICT COMMUNICATION
DAO DE JING: A QIGONG INTERPRETATION
DAO IN ACTION
DEFENSIVE TACTICS
DIRTY GROUND
DR. WU'S HEAD MASSAGE
ESSENCE OF SHAOLIN WHITE CRANE
EXPLORING TAI CHI
FACING VIOLENCE
FIGHT LIKE A PHYSICIST
THE FIGHTER'S BODY
FIGHTER'S FACT BOOK 1&2
FIGHTING THE PAIN RESISTANT ATTACKER
FIRST DEFENSE
FORCE DECISIONS: A CITIZENS GUIDE
INSIDE TAI CHI
JUDO ADVANTAGE
JUJI GATAME ENCYCLOPEDIA
KARATE SCIENCE
KEPPAN
KRAV MAGA COMBATIVES
KRAV MAGA FUNDAMENTAL STRATEGIES
KRAV MAGA PROFESSIONAL TACTICS
KRAV MAGA WEAPON DEFENSES
LITTLE BLACK BOOK OF VIOLENCE
LIUHEBAFA FIVE CHARACTER SECRETS
MARTIAL ARTS OF VIETNAM
MARTIAL ARTS INSTRUCTION
MARTIAL WAY AND ITS VIRTUES
MEDITATIONS ON VIOLENCE
MERIDIAN QIGONG EXERCISES
MINDFUL EXERCISE
MIND INSIDE TAI CHI
MIND INSIDE YANG STYLE TAI CHI CHUAN
NORTHERN SHAOLIN SWORD
OKINAWA'S COMPLETE KARATE SYSTEM: ISSHIN RYU
PRINCIPLES OF TRADITIONAL CHINESE MEDICINE
PROTECTOR ETHIC
QIGONG FOR HEALTH & MARTIAL ARTS
QIGONG FOR TREATING COMMON AILMENTS
QIGONG MASSAGE
QIGONG MEDITATION: EMBRYONIC BREATHING
QIGONG GRAND CIRCULATION
QIGONG MEDITATION: SMALL CIRCULATION
QIGONG, THE SECRET OF YOUTH: DA MO'S CLASSICS
ROOT OF CHINESE QIGONG
SAMBO ENCYCLOPEDIA
SCALING FORCE
SELF-DEFENSE FOR WOMEN
SHIN GI TAI: KARATE TRAINING
SIMPLE CHINESE MEDICINE
SIMPLE QIGONG EXERCISES FOR HEALTH, 3RD ED.
SIMPLIFIED TAI CHI CHUAN, 2ND ED.
SOLO TRAINING 1&2
SPOTTING DANGER BEFORE IT SPOTS YOU
SPOTTING DANGER BEFORE IT SPOTS YOUR KIDS
SPOTTING DANGER BEFORE IT SPOTS YOUR TEENS
SPOTTING DANGER FOR TRAVELERS
SUMO FOR MIXED MARTIAL ARTS
SUNRISE TAI CHI
SURVIVING ARMED ASSAULTS
TAE KWON DO: THE KOREAN MARTIAL ART
TAEKWONDO BLACK BELT POOMSAE
TAEKWONDO: A PATH TO EXCELLENCE
TAEKWONDO: ANCIENT WISDOM
TAEKWONDO: DEFENSE AGAINST WEAPONS
TAEKWONDO: SPIRIT AND PRACTICE
TAI CHI BALL QIGONG: FOR HEALTH AND MARTIAL ARTS
TAI CHI BALL QIGONG
THE TAI CHI BOOK
TAI CHI CHIN NA
TAI CHI CHUAN CLASSICAL YANG STYLE
TAI CHI CHUAN MARTIAL APPLICATIONS
TAI CHI CHUAN MARTIAL POWER
TAI CHI CONCEPTS AND EXPERIMENTS
TAI CHI DYNAMICS
TAI CHI FOR DEPRESSION
TAI CHI IN 10 WEEKS
TAI CHI PUSH HANDS
TAI CHI QIGONG
TAI CHI SECRETS OF THE ANCIENT MASTERS
TAI CHI SECRETS OF THE WU & LI STYLES
TAI CHI SECRETS OF THE WU STYLE
TAI CHI SECRETS OF THE YANG STYLE
TAI CHI SWORD: CLASSICAL YANG STYLE
TAI CHI SWORD FOR BEGINNERS
TAI CHI WALKING
TAI CHI CHUAN THEORY OF DR. YANG, JWING-MING
FIGHTING ARTS
TRADITIONAL CHINESE HEALTH SECRETS
TRADITIONAL TAEKWONDO
TRAINING FOR SUDDEN VIOLENCE
TRIANGLE HOLD ENCYCLOPEDIA
TRUE WELLNESS SERIES (MIND, HEART, GUT)
WARRIOR'S MANIFESTO
WAY OF KATA
WAY OF SANCHIN KATA
WAY TO BLACK BELT
WESTERN HERBS FOR MARTIAL ARTISTS
WILD GOOSE QIGONG
WING CHUN IN-DEPTH
WINNING FIGHTS
XINGYIQUAN

AND MANY MORE . . .

Printed in the USA
CPSIA information can be obtained
at www.ICGtesting.com
JSHW062002260424
61997JS00002B/3